Yorkshire Encounters

The author and the publisher acknowledge the assistance of
Black Sheep Brewery in the production of this volume.

BLACK SHEEP BREWERY

YORKSHIRE ENCOUNTERS

Lin Watts

MAINSTREAM
PUBLISHING

EDINBURGH AND LONDON

in conjunction with
BLACK SHEEP BREWERY

First published in Great Britain in 2003 by
MAINSTREAM PUBLISHING (EDINBURGH) LTD
7 Albany Street
Edinburgh EH1 3UG

ISBN 1 84018 710 7

A catalogue record for this book is available from the British Library

All the photographic material in this book is the work of the author,
her husband David, and daughter Amanda

Typeset in Baskerville MT and Caslon
Printed in Great Britain by
Mackays of Chatham plc

Cover photographs: front right – Whitby Abbey; front bottom left – Wensleydale;
front top left – Haworth Church; back top – Ainderby Myers;
back bottom – The Heritage Coast

Front endpaper: Ribblehead Viaduct
Back Endpaper: View of Wensleydale

To David and Amanda,
with love

Also the late Alf Wight (James Herriot)
and my beloved cat, Moses,
who together inspired me
to write about my
Yorkshire Encounters

Acknowledgements

First and foremost, I would like to thank my husband, David, and daughter, Amanda, for their unfailing support and patience whilst I took forever researching and working on this, my first literary effort. Without them it might never have been written.

My heartfelt appreciation to our dear friends, Val and Graham, at Ainderby Myers, who provided me with, amongst other things, so much help when researching 'A Feudal Manor House'. Chris and Brian for their friendship and enthusiasm, without whom some of the events within this book would not have been half so much fun! My special thanks to Paul Theakston of the Black Sheep Brewery for his proven confidence in me and understanding of what I wanted to achieve. Thanks must also go to our friends in Thirlby, the talented woodcarver Bob Hunter and his family, who gave me so much of their time (and tea) whilst I got to grips with the basics of his skills (literally). Bob was also the source of so much fascinating information on the late Robert Thompson.

I would also like to thank all those knowledgeable individuals employed at the various sites mentioned within my book who either deliberately or inadvertently supplied me with so much material. In particular the archivists in York Minster as well as many other heritage sites; the Whitby Tourist Centre; the Staithes Heritage Centre who helped my research into the mining communities and the effects of mining on the area, and provided background on Captain Cook; the ladies of the Brontë Birthplace in Thornton who were not only informative but entertaining too; the staff at Norton Conyers; the vicar at Masham, the staff of the North Yorkshire Moors Railway who indulged me; Mike Milner (one-time manager of the Saltersgate Inn); the historical records librarians in Slough, Reading, Leeds and Durham; the staff of the Northallerton County Records Office; and many, many others just too numerous to mention but not forgotten or less appreciated, as I hope the following text proves.

Contents

Foreword by Michael Parkinson

I have always considered Yorkshire to be a country rather than a county. It is as much set apart by virtue of its language and culture as Scotland or Wales. Its humour and attitudes are specific, and in terms of natural resources and variety of landscape it wants for nothing.

Lin Watts has written a fascinating account of the county, but I wouldn't be a Yorkshireman if I didn't find something to bellyache about. What is missing is my Yorkshire, the landscape of pithead gears and smoke-belching steelworks of South Yorkshire where I grew up. It might not be pretty and touristy but it has a certain grandeur. What makes it important are the people who live there. A common mistake is to assume there is a single tribe called 'Yorkshiremen'. In fact there are 20 or more separate tribes – many of whom are at war – making up the whole. My tribe occupies what used to be the coalfield around Barnsley and I think they are the funniest and most engaging people I have ever encountered.

One day Lin Watts might spend some time among them and write a different kind of book, a funny one. What she has achieved in this book is more than enough for the present. Her account is diligent and loving and that it doesn't tell the whole story only serves to illustrate how varied, intriguing and complex Yorkshire really is and why it stands alone.

Preface

Tourism may be a comparatively recent phenomenon that has its origins in a modern transport system and the lure of that great escape mechanism called a holiday, but there have always been travellers. Albeit in the distant past they only had their own two feet or maybe a horse and possibly a cart to rely on, but they ensured the paths of old England were well trod and, just like the tourist of today, they too sought food and shelter and warmth and company during their long journeys. Of course, in those far-off times most people only took to the road out of necessity – tradesmen selling their wares, noblemen going about their business, men off to do battle or folk simply looking for somewhere to settle. Few were afforded the luxury of travelling for pure pleasure until the relatively comfortable age of the stagecoach arrived.

Over the past 1,000 years, Yorkshire has become well used to welcoming such strangers to its soil and most have been truly grateful. However, throughout that time there have also been those who have sadly abused its hospitality and violated its peace, such as the hostile armies who trampled its rich and fertile lands, leaving them stained with the blood of men who fought for political, royal or religious supremacy. During these times Yorkshire's suffering was great and so were its losses, but there were always those who believed in the county, appreciated its virtues and stood by it, enduring with it. To them it had become 'home' and they were its people. Together they not only survived but flourished and the Yorkshire of today is justly proud of its heritage – a fact that is immediately apparent to the thousands of visitors it continues to welcome into its fascinating world each year. Yorkshire's past is all around them – an integral part of its present, and, in this new millennium, there is little doubt it will continue to be very much a part of its future too.

Whether it is Yorkshire's history or its spectacular landscapes, its natural ability to suit such a wide variety of interests or simply its popularity, whatever inspires the majority of visitors to come to Yorkshire and from whichever corner of the globe they come, invariably their lasting impressions far exceed their initial expectations. For those, and indeed anyone with an interest in this magnificent county, I have written this book and I sincerely hope it will not only be enjoyed, but inspire others to discover and appreciate a little more of that which is Yorkshire for themselves – just as I did all those years ago.

I will now leave you to judge for yourselves . . .

Introduction: A Brief Encounter with the Three Ridings

The largest county in England, Yorkshire straddles our island from the North Sea in the east to within a few miles of the Irish Sea in the west. Originally split into three areas by the Danes, for centuries the divisions were known as North Riding, West Riding and East Riding (Riding being derived from the Norse word '*thriding*', meaning 'a third part'). Today, for the purposes of administrative convenience, the powers that be have seen fit to redefine the areas of Yorkshire and sadly the word 'Riding' has officially fallen into disuse. I use the word 'officially' because it is an inescapable fact that the Ridings are synonymous with Yorkshire's long history and will forever be so.

Here I would like to apologise to those vast expanses of Yorkshire not covered by this book. It is simply because there is only so much one can write in one volume and there is so much more to be said on the Yorkshire I have yet to write about. I can only say I hope one day I will get the chance to do these areas the justice they deserve.

Although much larger in area than either West or East Riding, the North Riding has a much smaller population. This vast area of sprawling scenic beauty, unspoiled by the ruthless gluttony of time since it was first conceived by the impact of the Ice Age, holds within its grasp a host of different, but equally captivating, landscapes. From its western reaches of the high Pennines, this rugged and often bleak country gradually gives way to the more gently undulating curves of the foothills, rolling down to the green pasture floors of the Dales with their farms and attractive villages. Beyond the Dales is the great Plain of York, better known as the Vale of Mowbray. This huge expanse of fertile lowland is overlooked at its eastern extremity by the buttresses of the Hambleton Hills that lead onto the western fringes of the North York Moors. Interspersed with towns and villages, such as television's Aidensfield from *Heartbeat*, the North York Moors encompass the largest expanse of heather-clad moorland in England; legend and history are in abundance here – and so are steam trains! And so to the sea and the many fishing villages and towns that span the Heritage Coast. Such are the contrasts offered up by the differing landscapes of North Yorkshire.

West Yorkshire too has its fair share of variety, with hills, dales and moors providing a dramatic backdrop to its busy industrial towns. Leeds, Bradford, Halifax and Huddersfield were once home to the textiles industry, with weaving being rapidly transferred from the cottage to the mill, using wool mainly from North Yorkshire. The Industrial Revolution, however, led to a reduction in the workforce and local people once again had to face unemployment and poverty; thus followed the Luddite uprisings in 1812. However, West Yorkshire survived its times of real hardship and prospered. Although today there is still much of West Yorkshire's historic past preserved for us to relish, the dark satanic mills that once dominated the skyline are mostly gone. Only their surrounding moorlands remain, areas that have provided so much pleasure to so many local people over the generations – including the Brontës.

This Brief Encounter is about the Three Ridings, and South Yorkshire is very much a part of the old West Riding, so I make no apology for including it under that heading. It was not only the chattering of the weavers' frames that filled the air in the West Riding, but also further south the clanking and rumble of the pitmen's cages as they descended to the dismal workplace several feet below ground. Sheffield, Barnsley, Rotherham and Doncaster became lands of coal mines, foundries and blast furnaces. Today the horizons of these important areas of Yorkshire are as busy as ever, with industrial regalia such as power stations, chimneys dominating large factory complexes, towering office blocks and, of course, there are still a few of those majestic steel skeletons standing watch over the pit entrances.

Although I have centred my book on seven journeys through the North and West Ridings of Yorkshire, in this Brief Encounter I could not possibly omit the equally important landscape of East Riding.

Generally regarded as essentially less scenically dramatic than its counterparts, being mostly lowland country, it is easy to overlook some of its more spectacular aspects, especially since it boasts a substantial North Sea coastline. Its chalk cliffs at Bempton, near Flamborough, and at Flamborough Head itself, must surely dispel any doubts that East Riding does indeed possess some very different but equally aggressive landscapes of its own. The East Riding as part of its heritage is also justly proud of its long association with maritime trade. Kingston-upon-Hull has been a major seaport on our island since time immemorial. On the banks of the River Humber, within the southern boundaries of the county, the port was essentially a gateway to overseas trade with the known world when enterprising merchants first acknowledged the potential of plying their business ventures on foreign shores.

These are the briefest of sketches of the three Ridings of Yorkshire which, although at variance to one another of necessity because of their geographical and geological situation, each form an integral and essential part of the whole. Together they are one Yorkshire.

❧ ONE ❧

A Feudal Manor House *circa* 1066

Ainderby Myers in North Yorkshire is situated in the ancient parish of
Hornby. Approximately four miles from the nearest market town of
Bedale, which is often referred to as the gateway to the Dales, the old
grey manor house still dominates one of the finest settings in England
as it has done for nearly 1,000 years. Fondly referred to by myself and
my family as our 'second home', it was from here many years ago I first
began to explore and fall in love with Yorkshire. It didn't take much to
convince me how truly remarkable and fascinating this land and its
people really are and it didn't take long for Val and Graham, who live
beneath Ainderby's roof, to realise that they were going to have to
accept we would never be away for long!

First recorded in the Domesday Book of 1086, despite our not quite
so long association with the place I could never take it for granted nor
cease to be intrigued by the atmosphere it evokes. To me, Ainderby
Myers is steeped in echoes of its past – a past which travels back in time
to before the Norman Conquest – and I can well visualise part of this
stoic building as once being the feudal manor house central to the
community who lived on this land. The village has long since
disappeared into the archives of local history, but Ainderby, with its
ancient house and lands, still survives as a working farm, which has
always been its primary function.

There are many such properties all over England that have not outgrown their usefulness. Notwithstanding their age, they have continued to provide a home for generation upon generation of various occupants down through many centuries of our history. Remarkably, most of these properties remain virtually unheard of, their only claim to fame being the longevity of their lifespan or perhaps an obscure reference in a local history book. This is a pity, but perhaps just as well since doubtless the occupants of these valued properties would not want to be inundated with sightseers tramping through their back kitchens at teatime. Anyway, the sightseers would probably be a little disappointed to find the old house would have had to relinquish many relics of its past. Each era of our history has called for change of some description both in our homes and socially – so what can any of us expect from a house like Ainderby Myers, that came into existence in the eleventh century and has survived into the twenty-first? However, looking beyond what we can see today, to me these old houses are an essential part of our heritage. They are as much a part of our past as castle ruins, famous landmarks and important artefacts in our museums or historical characters from our history books. The difference is they endure. They are not static exhibits which, of course, have a valued place, nor have they been time-stamped.

Bearing this in mind, Ainderby's potential as a perfect time capsule through which to recapture what life may well have been like for all who had lived and worked on its soil for an entire millennium was just too tempting a project to be ignored. I began by researching as much documented evidence as I could find on Ainderby Myers in particular, and this area of North Yorkshire in general. All too soon I discovered Ainderby's story was inextricable from that of the ancient parish of Hornby and, more importantly, reflected the effect some of the most dramatic events in our history had on its people of the time. It also provides an interesting portrayal of how North Yorkshire itself evolved and how so many of its farming communities today owe their origins to the end of the feudal system and the establishment of yeoman farming or freeholding. Of necessity, apart from documented evidence from essential records, local and general historical fact and architectural proof, I have had to use a sprinkling of conjecture. However, the results of my findings, I believe, make at least Ainderby and indeed the ancient parish of Hornby well worthy of note.

⁂ A Feudal Manor House *circa* 1066 ⁂

At this point it is worthy for you to note I am no professional historian and I do not even try to be an expert. Despite the fact I have used proven fact to guide me along the way, this is history at its best or worst with the 'common touch' and I make no apologies for the fact that at times I could not resist the more light-hearted touches that go with my observations.

The deforesting of large areas of land not only in this area of Yorkshire but all over England, and the establishment of substantial areas of farmland, known simply as 'estates', had already happened by the time of the Viking invasions (*circa* 800). The origins of these 'estates' are debatable, but whether they evolved from Roman or Anglo-Saxon times, they ultimately belonged either to kings, lords or the Church. Generally they were overseen by estate managers and farmed by the people, but individuals were rarely allowed to own their own land. This remained the norm until just prior to the arrival of the Vikings, when Anglo-Saxon kings decided to start granting portions of their lands to loyal followers who had done them good service – usually on the battlefield. Thus the innovation of private land ownership had begun, but was to be very much accelerated during the Viking age (*circa* 800 up until the Norman Conquest).

Sporadic raids and looting by the Vikings are well recorded in our history books. At this time England was divided into four independent kingdoms – East Anglia, Wessex, Mercia and Northumbria – the latter encompassing the Yorkshire we know today. All in their turn suffered from the havoc rained on them by the Vikings. Northumbria was notorious for being a kingdom of unrest at the hands of feuding rulers and suffering from constant hassle from the Scots. The Vikings took advantage, including the capture of York in 866. By this time, however, the Vikings arriving on our shores did not purely come with violence in mind. Many came purposefully to set up colonies and settle here with their families, either on the lands they had conquered or, not so well known, on land legitimately purchased from the Anglo-Saxons by the Viking leaders, who in their turn wanted to reward their loyal followers who had fought for them by subsequently dividing their new lands amongst them. By the end of the tenth century, Viking colonisation was established in England and, through the seizing and selling of parcels of land, numerous individual manors evolved with their related villages and parishes. Thus the forerunner to feudal England was born and the Vikings and the Anglo-Saxons learnt to live side by side within peaceful communities.

During the Viking age the population in England had increased from about 1,000,000 people to around 2,000,000 and more food was needed. On top of this, far more people now lived and worked in towns. It was time for agricultural expansion, which was aided by the fact our climate had also been slowly changing. Winters were becoming shorter and milder and summers longer and warmer. There is no doubt that a self-sufficient farming community had established itself at Ainderby by the time the Vikings arrived and was one that would in many respects survive long after they had left. Whether these settlers were of Anglo-Saxon descent is not known but is likely.

By 1000, for administrative purposes, England had been divided into the much more familiar (to us) shires and Ainderby Myers was firmly placed in the parish of Hornby in Richmondshire in the North 'Thriding'. The fact that a new millennium had dawned – according to the Christian calendar – would have meant little. At the time, King Ethelred Unraed, or 'Unready' as he has been nicknamed, was rocking unsteadily on his English throne and it is probably just as well that no great fuss was made of the occasion, since as the great moment arrived doubtless he would not have been ready – and by the time he was, it would have been too late! The poor man was plagued by ill-counsel and treachery, which is what 'Unraed' means. His people despised him. Maybe they had just cause – he is supposed to have ravaged the lands of his own subjects.

England, like its king, was in a precarious state. He ruled from 978 to 1016 and from 991 recurring heavy Viking raids again persecuted his people, but Ethelred did little to help. In fact, he made matters worse. First he tried to bribe the Vikings by paying them Danegeld but over the next decade these payments became astronomical. He then resorted to ordering the massacre of those Danes that had chosen to live peaceably within his kingdom. This unfortunate slaughter took place on St Brice's Day in the year 1002. Whether it affected the people at Ainderby is not clear, but it is understood that the massacres did not include those settlers within the Danelaw. These were areas of England which were under Scandinavian control and so followed the Danish law. Since Ainderby may well have come within the Danelaw region of the north-east, it was possibly spared any confrontation. Ethelred's irrational solutions solved nothing. England was battle torn and weary – a land where the poor struggled and the powerful also struggled – the former to survive, the latter for more power. (Nothing new there!) However, as usual, the latter always seemed to reign supreme and trample over the hard workers who helped line their pockets. Ironically, after the demise of Ethelred, came the rise of Cnut and England warmed to their new Danish king, who by immediately putting his kingdom in order – entrusting the Saxons with their own government, dispersing his Danish armies and even marrying Ethelred's widow, inspired a united kingdom as well as being King of Denmark and Norway. He died in 1035.

However, despite Cnut's valiant efforts and the relatively peaceful 24 years under the reign of good King Edward the Confessor, a new force was abroad to claim the lands that had been cultivated by the peasants so they could thrive – claimed in the name of a king and lorded over by his barons, and although the same hands rutted the earth and planted the seed and harvested their work, it would no longer be theirs.

It was 1066, the Battle of Hastings had been fought and poor King Harold II, who never had the chance to polish his crown, had been slain, noted more for the legendary arrow that felled him than for the brief time he sat on the royal throne. William the Conqueror was now proclaimed King of England and crowned in a very new Westminster Abbey on Christmas Day, 1066. He immediately confiscated the estates of England's aristocracy, who not only lost their homes, but their political power and privileges. In gratitude for the services rendered him by his own faithful Norman and other French barons, knights, bishops and abbots, the king partitioned off his new lands and rewarded this formidable body of men with huge estates to preside over in his name. The Norman feudal system had arrived and life in England was about to change radically for everyone – not least the people of Ainderby. The same peasant farmers and crofters would still work the fields, graze their sheep and traverse the familiar stony pathways, but they would have a new master – a lord of the manor – who would speak in a foreign tongue and dominate their way of life. All this and a necessity for them, the peasants, to swear fealty to a new king who they already detested for his known cruelty and obsessive dominance of all he surveyed.

Those pathways at Ainderby have long since been obliterated by the soil. The wells too have vanished with time, where once they were served by underground streams to ensure all who dwelt here had water. One thing has not changed: the eastern boundary of the old Roman Road (now the A1), way over in the distance, still remains, although now it hisses with the sound of wind rush and rubber on tarmac as opposed to the clump of horses hooves and rumble of cart wheels. With its relatively close proximity to the road, Ainderby, from its creation, would have been a welcome sight to travel-weary strangers and indeed a place for them to rest a while and renew their strength for their onward journey. In this respect I often wonder: what if some of our old kings, such as William I, their courtiers and great armies could awaken from their eternity for a short time? Would they not marvel at the ease with which we now travel the length and breadth of this country of ours?

For them a journey from London to York, for example, would have meant days of travelling. Mostly the roads would have been little more than cart tracks and much of their food would have been 'on the hoof' – so to speak! – or DIY with a bow and arrow. Whether moving huge armies off into battle or travelling about their lands, just imagine those long winding columns of mounted nobles and knights, followed by their foot soldiers and servants, bravely ignoring searing blisters on their ill-shod feet, escorting rickety carts carrying supplies and almost certainly most, if not all, of the noblemen's treasured possessions, as was the custom back then. A fact well known not only to the Robin Hoods of the wayside but men of more evil intent who, no doubt, grasped their opportunities whenever the chance came their way. Somewhere in this great entourage there may well have been the Ladies of the Court, travelling 'in style', in uncomfortable horse-drawn litters which provided little protection from the elements or the grime and the dust as they made their slow progress. There must have been many folk who fell by the wayside on these arduous and often perilous journeys, if not from unexpected ambush, then from sheer exhaustion or sickness. No wonder there was usually a sense of urgency to reach a safe haven before nightfall, be it castle, manor house, inn or riverside encampment.

❧ A Feudal Manor House *circa* 1066 ☙

Of course, since man's creation, he had traversed his lands much as I have described and knew no differently. That is until the arrival of the stagecoach in the eighteenth century. Remarkably, from that small beginning it was to take us only two and a half centuries to achieve the ability to travel not only within our own kingdom, but virtually anywhere in the world by whatever means we preferred. The stagecoach was our first inland public transport service and it was welcomed by those who could afford the rather exorbitant fares as a (comparatively) more comfortable, reliable and safer way to travel. It was also far more convenient and efficient for the longer, more tedious journeys, with coaching inns providing not only the necessary changes of horse teams at regular intervals but also the added luxury of refreshment or overnight accommodation for passengers. However, travellers still had to allow days for the majority of their journeys, that is until that great innovation of the Victorian age – the steam train. With an ever-expanding network of railways and more powerful locomotives not only was a great new transport system born but so was a means by which to improve our industrial, economic and social growth. However, competition was already on its way. It was also towards the end of the nineteenth century that a couple of German fellows by the familiar names of Daimler and Benz developed the petrol-fuelled internal combustion engine and introduced us to the motorcar. Today, 100 years on, I think many of us are convinced that it is the only way to travel.

Thus, using our car as our trusty steed, within four hours of leaving our home in Berkshire we are usually taking the Hackforth turn-off from the old Roman Road (the A1) in north North Yorkshire, roughly six miles south of Scotch Corner. Here, down the familiar winding country lane, our journey nears its end. A few minutes later we are turning left through the familiar white gates of Ainderby Myers and over the cattle-grid. Ahead lies the old cart track that guides you down to the ancient house below, its red pantile roof just visible through the trees that edge the fields flanking the track. Sheep are often grazing in the pasture through which the track is set and although they add much to the charm of this entrance it is wise to proceed with caution since their antics are not always predictable.

They are prone to gathering on the path itself and appearing completely oblivious to your approach. They will only move at the last minute and at their own speed, which usually varies between dead slow and stop! If lambs are about, they present their own set of problems. Mum is often one side of the path and the lambs the other, but if the youngsters sense impending danger – i.e. humans approaching in a ton of metal – they have a nasty habit of deciding at the last minute to tumble over and join her for safety. Of course, there is no option but to stop and enjoy the view. A view that has little changed down through the ages, since sheep have been grazing these pastures for nigh on 1,000 years (no, not the same sheep! By the way, it was carts passing by that interrupted their peace then – that's why it is called the 'cart track'). At the end of the track, which is approximately a third of a mile long, there is a second cattle-grid which takes us onto the wide stony forecourt in front of the house which, together with its various farm buildings, appears to nestle in a great hollow surrounded by field and pasture as far as the eye can see – an aspect which has changed little with time according to the Domesday Book.

It is important to note here that those who are far better qualified to comment on this valuable document than myself have concluded that bearing in mind the attention to the most intricate detail afforded all the other shires, Yorkshire is possibly the least satisfactory. They partly base their observations on the fact that extensive portions of land within the shire have simply been described as 'waste', which means land that is unusable or uncultivated and therefore cannot be taxed. Having read extensive entries concerning other counties, I did notice the surprising lack of the same informative detail for this, the largest county in England, which certainly seems at variance with the fact that in the years prior to William's reign, evidence shows this to have become a prosperous shire of extensive and valuable farmlands and pasture. Historians, however, record that William's 'harrying of the north' in the winter of 1069–70 may have been partly to blame for the lack of inventory detail compared to the other shires and that Yorkshire had also suffered much at the hands of the Vikings and the Scots for some 20 years prior to the survey, which probably devastated substantial areas of the county.

From the records for such a vast area there were also surprisingly few tenants-in-chief. These were the landholders or lords holding land directly from the King and there were only 28 of them. Only eight, including the King himself, the Archbishop of York and Count Alan of Brittany, being major landholders. The count was a man obviously much favoured by William I since the King had not only bestowed on him sprawling lands in Yorkshire but in 12 other counties too. Head of the Bretons in England, he also carried the title of Earl of Richmond and his holdings in the North Riding included Ainderby Myers (or Endrebi as the name is recorded in the Domesday Book) and the surrounding area. The king had also bestowed one more favour on the count: he was married to William's daughter Constance, which meant that since the Conquest, Ainderby had come under the direct jurisdiction of none other than the King of England's son-in-law, who probably trod its soil many times on routine visits around his estates.

Ainderby, at the time of the Domesday in 1086, already had a two-storey stone block house, now the east wing of a far larger house, which was occupied by a fellow by the name of Landric who was probably one of Count Alan's trusted men. The major landholders divided up their huge lands into manageable manors or estates and installed their loyal followers to administer these on their behalf. No doubt Landric presided at Ainderby for this purpose and it is not hard to imagine the effect his arrival had on the villagers in these parts. After Landric, the lordship of Ainderby, as well as Hornby just two miles away, apparently came into the hands of Conan, son of Ellis (sorry, but that's what the archives say), before being passed on to the Fitton family (what wonderful names they all had). Then we come to a 'supposed' Frenchman called Robert (de Endrebi) in 1286 who held land here directly of the Earl of Richmond – no, not the Count (he had been dead nearly 200 years). Anyway, I say 'supposed' because whether this new incumbent's name did include Endrebi or whether he took it from the manor is not clear but knowing it was often the case for such gentlemen to take their name from either their origins or from where they presided it could well suggest that by 1286 Endrebi (Ainderby) had become of sufficient importance for Robert to adopt its name as his status symbol. However, the 'de Endrebi' or 'of Endrebi' probably confused record keepers after the property became known as Ainderby and thus the easy assumption was made that the gentleman was French. I believe this latter explanation to be the truth since I found nothing to substantiate his origins, although he may well have had French ancestors, of course, as did many at this time in our history.

Robert and other such men were deemed worthy of their privileged positions primarily because of their actions on the battlefield in support of their respective barons and of King Edward I. Edward had been on the throne since 1272 and had certainly needed all the help he could muster in the ten turbulent years prior to Robert taking up the occupancy of Ainderby. Despite William the Conqueror and his various successors' substantial attempts to put England firmly in order, battles still raged throughout the countryside, which constantly resounded with the drumming of horses' hooves as they thundered over the sod taking their riders to glorious victory or involuntary death. Armour was for the privileged few, as indeed was the horse, but still great vanguards of valiant champions (such as Robert) followed the fluttering, colourful banners of their knight (such as the Earl of Richmond) and willingly sped forward to meet their opponents in the heartfelt hope that today their name would not be written in God's great register of men who had fallen.

Before leaving their tents that morning they had prayed – surely that would be enough. But as the battle raged out of control and all around them greater men than they lay disfigured and torn, their horses cast from under them, sometimes crushed down upon them, after they too had been slain by a stray lance cracking into their once sleek and supple flanks, how could these poor souls try to hold out? But they did. They had to. Still, somewhere in the distance their lord's banner floated on the air, above the dust and blood, and sight of it gave them hope. That was all they had now since all around them, beneath the noise of clanking swords, reeling axes and clashing pikes, men shouting oaths of defiance and the horses' high-pitched responses to their own fear, there was that constant groaning and weeping of men who could no longer hold out – their battle was fought, their eyes agog with the fear of that last fatal blow; they surrendered themselves to God. Such was the price paid by so many of the knights and lords who had sworn fealty to their king in return for their lands and respective privileges which were of no use to them now. Such was the price paid by the ordinary men who had sworn fealty to their respective lord. Such was the dark side of feudalism. Freedom was for the privileged few – or the dead!

❧ A Feudal Manor House *circa* 1066 ❧

And so no doubt Robert was summoned to support his lord in battle for their king, who had one major thorn in his side – Wales. He was determined to put an end to the ceaseless feuding between the Welsh and the English once and for all. Eventually, Edward defeated Llewelyn and the princes of Wales and annexed Wales to the English crown in 1284. He honoured his conquest by bestowing his newborn son and heir with the title of the Prince of Wales at Caernarvon Castle to secure the unification – a tradition that continues to this day. As for Robert, the Earl of Richmond undoubtedly showed his appreciation in the customary fashion by bestowing on him the lands of Endrebi, an established and substantial estate, which he would now control.

Notwithstanding the unrest in England that followed the Norman Conquest and which saw such kings as Stephen, Henry II, Richard the Lionheart, his brother King John (of Magna Carta fame) and Henry III being forced to fight even their own barons who rebelled against them, Christianity had well and truly infiltrated the kingdom. These great men of history and their loyal followers were all born into the faith and lived by it. Although the numerous castles and fortresses that dominated the English landscape were grand and formidable enough, nothing compared with the architecture of the many fine abbeys and churches that were now appearing all over the land. In these unsure times, people from all walks of life were deeply superstitious. Christianity brought them hope and through the psalms, which formed an important part of their teaching, they truly believed their merciful God would deliver them from the torment of servitude and temptation of evil that was so much a part of their daily lives. The finely illustrated psalters, manuscripts and books of hours, were laboriously reproduced by the scribes and held by those who could read them – mainly the privileged lords and their ladies, as well as the monks themselves. Others just listened, but they still believed. Matins at midnight, Vespers and Compline were part of daily life – especially for the monks – when prayers were said and faith renewed. Christmas was a great feast time when lords entertained their guests at the manor on a magnificent scale and their serfs also celebrated to a lesser degree and were allowed a holiday from their labours. They had special treats to eat, such as a goose or capon and – believe it or not – mince pies, made from minced pork and herbs. Easter too was welcomed as a time of holy reflection.

After the statutory 40 days of Lent, when everyone kept to a strict diet, a huge feast was arranged and oxen were cooked on the spit. Apart from these special dates in the Christian calendar, weddings were held in church and baptism was regarded as crucial, since it was believed that to remain unbaptised meant you would never go to heaven.

Well before Robert arrived at Ainderby in 1286 – from around 1160, in fact – monks had lived here side by side with the occupants of the manor. Richmond Priory held land here and the monks used the rich pastures to graze their sheep. (I told you those sheep had been around a long time!) As Saxon lords and Viking settlers began to firmly acknowledge Christianity, it became important to them to establish a chapel within their manors or estates to symbolise their status and be used for burials. Their successors, the Normans, followed suit and it seems Ainderby was no exception, since long before the monks arrived there was in fact a small chapel within the confines of the manor house on the ground floor, although whether any burials actually took place here is open to conjecture. However, with the onslaught of plague, high death rates amongst the newborn and young children, as well as women in childbirth and peasant workers, it is highly probable that interments were carried out. One fact is beyond probability and that is that the chapel determined the house to be described as 'a religious house' in all future reference. Four hundred years later this was to prove a great danger to all who dwelt here.

In reality, the monks at Ainderby were lay brothers and as such, unlike their counterparts – the choir monks – were not in holy orders and not given any intellectual duties, such as learning, teaching and reading. In general the majority of lay brothers of this period could not read or write anyway, but were a band of men who wanted to live pious lives and help the community.

In 1286, apart from the monks, that community would have consisted of numerous peasants, who worked mainly on the land, their families and Robert's family and his various servants. The latter would have probably included a steward, a bailiff and a reeve, who was the middle man between the peasants and the administrators and ran the estate as per instructions from the bailiff. The bailiff also hired skilled workers such as the miller, the blacksmith and carpenters.

Almost certainly, the village itself was concentrated to the north of the manor. The tiny daub-and-wattle huts that housed the peasant farmers and their families, with turf or thatching on the roofs, probably spanned the fields either side of the present cart track. These peasant dwellings, which would have hardly been adequate against the cruel northern winters, consisted of little more than one main room where the family ate and slept. Food would be cooked over an open fire in a central stone hearth and there would have been no sanitation or privacy. The discomfort of such inadequate living quarters was often intensified by the fact that the families had to share them with their animals – and not just a friendly cat or dog. Just imagine those poor souls after their meal huddling around the remains of their fire whilst the northern winds whistled in through every crack. To go to the loo must have been an adventure into the Arctic which needed at least an hour's warning to summon up the courage. Then, those who had had the misfortune to have to answer the call of nature had to risk the total annoyance of the rest of their family by bringing the mud, snow or whatever else back in with them when they returned. Then there was bedtime – no cleaning your teeth, no bedtime comforts – just curling up around the fire with probably a goat muzzling you in the ear to make you feel loved! In other words, in the ensuing 300–400 years since those first settlers had come to this beautiful land, there had been little or no improvement in the standard of living.

In fact, with the arrival of the manors, which at this time in their history were run as profitable businesses, life had become a good deal harder for the majority of people who had to support themselves as well as their lord. He presided over all and, when the need arose, he also acted as judge and jury for petty crimes committed against his estate. Many of the poor workers were often tempted to take an apple from the orchard or some corn from the fields, but this was a serious abuse of the lord's trust and the punishment often far outweighed the crime so as to set an example for other would-be offenders.

Thus, in principle, life at Ainderby differed little from the rest of England under the feudal system that had prevailed here (and for that matter many parts of Europe too) for 200 years. In sharp and cruel contrast to the peasant workers, whilst all lands still ultimately belonged to the King, his leading courtiers, to whom he had granted huge estates, lived like princes. The Earl of Richmond, from whom Robert held his lands, resided in his castle at Richmond, rising high above the picturesque River Swale, approximately 15 miles from Ainderby. Today the ruins of this once-splendid fortress still dominate the old market town and provide us with little doubt as to just how grand his residence once was. Built in 1071, following the Norman Conquest, by the Count Alan of Brittany, it is said to be the oldest stone-built castle in England and unusually had no timber predecessor. Nearly 100 years later the magnificent 100 ft-high stone keep was begun by a later successor to the earldom, Conan – also a duke of Brittany – but, alas, he never saw his work finished and it was left to his daughter's guardian, King Henry II, to oversee completion in the 1180s. Notwithstanding the grand lifestyle of such honoured gentlemen, even in those days nothing came for free and the kings of those far-off times weren't stupid. (Well, not all of them anyway!) To ensure they had the right men on their side, those privileged high-ranking nobles who were great warriors, whether they wanted to or not, had to swear fealty to their king and undertake to support him in war and to discharge other dues and services. As explained, there was no way all these men could possibly manage holding so much land by themselves and so they, in their turn, granted various portions of their estates – thus the manors – to their leading men, who were normally lords or knights, on similar terms to the terms they held with their king. As I have illustrated, Robert was obviously favoured by the Earl to hold the manor at Ainderby and, living in such close proximity, it is reasonable to assume his baron was a frequent unannounced visitor, whether his host approved or not. All these aforementioned gentlemen 'held land' and were duly expected to administer their estates and pay the appropriate taxes to their king, which in itself was doomed to cause problems for individual monarchs throughout history.

In this great scheme of things, we then come to the poor villeins (peasant workers) on the farms and manors, many of whom became 'serfs' to their respective lords who undertook to protect them all in return for their free services. Their subservient lives were guided by the hand of nature. They rose with the sun and slept as it set. Their work on the land was as the season demanded. That was all they knew. They were mostly ignorant of the intrigues of court or any other matters that concerned the world outside their village.

❧ A Feudal Manor House *circa* 1066 ❧

It is hard for us to imagine a world where little or nothing is known of what is happening in one's own country from one day to the next, but that is how it was. The BBC was definitely not on the map yet – at home or abroad – so word of mouth was the only reliable source of communication. Travellers, therefore, were very welcome for they often came bearing news of some importance, but apart from these accommodating strangers, the only other likely sources of current news were the local ale houses or marketplaces. The nearest market town to Ainderby was – and still is – Bedale, which was granted its right to hold a market by King Henry III in 1251. Market day was – and still is – Tuesday. It is to here the peasants of Ainderby would have come to sell their vegetables or cheese. Mind you, they had to pay a tax for the privilege of standing in the square. It was only more wealthy traders who could afford to set up a stall. It is also from here they would have purchased their provisions, such as pots and pans, knives and livestock. Entertainers would do a turn whilst people gossiped with friends and enjoyed a moment's freedom from their busy lives.

The market of today is a much more orderly affair and although Bedale is referred to as a town, in shopping terms it has only one main street. However, it is so attractively arranged you cannot help but be impressed by its old-world charm. Many of the shops are of the quaint old-fashioned kind and the shop fronts have not been ruined by lots of glass and modern heading signs, but most still have their bay windows and time-weathered brick and stonework. There is no uniformity within the buildings and this only adds to the overall pleasing aspect wherever you look. Some are two storey, some are three, some have slate roofs and some have tiled, some are straight and some are higgledy-piggledy, there are even a few Georgian-fronted houses with their doors opening directly onto the street, and just here and there, blended well, a few buildings of a more modern nature, but taking all into account with their rows of undulating chimney pots, the whole effect is a picture waiting to be painted. The old market cross is still here and doubtless those ancient traders who sold their wares beneath it would have heartily welcomed our friend Brian Dobson into their midst. Brian is renowned in the area for his particular talent – making succulent sausages in the traditional way. He is not alone. Many purveyors of good-quality food in Yorkshire follow the long-established traditions of their ancestors by providing their customers with their own particular brand of good-quality 'home-made' produce.

Bedale's main street is dominated at the northern end by the projection of the 98 ft-high tower of St Gregory's Church. It is one of the best examples of a fortified church tower in the north of England and the three lower stages were probably built around the early fourteenth century whilst the fourth or belfry stage was added in 1400 – work was probably delayed due to the Black Death, which sabotaged so much in England at this time. The parapet is battlemented. In the second stage there is a living room – the refuge – with window seats, a fireplace and *garderobe* – medieval loo to you – and the blue-faced clock of the tower is housed in the third stage. The chime of eight bells includes the Tenor Bell, which dates from the fourteenth century, making it one of the three oldest bells in Wensleydale.

However, long before the sound of St Gregory's bells rang out over the town, or indeed before the church itself was built, towards the close of the thirteenth century, gossip mongers in Bedale's marketplace would have been having a field day speculating on the latest political intrigues. In 1296 and again in 1298, huge armies were making their way north to Scotland under the command of Edward I. It is more than likely that the Earl of Richmond and Robert de Endrebi would have joined their king and ridden with him over the border. He now had Wales but he wanted Scotland too. He did have some modicum of success, but all he acquired in the end was the Scottish coronation stone of Scone, which has recently, graciously, been returned – nigh on 700 years later.

Edward I died on his way to yet another battle against the Scots in 1307. The reign of his son, Edward II, was disastrous and in 1322, having finally driven his barons to openly defy him, civil war broke out. How this affected the Earl of Richmond or Ainderby is not recorded. By 1327 it seems enough was enough and none other than Edward's wife, Queen Isabella, conspired with other nobles to have him deposed and eventually murdered in Berkely Castle. He was succeeded by his son.

During the 50-year reign of Edward III in the fourteenth century further radical changes, both socially and politically, placed another landmark in England's history. Parliament had developed to the extent that it was acknowledged it should be consulted in the general affairs of the country, especially where taxation was concerned. The assembly had consisted of upper-, middle- and lower-class representatives of the social ladder. Now this assembly was to be divided into the much more familiar 'Lords' and 'Commons'. The former speaks for itself (and still does) but the latter was made up of knights of the shires and the town representatives. Talking of speech, the good old English language was also back in fashion in the upper classes and, as if substantiating the fact, the first translation of the hitherto Latin Bible was made into English.

The ancient parish of Hornby at this time was divided into three townships: Hornby to the west, Hackforth in the centre and Ainderby Myers with Holtby to the east. For some years now the residence of Hornby's lords of the manor would have dominated the skyline for miles around and been easily visible to Ainderby some two miles away. A prestigious fortified castle, which, although not on the scale of its counterparts such as that at Richmond, would still have presented a foreboding front to any would-be adversaries. Set in rich grazing lands it was the home of the St Quintin family in the fourteenth century who were the lords of the manor at Hornby at that time. Today it still presents an imposing picture on the landscape, despite the fact it has undergone considerable alteration over the years. Surrounded by attractive parkland adjacent to Hornby Church, it is now a private family home and not open to the public.

In the first half of the fourteenth century, whilst Edward III rained havoc on the Scots and the French and founded the Order of the Knights of the Garter, a Thomas Covell, Lord of Holtby, (who had lived in the manor at Holtby since 1288) had also held land at Ainderby Myers. Robert must have known him well. (I wonder what became of Robert? Nothing is recorded.) Anyway, after the devastating Black Death, which reduced England's population by approximately one-third within ten years of its initial outbreak on our shores at Bristol in 1348, Thomas Covell's descendants decided to vacate Holtby in favour of the manor house at Ainderby, which was unoccupied. Around this time, it seems the lord of the manor at Hornby – Anthony St Quintin – had died, since he left his sole heir, a daughter called Margaret, in the care of the first Lord Scrope of Castle Bolton in Wensleydale. Lord

Scrope, who had served with John of Gaunt and been Lord Treasurer of England, also had the wardship of a John Conyers to further educate that gentleman in the graces of the elite. The Conyers were, in their own right, a wealthy, influential family with a good pedigree. Whether John and Margaret fell in love or Lord Scrope decided it was a good match will not be found in any history book but he arranged for the couple to marry and hopefully they lived happily ever after at Hornby Castle. Sir John was not only a knight but a chief justice and now lord of Hornby, whilst another branch of his family moved into the newly vacated manor at Holtby. Throughout the long history of the landed gentry of England these powerful and privileged ranks of our society have so consistently intertwined their families through marriage that their respective family trees read like an advertisement for *Who's Who* and together bear an uncanny resemblance to one another. The Conyers of Hornby, as we shall see, were no different.

However, despite the comings and goings at Ainderby Myers, Holtby and Hornby, the latter part of the fourteenth century was a bleak time for everyone. The Black Death, which had infiltrated our island from the Continent, reduced labour forces to a minimum and consequently had a near catastrophic affect on our farming and cloth manufacturing industries. Of course, these two essential areas of production were inextricable from one another and Yorkshire was a county of paramount importance on both fronts. It had become a land of thriving sheep farming communities who provided a large proportion of the wool for the cloth, much of which was exported. It was also widely exalted for its arable farming. Trade for our cloth plummeted and economically the country was at a dangerously low ebb. The lower classes saw their chance and took it. They weren't interested in economics. They were now a force to be reckoned with and with their services in desperate demand, they decided they could name their price. The landed gentry had no choice – they now had to pay for hired help. Parliament tried to intervene with official guidelines, but failed. The workers had a voice at last and the class struggle had begun. Life would never be the same again for either the upper or lower classes . . . and this applied to all those who lived in the parish of Hornby.

There is little doubt the majority of the inhabitants of Hornby, Hackforth and Ainderby fell victim to the dreadful plague, if for no other reason than their geographical situation. What chance did they stand against an invisible and deadly enemy? Of course, once it hit a small community such as Ainderby, the effect was devastating. The monks would have done their best to tend the sick, but apart from prayers for their patients' souls there would be little comfort. Here at Ainderby, as at Hackforth and Hornby, doubtless the inadequate dwellings of the peasant victims would have been torched whilst a communal grave would have been used for the dead. The ultimate effect on these villages would have been near extinction while the plague also struck men of nobler rank.

Some 70 years later, in 1434, the presiding Earl of Richmond's days were also numbered. That esteemed gentleman's title and estates, including the parish of Hornby, reverted to the Crown when the young King Henry VI, aged 13 years, decided to reclaim his lands – or at least his advisors did. His country was being badly managed by a council of ever-quarrelling lords and with the wars in France being lost, his people were becoming sorely divided. This resulted in many of the high-ranking nobles being forced to relinquish their power and their lands with it. It appears the poor Earl of Richmond was just one of the victims of the great upheaval who lost his castle, his status and probably his head (as was the custom then)! However, being a valuable asset it was essential this prestigious and extensive estate of Richmondshire, as it had become known, in the North Riding of Yorkshire, be kept in the royal family for safekeeping and so Henry VI's half brother, Edmund Tudor, was bestowed the honour.

Ah, Tudor, there is an interesting name. He was the son of Henry V's widow queen – Henry VI's French mother, Catherine – and Owen Tudor, who had been Henry V's squire and, after his sire's death in France, had raised himself to, firstly, clerk of the Queen's wardrobe and then her legal but unauthorised husband. They had three sons and a daughter. Henry VI, being a pious man, fully recognised his responsibilities despite the fact he had not given permission for his lady mother to marry, which was his right. After her death, and the dispatching of Owen Tudor to the Tower for his misdeed in marrying the Queen, he brought two of his half-brothers, Edmund and Jasper, to court (what happened to the others is not certain) and they were brought up according to their status. Jasper was later made Earl of

Pembroke. Their father did escape from the Tower back to Wales and fought on the side of the Lancastrians in the wars that were to come. Meanwhile Edmund, destined to become the father of Henry Tudor – founder of the Tudor dynasty as Henry VII – ventured north to take up residence in Richmond Castle.

Of course, the new overlord would have taken his new responsibilities very seriously and taken every precaution to ensure that his new domain continued to be both efficiently and profitably run by the various incumbents of his lands, which extended far beyond the comparatively small bounds of the parish of Hornby. Nevertheless, the estate he inherited would have been a far different one to that originally overseen by his predecessors. The King's move to reclaim titles and estates all over the kingdom precedented not only great upheavals in overall management, but marked the beginning of a new era for old England – the seeds of which had been sown some 50 years earlier – in what became known as the Peasants' (albeit unsuccessful) Revolt – a result of the lower classes' demands following the backlash of the Black Death, which had left the country in crisis. Basically, it was a cry for equal opportunities: the peasants had something to offer and the country needed them.

Now along came the young Henry VI, whose main interests were in architecture, scholarship and music. He founded King's College, Cambridge, and Eton, and was also devoted to the worship of God. Despite his preoccupations, however, he also had one great desire, which was for his common people to live in ordered communities and have regular lifestyles. Whether by accident or design, in this aspect he achieved some modicum of success, since there were changes taking place that had a revolutionary effect and were virtually to eradicate the feudal system from England's soil once and for all. Now the Covells at Ainderby, the Conyers at Hornby and all other holders of manorial estates throughout the kingdom had become employers and were obliged by new laws to pay a wage of some sort to everyone in service on their lands. In other words, the demands of the much needed workforce at the end of the previous century were now made law for all the lower classes. Some farmers even began renting two or three fields from their lords, setting themselves up as free yeoman farmers. Many also built themselves a decent house and employed one or two peasants to work their land. Although they still had to provide the lord of the manor with a good helping of the produce from their efforts, they had risen from the lower ranks to form a new middle class. The lower classes gained recognition at last.

The manor house at Ainderby had also undergone subtle changes. The Covells had decided to expand and now a second stone block house had purposefully been built parallel to the original. The original's upper storey continued to house the main hall where all the administration of the estate was dealt with, but the Covells no longer slept at one end of it within a small space partitioned off for the purpose. No, they now had private chambers in the upper storey of the second block house with room for guests as the occasion demanded. The floors of both these buildings were constantly strewn with rushes, mixed with herbs to give a sweet smell that masked the stench of medieval England. Although I admire the initiative, I could well imagine this early form of potpourri being a danger to your health, bearing in mind the only source of illumination in those days was the burning of tallow candles, which would often be carelessly placed amongst the rushes at night. Hmm. Perhaps that's why some 'bright spark' invented the forerunner of the chamber pot – a bucket strategically placed under or by the bed – which at least saved 'hot footing' it to the nearest well, even if it did dampen the ardour of the occupiers of the bed! However, the lower classes on the manor would have had none of these problems. That is, they may have progressed to using a bucket by this time, especially at night, but they still didn't have the comfort of a proper bed or the luxury of tallow candles burning well into the night. Instead, when the sun went down they curled up on their wooden pallets or rush mats around the dying embers of the fire that had cooked their supper, the aroma of which would still prevail on the air since sweet herbs too were a luxury they could never afford. (Let's hope they kept their bucket outside!)

Although life at Ainderby was improving in all directions and it was now a far more organised country estate, King Henry VI was having problems. Within 20 years the country was to be divided again, this time for his very Crown. Richard of York put down the challenge and in 1455 the Wars of the Roses began. Richard had acted as protector when the King had been indisposed with 'sickness', and as a direct descendant of Edward III, many believed him to have more royal blood running through his veins than the King. During the ensuing six long years the hillsides of England's various landscapes were often littered with the glowing embers of camp fires in the opposing camps of York and Lancaster, whilst barons and their knights discussed their strategy for the coming conflict within the relative security of their tents. In the morning before the first hint of dawn lightened the darkened earth, the squires would stir, knowing well their masters had not slept but spent the night in silent deliberation on whether the morrow would bring them safe to victory or a sleep, very different from the one that evaded them this night, from which there would be no awakening in this life. The squires would make no comment, for by now the camp would be bustling with the sound of men preparing for battle: the clink of chain-mail and the clank of armour; the echo of pikestaffs being playfully clipped between friendly comrades; the scratch of metal as swords were honed; and the clump of horses hooves on the sod as they were led to where their heavy load waited under the paling sky that stirred the shine of glistening metal and proved that time waits for no man. Then with prayers said, stallions mounted and the foot soldiers filed, with banners high and minds focused, the procession left to take up its relevant position on the waiting battlefield.

Grandson of the first Sir John at Hornby, Sir John Conyers, lord of the manor of Hornby Castle, nearby Langthorne and Crakehall and many others, rode for the Yorkists. He had married Margerie Darcy in 1431, and so linked his name with one of the most powerful families in the north of England, but that didn't matter now.

With yet another battle to fight, no doubt Margerie and all the other soldiers' women were united in one thought: would their men-folk come home safely? Sadly, within a few short years, Margerie would know the pain of losing a son in battle.

Families had of necessity become divided. If one brother had worked for a knight or lord whose loyalty was with Lancaster and the other brother worked for a knight or lord whose loyalty was with York, so the brother would have to fight brother when it came to battle. So it was during the wars. Both the Yorkists and the Lancastrians had their share of victories and defeats. Henry bribed Yorkist soldiers with a pardon if they surrendered. Ironically, Henry's battle commander at

🙞 A Feudal Manor House *circa* 1066 🙜

Northampton deserted to the Yorkists, which resulted in the King's capture. Richard of York managed to convince Parliament to give him the right of succession on Henry's death. It was a time for reflection when, as the flickering flame of burning wax lingered long into the night, the people of England deliberated on the outcome of such turbulent times. Then Richard made the mistake of venturing north to where Henry's wife had gathered an army of 150,000 men. He was slain at the battle of Wakefield in December 1460, as was his second son, Edmund. Richard's eldest son, Edward, was devastated and in the mood for revenge. Towards the end of March 1461 it came in the shape of the Battle of Towton, near York – only 40 miles from Ainderby. It was here, with his cousin, the Earl of Warwick, by his side, that Edward fought his greatest battle. It took place during a violent snowstorm and was the bloodiest of the wars. He had already had victory in the south and had marched on London to claim his Crown. But Towton was different. The battle raged on until the earth was strewn with the bodies of 28,000 men and the victorious King Edward IV of England then rode triumphantly into York, once a city that held fast for the House of Lancaster, but was at that time divided. Sir John Conyers of Hornby survived and was there to witness the tumultuous welcome for their new king when no one dared question his right to the Crown of England. As for the poor deposed Henry, he was imprisoned.

It has to be assumed, since there is no reliable evidence, that the Covells of Ainderby were also unable to detach themselves from the political intrigues of the wars. It is difficult, however, to assess whether they would have expressed allegiance to the house of Lancaster or shown preference for the house of York, just as their neighbours the Conyers did. It must be remembered that Henry had reclaimed his lands and, being that the presiding Earl of Richmond was of royal blood, it could be easily assumed their loyalties were to their Lancastrian king. Perhaps they were, but any such allegiances were soon to be dangerous and somewhat pointless as far as the Covells were concerned. No doubt it was around this time that Richmond Castle was vacated by the Tudor offspring, Edmund, who retired diplomatically to France, to view the Lancastrian fate from a distance. The new king, Edward IV, wasted no time in making his presence felt in their absence. Realising the importance of the northern stronghold at Richmond, he bestowed the title and the castle on his brother George, Duke of Clarence, and so the residents of Richmondshire had a new royal personage in their midst, this time a Yorkist. What impact this had on the local gentry is not recorded but doubtless any adversity to the new king or his kin would have been considered extremely unhealthy. Although the Conyers, of course, had nothing to fear.

Unlike his brother, however, George was weak and gullible. Eight years later in 1469, there were uprisings in the north instigated by the one time 'Kingmaker' – the King's 'loyal' cousin – the Earl of Warwick. A member of the powerful Neville family, his family seat was Middleham Castle, not far from Ainderby – or Hornby Castle, for that matter. Anyway, he may have had much influence in the crowning of Edward but then he turned traitor, partly due to Edward's secret marriage to Elizabeth Woodville but also in protest at the heavy taxes levied on the northern landowners on their extensive estates – taxes raised by Edward's advisors but sanctioned by the King and his unpopular queen. The Nevilles and the Woodvilles were known rivals. Warwick openly declared he'd switched his loyalty to Henry VI and his partner in crime was none other than the King's easily influenced brother, George, Duke of Clarence (nice family, weren't they?). Now here's the best bit. With George holding the manor at Catterick as well as Richmond Castle he was a near neighbour of Hornby Castle and its residents. Guess who marched south with the armies in rebellion against their king alongside George? Sir John Conyers, ex-loyal and victorious soldier of his king, together with his eldest son – also Sir John – another Conyers who had made a powerful match. He had married into the powerful Neville family by way of Alice Neville, daughter of William Neville, brother of the King's mother, Cicely, and therefore cousin to the King. However, this was only part of her pedigree. Through another of Cicely's brothers she was also cousin to the rebellious Earl of Warwick. What a dangerous position these Conyers found themselves in. At the famous Battle of Edgcote in Northamptonshire in 1469 they paid the price. Alice Neville was widowed and Margerie Conyers mourned a son when Sir John the younger was slain 'in his stirrups', despite the fact his father, Sir John the elder, was victorious.

The result of this uprising was that poor Henry was now brought out of 'mothballs' and reinstated as king, although now virtually mad, whilst Edward was held in Middleham Castle as 'guest' of his errant cousin, the Earl of Warwick, before being forced to flee to France. Later, he returned to do battle with Warwick, who met his end at Barnet. Henry's formidable wife, Margaret, was captured after seeing their son killed at the Battle of Tewkesbury. She languished in prison for four years before being ransomed. As for poor Henry, he ended up in the Tower where he was murdered in 1471. Sir John Conyers senior survived by not using his real name during these troubles – talk about hedging your bets! A year later, when King Edward was in the north, Sir John made his peace with his king and was made sheriff of Yorkshire. Not only that but in 1478 – only eight years later – George of Clarence, the King's rebel brother, forfeited his estates, which included the Manor at Catterick, and guess who was granted it for life by the King? You've got it: Sir John Conyers. Mind you, I don't think George had a choice about losing his estates, since he was held prisoner by his brother, King Edward, for treason. George subsequently drowned in a butt of malmsey wine whilst being held captive. Hmm. That meant the Conyers now had Hornby, Holtby and Catterick as well as many other manors and estates in the area and beyond. As for Richmond Castle, the title and the castle were bestowed on Edward's youngest brother, the future Richard III, who on the Earl of Warwick's death had also been given Middleham.

From records that are available, a Richard Covell was living in the manor house at Ainderby at this time with a wife and family and there is also evidence that, as with the Conyers, other members of the Covell family lived within the area. After all, we have to remember that by now both families had occupied their residences for nigh on 200 years – pretty old, weren't they? – and were therefore well established. However, whether the Covells were aware that the Conyers had ridden with the King's brother and Warwick or not, they certainly weren't as well connected or as powerful and influential as that family, and after eight years of relative peace under the reign of Edward IV, and with little to gain and much to lose if Henry VI was reinstated as king, it is doubtful that they, like many others in their position, would have become involved in what seems to have been a rather personal uprising on the part of the Earl of Warwick at Middleham. Instead, keeping their heads down, their eyes open and their mouths shut might have been the best policy. It is probable that the final overthrowing of Henry may well have been regarded as a blessing in disguise by the majority, bearing in mind the disruption his reign had brought down on them, although it is also probable that they were justifiably grateful that the Wars of the Roses had finally come to an end, whatever the outcome.

King Edward IV died in 1483, leaving his two young sons, Edward V and the Duke of York, in the care of his infamous brother Richard, who had become known as 'Lord of the North' and was loved by the Yorkshire people. Richard became king in 1483, but for only two brief years. He lost his crown and his life at the Battle of Bosworth Field and Henry Tudor, son of Edmund, was now on the throne. England had arrived at the Tudor dynasty.

Henry VII was a diplomatic man. Of the Lancastrian lineage, he married Elizabeth of York, Edward IV's daughter, to ensure the two houses were reunited. The Wars of the Roses had decimated the old feudal nobility, who Henry didn't want back. To make sure they never recovered their power he replaced them with wealthy merchants, country gentry, the yeoman farmers and other suitable sections of the community. Collectively they now formed the new middle class. The old ways had gone for good – or had they? – and to see that justice was fair in his new kingdom, Henry delegated more responsibility to justices of the peace, or local magistrates, as we know them today. How Henry's new policies affected the Covells personally is unclear, but they continued to hold the estate at Ainderby, although with all the various changes in feudal laws throughout this century the lives of the peasants of this small community, whose livelihood and homes were dependent on their continued employment on the manor, were made more tolerable and they were truly thankful – for a while.

By 1490 William Conyers had inherited the Hornby estate from his grandfather but he was not knighted until 1497. Henry VIII succeeded his father in 1509 and summoned William to Parliament in the same year. Thus William officially became the first Lord Conyers as well as constable of Richmond and Middleham castles. William's first marriage to Mary Scrope had been pre-arranged, but when he died in 1524 he was succeeded by his son Christopher, from his second marriage to Anne Neville. Thus Christopher became the second Lord Conyers.

✸❦ A Feudal Manor House *circa* 1066 ❦✷

Henry VIII, like his father Henry VII, served his country well, but after 20 years he grew restless for a male heir and wanted rid of his wife, Catherine of Aragon, in favour of a much younger and more attractive mate in the shape of Anne Boleyn. Henry deliberated on an English divorce after the Pope withheld his consent to dissolving the King's marriage to Catherine on the grounds that she had been his sister-in-law and in 1529 summoned what became known as the Reformation Parliament – an indication of his desperation. Christopher Conyers, who had been knighted in 1523, was amongst those summoned and attended this Parliament from 1529 to 1536, where he was to bear witness to some of the most controversial and dramatic years of England's history.

The Reformation had originally broken out in Germany when a friar, Martin Luther, attacked the supremacy of the Pope and the powers of the priests, simply believing that by faith in God and the reading of the Bible man could be saved. Henry had decried Luther's teachings and the Pope had rewarded him with a new title of 'Defender of the Faith'. Now Henry was obviously finding it useful to reconsider Luther's teachings and their merits. His new Parliament at last concluded he should approach the high bishops for their consent. However, the clergy supported Catherine, falling in line with the doctrine of the Church of Rome. He then became more forceful and instructed Parliament to put pressure on the clergy – in other words threaten them! The result was the Submission of the Clergy which gave Henry exactly what he wanted: control over the clergy's power to make laws for the Church.

The granting of his English divorce was in sight but he now needed the judicial ruling of his ageing Archbishop of Canterbury. It was not forthcoming. But Henry had been far-sighted. He had also obtained the prerogative to choose his own bishops and archbishops without papal consent. The archbishop conveniently died and Henry replaced him with the amicable Thomas Cranmer. Finally, in January 1533, he married the now pregnant Anne, feeling firmly confident that his first marriage to Catherine was invalid. In April, Cranmer completed the final details to grant Henry his long-awaited official English divorce.

However, Henry could not afford controversy. He needed the blessing of his churchmen in England but asking the reverend gentlemen to choose between loyalty to their Pope and loyalty to their king was not as straightforward as he had hoped. When it came to signing their approval to the Act of Supremacy, many faltered, which infuriated Henry. These holy men, many of whom were not without substantial wealth and power of their own that had been bestowed on them primarily to ensure their total unquestioning loyalty to their various monarchs down through the centuries, were now reluctant to acknowledge him – Henry – as head of their church in England and thereby risked losing his favour and their privileges out of loyalty to the papal seat. Henry was speechless. But not for long. If these devout men of the Church couldn't be persuaded by reason then he would threaten them. He decreed that those who did not sign the act would be found guilty of treason against their king; he was confident that they would then sign since such a crime demanded only one inevitable punishment.

Many of Henry's friends, including Sir Thomas More, chose their God over him. This dreadful sacrifice was the final price that Henry had to pay to secure his undisputed supremacy over the church and his divorce from the Pope, as from Catherine, would be absolute. Ironically, Henry's new position was decreed only months before he was to sign the death warrant of his second wife, Anne Boleyn. She had been unable to give him a male heir and worse, she would not renounce her daughter's claim to the throne. Falsely accused of incest with her brother, she was executed in May 1536. Her legacy to England was a daughter who was to become one of England's most respected monarchs: Queen Elizabeth I. In the same year Catherine also died. Henry did not mourn. Instead he married Jane Seymour. As for the Reformation Parliament, it had done much to try to placate a monarch whose will had alienated most of his once loyal and trusted followers, but it no longer served a purpose. Henry was now listening to voices other than those who had his and England's best interests at heart.

All these intrigues at Henry's court in London may seem far removed from the comparatively peaceful haven of Ainderby Myers, but they created insecurity in his people throughout the kingdom. The thoughts and fears of Henry's subjects, however, were of little consideration to him at this time. He was indeed possessed and, although an intelligent and talented man, many were genuinely fearful for his sanity. His advisors at court had the same fears as his people, but learnt to hide them well. That is except for Thomas Cromwell, who succeeded Cardinal Wolsey as Henry's principal minister and had the King's confidence. He reputedly abused his privileged position by often manipulating the vulnerable Henry's decisions at this time, not only to enforce his own ideals on the reformation of the Church, but also to further his political powers. Cromwell's religious tendency was definitely inclined to the new and unpopular Protestant faith. He was not alone. The new Archbishop Cranmer also shared that belief, as had Anne Boleyn. The people at court and outside it mistrusted Henry's closest confidants and they mistrusted Henry.

As well as the priests, the monks too had always been greatly revered. They were regarded by their power of prayer and other known talents to be another source of direct contact with God and thereby of upmost importance to the spiritual welfare of the community. Henry was never foolish enough to tamper with the priests' role in the Church but, with Thomas Cromwell sowing the seed, he now ordered the dissolution of the monasteries – an act that was to secure his notoriety in his own time and for future generations.

The people were horrified as between 1535 and 1539 the King's men ransacked the abbeys, taking all that was of value, and stone by stone destroying years of hard labour and toil. Scars of their work are still scattered all over England and a fair number are concentrated in North Yorkshire. The King then sold off these vast estates to laymen. The monks were spared nothing and many lost their lives trying to protect the treasured possessions of their faith. Most fled, taking what little they could carry and went into hiding, others became priests or just ordinary laymen. There were numerous uprisings against the King's actions, particularly in the north. The most well-known of these, in which the monks played a vital role, was led by Robert Aske in 1536 and became known as the Pilgrimage of Grace. Sadly, it ended in the death of the rebels.

But it was not only his religious orders that Henry had problems with. In 1537 his most prominent northern lords and churchmen attended a meeting at Pontefract Castle. They were enraged and preparing, no doubt, for their own rebellion against their monarch. Whether their concerns were based on religion or self interest cannot be known for sure, but judging by the prestigious guest list which represented more or less all the major landholders in the north, the latter option may have given them the motivation. Among the celebrities in attendance were the lords Scrope, Neville and Darcy, whose family trees by this time all made mention of a Conyers and yes, he was there too – Christopher, second Lord Conyers of Hornby. In 1531, as one of Henry's loyal peers, he had willingly signed his agreement that the Pope should not have supremacy over the King if he refused his papal consent to the much-wanted divorce. Now here he was, yet another Conyers, involved in yet another treacherous act against yet another monarch! But yet again fate decreed that a Conyers would get away with treason. The lords were betrayed and most were hanged or worse. Thomas Darcy was executed on Tower Hill but Christopher Conyers escaped, only to die of natural causes two years later. Meanwhile, there was no hope for the poor monks either, despite attempts to stem the tide of the dissolution. Of course, they all had the sympathy of their various communities but to help them was tantamount to treason against Henry, both as king and head of the Church, and the price for such an act was just too high.

After 400 years, it was now time for the monks at Ainderby to leave too – or at least appear to. They may only have been lay brothers but the land they worked at Ainderby still belonged to a holy order and as such would have to be relinquished to the Crown with vacant possession, otherwise its reputation as a 'religious' house could put Ainderby and its community in great jeopardy, notwithstanding the fact they no longer used the private chapel but undoubtedly attended Hornby Church for regular services. Furthermore, once the Crown had obtained possession of the land, it would then make the Covells an offer (they couldn't refuse!) to purchase it. Not being attached to the main religious estates, this was an easy and profitable option for dealing with such remnants of land all over England as far as the King's coffers were concerned. No such options were likely from the Crown for the lay brothers. They had taken no vows but that was of no concern to Henry. If they stayed, by definition, they represented the monasterial establishments that he wanted dissolved and they would risk their lives and the lives of those who supported them. Their faith and their habit were against them. To flee would have meant they had nowhere to go, except their priory, which would have probably already been demolished. But they did have a third choice and one that many lay brothers in their position would have opted for. To discard their habit and become part of the community where they could at least live out their days in familiar surroundings, doing the work they had always done. Whether this is indeed the choice the monks at Ainderby made is not recorded (well it wouldn't be, would it?). However, what is recorded is that the title of the lands owned by Richmond Priory at Ainderby was transferred into the name of Covell during the period of dissolution, which conveys the intended message that the monks also 'left'.

However, people were wary and so were the King's men. The latter would not have dared leave a stone unturned – particularly in the north, where rebellion was rife. And so the dreaded day would have come when the Covells of Ainderby would have found themselves hosts to these trusted messengers of the King. Instinctively they would have known where the sympathy of the Covells would lie, but with the monks having made a tactful exit by this time, the Covells would at least have been in a more favourable position to convey to their formidable guests that their loyalty to their king was beyond question and that there were no monks hiding in the stonework, nor any monasterial valuables concealed about the place. Since the family survived they must have been convincing but was their faith so easily shaken, or were they, like so many of the King's subjects, purely acting out a charade for their monarch's benefit and secretly holding onto their old loyalties and beliefs (i.e. their association with the Church of Rome)? The answer to this will become clear soon. As a footnote, despite provocation and much to the amazement of many, there were no reprisals from Catholic powers and the Pope did not fully excommunicate Henry, or England for that matter. The door was always left open.

Eight years later, in 1547, having married six times and leaving his one sickly son of nine, King Edward VI, to rule after him, old 'enry died. Although he achieved much to the good of England during his reign, not least the establishment of the Royal Navy with a substantial fleet of ships, Henry VIII primarily maintains his prominent place in our history books for three main reasons, each of which is inextricably linked to the next: his six wives, the creation of the Church of England and the religious unrest he inflicted on his people, the scars of which were to criss-cross the reigns of many of Henry's successors for generations to come. After Edward's six brief years, during which time the Catholics and Protestants jostled for supremacy, Catherine of Aragon's daughter Mary became queen. She became known as Bloody Mary after marrying King Philip of Spain and resolving to have all confirmed Protestants burnt at the stake in her attempt to re-establish the Catholic faith as the sole religion of England. In doing so she drove England to more or less a complete conversion to the Protestant religion and, alas, even her husband left her. Within five years she too was dead and at last Elizabeth I, Anne Boleyn's daughter, was Queen of England and remained so for 45 years.

She was born and crowned as a Catholic, but was not an extremist so she caused Parliament to reverse Mary's return to Roman Catholicism and revived the Protestant Laws, with some modifications to please moderate Catholics. So the new independent Anglican Church was born and became firmly established, much as it exists today. Unlike her father, Elizabeth was not susceptible to manipulation via flattery or anything else. She let neither her advisors nor her heart rule her common sense. As much as her father had desired frequent matrimonial interludes, she desired none. She vowed to rule as a Virgin Queen, only married to her people. Notoriously strong willed, she brought order to her court and her country. Her father's great foresight in founding a substantial Royal Navy proved to be one of Elizabeth's greatest assets – not only to defend this country against such onslaughts as the legendary Spanish Armada in 1588, but to enhance trade and encourage business. To this end her ships ploughed the remotest seas even as far as the Far East and Russia. However, this also gave birth to a new aristocracy, the enriched traders. Now the remaining crude barons of earlier times were gradually being replaced by more polished and elegant courtiers. But the poor were getting poorer under these new social changes, and this poverty and degradation of the lower classes was becoming a desperate problem since it affected approximately half the population. The feudal system was all but gone and no longer offered them any stability or protection. The Poor Act was introduced to assist those looking for work, but there were also those new innovations, the almshouses, for those who could no longer support themselves, either through circumstance, health or age.

Meanwhile, the physical evidence of the late medieval and Tudor dynasties enhanced, or not, the landscape of rural England, which was now impregnated with the vanity of their age. Having discovered that materialistic attributes such as the length of an upper gallery, the number of windows, the grandest of entrances, the addition of wings and even the height of the chimney pots could positively make a statement to the undiscerning eye about the owner and the extent of his financial worth, these vast brick or stone structures were imposed on our countryside whether we wanted them or not. Many villages and towns also received a facelift in this age of modernisation but here the addition of more modest and more tasteful timber-framed buildings did for the most part make a pleasing contribution to the overall appearance of the place and in many cases still does. Modernisation visited Ainderby too.

By the second half of the fifteenth century it was obvious the two-block houses were no longer adequate or convenient for yet a further generation of Covells and subsequently for impression and convenience they were now connected by a new ground-floor main hall which was probably initially open to the roof. Here the Covells could receive guests and entertain in style. To the western end of the hall a large arched fireplace was installed in bold stone – the chimney of which, lined with brick, abutted the wall of the west wing and rose to the roof. It is still there today and grandly presides over Val's son's lounge. There was another fire on the other side of this wall in the west wing itself and the double-backed chimney still dominates the pantile roof of the house. As for the first-floor solar or main hall in the east wing, now redundant, it was subsequently divided into individual chambers which were mainly used for sleeping or private entertaining. Perhaps Richard Covell would have held confidential meetings with some important conveyor of news on the political issues of the day in these rooms. The kitchens, dairy and other utility rooms remained at ground-floor level with one or two private rooms off the main hall, known as parlours – my granny had one of those! Of course, there was one added luxury: the installation of an indoor staircase (no, not a loo – yet). It led from the hall to a new first-floor narrow hallway or gallery which also linked the upper floors of the east and west wings of the house. This gallery had small sliding casement windows which faced out northwards whilst the

51

inward side had a wooden gallery rail providing a good view of the hall below. These changes were well in keeping with the fashion of the day. (I suppose you could say it wasn't so much keeping up with the Joneses as keeping up with the Tudors.) Anyway, eventually at Ainderby another chamber was added over the hall, leading off the gallery which then became enclosed, much as it is today. There is a whisper that it is haunted, perhaps because it conjures up pictures of the old tales – true or false – of haunted galleries. If it is I have never seen the ghost, but having said that I wouldn't walk down it in the dark either. Just in case!

Apart from the house, other changes at Ainderby were now taking place under the influence of the Elizabethan age. Records show a John Smelt held a portion of land here in 1579 that his son William apparently inherited after him. He died in November 1627 and was buried at Hornby. They were in the business of iron-smelting, which is probably how they acquired such an 'attractive' surname. It substantiates the theory that individuals of all classes were now in demand for their own skills in their own right and the Smelts, at least, obviously had a thriving concern on Ainderby land, providing their services to the area for a number of years. As well as new tradesmen, an increase in yeoman farming was also making inroads into the parish of Hornby and with the serfs having substantially been replaced by paid labour, much of the landscape of the area began to change. The peasant communities were gradually disappearing, forced to move on in the hope of finding work and shelter elsewhere, as the land they worked was sold off or given over to sheep pasture to feed a rapidly expanding wool trade. Their dwellings became vacant, and also began to disappear. These poor hapless people had once again become the undeserving victims of a new, more prosperous era which caused a population explosion in the middle classes and nothing but further degradation for the lower classes, who now reached a new level of poverty. It was the end of an era for them and the end of an era for Ainderby too. What the future held for this one-time feudal manor, now purely a substantial family home and estate, and the people that remained in the service of the ancient parish of Hornby is now written into the history books of England.

Few can deny that we owe much to the renowned Tudor dynasty. During their successive reigns, spanning 118 years, little remained untouched by their hands. However, as history was to show, the religious wounds Henry VIII had inflicted on England during his reign were slow to heal and many were to suffer the consequences for years to come. Despite Elizabeth's attempts to find a happy medium with her Anglican Church, where the Protestants and milder Catholics could regularly worship side by side, there was no peace. The Pope intervened in 1570, excommunicating Elizabeth and forbidding all Catholics to attend their parish churches, which contravened English law. Eventually fines were introduced for those who did not attend church, but many paid, preferring to hold secret masses, which were also against the law. All these problems finally culminated in an act in 1582 that decreed that all Catholic clergy found in England ran the risk of execution. But the Catholic clergy had many sympathisers who offered these holy men sanctuary from the authorities. There are many houses still standing in England today where priest holes are still very much in evidence, substantiating the fact that those who lived beneath their roofs remained, during these troubled times, fiercely loyal to the Church of Rome and were prepared to risk their own lives by helping a revered member of the Catholic clergy. Ainderby was one of them.

There is little doubt that the double-backed chimney I mentioned earlier had more than one use. It conceals a cavity that rises from behind the brickwork of the fireplace on the ground floor to the upper floor and roof level which would have been ideal, if a trifle hot in winter. It appears to lead to a wider area at the upper floor of the house, since a small area of wall adjacent to the gallery and directly in line with the chimney sounds hollow when tapped. Of course, it is tempting to examine it all more closely but the passage from the fireplace has obviously been partially filled in and Val and Graham wouldn't take kindly to us demolishing the walls. However, what it undoubtedly substantiates is that the Covells, like their ancestors, never relinquished their loyalty to the Roman Catholic faith, as dangerous as it was, though their previous generation did convince the King's men otherwise during the dissolution.

By 1625 the Tudors had long gone and James I was no more. His son Charles I was on the throne, but sadly had inherited some of his father's bad habits. He arrogantly thought he had the royal prerogative to rule England as he saw fit, without seeking approval from Parliament. His extravagant tastes and a war with France led to his constant demands for more money, making him very unpopular with the majority of his people. He levied taxes and subsidies on everything and anything to get what he wanted and even the landed gentry did not escape. Parliament tried to intervene but he defiantly dismissed it in 1629 and ruled the country alone for 11 years until he ran out of money again. A staunch Anglican, he also inflicted his religious beliefs on his subjects and, like his father before him, had no tolerance of Puritans who had been strongly represented in the Parliament he had dismissed.

It was during these unsettling times that the Covells were to leave Ainderby. Their family had held this quiet corner of the parish of Hornby for nigh on 300 years. The changes their many generations had borne witness to, mainly influenced by the monarch of the time to whom they had sworn allegiance, were now firmly embedded in the landscape and the lives of the people who lived here. Irrevocable change – from the vulgar domination of the Normans and the stench of medieval poverty to the zest for trade, free enterprise and a more cultured society under the Tudors – had wielded its often uncompromising sword and slain the patience and the trust of so many hitherto loyal and goodly servants of the Crown.

Richard Covell and his family may have pondered on this change at the time. Despite the honourable lineage from which they descended, however, theirs was a new generation with more freedom of choice. With consecutive poor harvests and a massive slump in trade plunging England into a deep recession, undoubtedly the Covells suffered financial losses via their estate at Ainderby and investment in trade. There was also the King's incessant and unreasonable financial demands on a people already facing an economic crisis of their own and the intolerable situation of having no parliament to help fight their cause. There was also the problem of religion. The Covells were Roman Catholics and Charles I was not only intolerant of Puritans, but as an Anglican, the Church of Rome too. Although I have to admit to a little supposition here in assuming that these historic facts were the main issues surrounding the Covell's departure from Ainderby, I do not believe them to be far from the truth from what little information was made available to me, especially since the Covells not only left Ainderby but England. They would have undoubtedly known George

Calvert, who lived at Kiplin Hall just a few miles from Ainderby. A Roman Catholic himself, he was a founder of the Catholic State of Maryland in America and positively promoted emigration to the New World. It seems the Covells decided they would take their chances with this New World too. As for their home, the records show Ainderby Myers manor house and adjoining lands passed, unsurprisingly, into the hands of the Conyers Darcys at Hornby Castle – I told you there was a connection, I just took a long time getting there. The year was 1632.

However, it appears that for the first time in its long history the house was destined to remain empty for 32 years once the Covells had gone – or was it? From the records it was not until 1664, after the restoration of the monarchy in the shape of Charles II, that a Darcy and his wife Margaret actually moved into the house. In the intervening period it is interesting to note that the Conyers Darcys also obtained the Manor at Hackforth, which meant that they now owned the entire ancient parish of Hornby – an area of some 4,000 acres.

By 1640, with the threat of invasion from the Scots looming, Charles had decided to restore Parliament, but his plan backfired. Parliament immediately banned his right to personal rule and declared many of his fines and taxes illegal, but then it too went too far and became divided. The Puritans wanted more monumental reductions in the King's power and the power of his valued bishops, whom they despised. Thus the question of the King's sole right to rule was finally to plunge England once more into a bloody civil war: a conflict between the King and his Parliament who wanted to rule the country independently of him. Nobles and Anglicans aided Charles I and were known as Royalists. As for Parliament, they had the support of the Puritans and the trading and artisan classes. However, the divisions were still by no means clear cut. For instance, the wealthy did not necessarily support the King – oh, no. He had already hit them hard where it hurt – in their pockets. Many rejected the King's right to rule alone, having disapproved of his constant levying of new taxes with the threat of imprisonment if they didn't pay up.

It was the army that fought the Parliamentarian's war for them under the leadership of that staunch Puritan and country squire from Huntingdon, Oliver Cromwell. His men became known as Roundheads. During the Civil War, Cromwell and his armies marched all over Yorkshire and the Parliamentarians found a lot of sympathy within its boundaries. They had many temporary garrisons within its landscape and one was sited in close proximity to Hornby. It is recorded that the son of the fifth Lord Conyers, an Oxford graduate in law living in the south, did his bit for the Royalist cause, but his father's loyalties are not so well recorded except that he and his wife remained in residence at Hornby Castle and presumably, since he died in 1689, he survived the ravages of the Civil Wars by placating whatever side he bumped into – not unlike his ancestors!

We should not be too harsh in our judgement, though. The Royalists and the Parliamentarians relied heavily upon local hospitality for their respective armies and their visits were often more dreaded than welcomed, even by sympathisers to their own cause. In general, it was accepted that those not involved directly in the wars had no need to express allegiance to either side. This was a political conflict of power. However, local people were fearful of the way they were treated by the various fighting forces and eventually peace associations were formed by bands of men to keep order by negotiation with the armies in their respective localities. In part this worked, but to some headstrong leaders of the forces these unofficial organisations had no authority to enforce restrictions on the armies, either politely or otherwise, and so their bid for calm was not always successful. The Parliamentarians in particular caused horrendous amounts of damage wherever they went – vandalism and theft were common and the Puritans ransacked churches, smashing the adornments. Notwithstanding these administrative problems, the Parliamentarians won many battles in Yorkshire and on more than one occasion gained victory over the whole county.

The battered Royalists suffered much at the hands of their opponents. Even their fine houses did not escape. They were often left unattended whilst their owners were off fighting for their king and many were known to serve as sanctuaries for the Royalists in hiding from Cromwell's men. Tunnels were often hastily dug under these buildings to provide further concealment or a means of escape, although some already possessed such assets from the days when Catholics lived in fear of their lives and priest holes, secret rooms and underground tunnels were all used to hide the truth from the authorities. Cromwell's men were not stupid. They knew that the torch was the only way of being sure that any occupants of such houses were completely dealt with and it was often applied without discretion. Occasionally a Royalist house would be taken over by a Parliamentarian official who would take up residence and do his duty as superintendent for a specific area.

I doubt the torch was ever taken to Ainderby in its vacated state, but then Hornby Castle, Holtby and Hackforth also appear to have remained comparatively unscathed. That does not mean they were not raided by the Roundheads – in fact it is almost certain they were, bearing in mind the close proximity of a Roundhead garrison and their mistrust of sympathisers. Although not officially recorded, the now sparse community of Ainderby Myers, with its, I assume, vacated manor house, might even have proved an ideal opportunity for the shrewd Lord Conyers to show the Parliamentarians his support. He could have offered the use of the manor to their commanders to pacify their curiosity as to his true loyalty, knowing, as he probably did, that his son was fighting for a very different cause.

Between the Civil Wars, Charles rallied much support, particularly from the Scots, who he had pacified with promises, and Independents within Parliament. Cromwell and the army were furious, and in 1649 the second Civil War broke out, but the Scots were defeated at Preston. Cromwell was now out for blood. The army marched on London, their destination the Commons, where they took their revenge on their opponents, leaving what became known as the 'Rump' Parliament. This body of men, mainly Independents, were now forced to suffer the trauma of putting their king on trial as a public enemy and tyrant. Of course, it made a mockery of the law and there could only be one outcome if they were to do their work according to the dictatorship of Cromwell. They found their prideful king guilty and, to the horror of nearly all Englishmen and the whole of Europe, Charles I was sentenced to meet his executioner on 30 January 1649. He met his death with dignity and sympathy for those who wanted no part of it. Cromwell earnt himself much contempt for his actions from a good many of his hitherto loyal supporters. Not least, it is recorded, from a Lord Fairfax of Yorkshire who had fought well and hard for Cromwell's cause. In the event, Cromwell became Lord Protector of England, which was now a republic for the first and only time in its history, and all the surviving communities of England and Wales, Scotland and Ireland shuddered at the cost in human life: it is estimated that 84,830 men were killed fighting in England, 27,895 in Scotland and in Ireland an unbelievable 618,000 – nearly half the population. If we also include the appalling loss of life attributed to bubonic plague and typhoid fever during this period, England alone lost 3.7 per cent of its population during the Civil Wars, whereas the Second World War claimed 0.6 per cent of her population.

It is probable the Parliamentarians continued to use the manor house at Ainderby during their further troubles with the Scots and afterwards, since Cromwell is known to have retained several administrative bases in the north. How the Conyers Darcys responded to the death of the King is not known, but bearing in mind Fairfax's response, it probably can be assumed they felt equal disgust. It was not until after Cromwell's death in 1658 and the subsequent restoration of the Crown in 1660 that life returned to anything like normal for England. By this time there is evidence that Ainderby had suffered considerable damage. It has to be assumed that when the Conyers Darcys took ownership in 1632 the manor had been in good order and that during the ten years that elapsed until the outbreak of the Civil Wars it was not totally abandoned, since it became an integral part of the Hornby estate. What is also well documented is that the manor house's main access had been from the south. Today it is entered from the north, via the cart track and the small court, which is spanned by an archway that bears the shields of the Conyers and the Darcys with the keystone, partially indiscernible, dated 16—. There is little doubt this archway once served the purpose of a fascia to a porch-way of the house. Obviously, however, having been found wanting it was thought precious enough to preserve and erect in its present position. More pointedly, the south ends of the east and west wings of the house also demonstrate new and altered stonework which suggest that Ainderby received some sort of damage from the south. It may have been sustained during the conflicts either at the hands of marauding Royalists taking their vengeance out on their opposing gentry in the area, or the Parliamentarians resident at the time. It is very unlikely that Cromwell's men actually did the damage, but not impossible to believe if the Darcys showed their reluctance to support the cause after the execution of Charles, when the Scots were still giving

Cromwell problems. Whatever happened, we shall never rightly know.

At last, as I mentioned earlier, in 1664 a Darcy did take up residence at Ainderby Myers. How long the Darcys lived there and what became of them is not known. The subsequent plague in London of 1665 and the Great Fire which wiped it and most of the city out in 1666 had little impact on Yorkshire in general or Ainderby in particular. As indeed did James II's three years of disastrous rule from 1685 to 1688. Part of his problem was his obsession with his new-found faith, which was Catholic to the extreme. England had been here before and now wanted to preserve the Protestant faith. In the end, a plot was launched to send James packing by inviting his Protestant daughter Mary and her husband, William of Orange, to invade England and depose him. Of course there had to be insiders on this plot, and one of them was none other than a John Conyers, son of the sixth Lord Conyers who had fought for the Royalists in the Civil Wars. Anyway, William and Mary arrived on our shores and met little resistance. Daddy fled to France, where he died some years later. Now England was to be ruled by a monarchy that was a parliamentary institution much as it is today.

Meanwhile, there was still a small community thriving on the Ainderby lands, as is proved by records I unearthed at the North Yorkshire County Records Office. These confirm that well into the Georgian age various families occupied the estate. Their names, such as Atkinson, Nilky, Midgley, Broad, Johnson and King, together with their entries, denote the very different environment now prevailing in this ancient parish. The records identify them as household servants and estate workers who were free to intermarry (and indeed did), produce their own family and have a home at Ainderby, in most cases, it would appear, until they died. In the absence of much of the documentation of the parish for this period (which was destroyed by fire), this importantly suggests a family of note still occupied the manor house at Ainderby Myers.

As for Hornby Castle, it appears that from the end of the seventeenth century through the eighteenth century its subsequent generations of incumbents either chose to live in it or not as their obligations allowed. After all, this celebrated family that had begun with a Margaret St Quintin and Sir John Conyers in the late fourteenth century now embraced, through marriage, some of the most prestigious families in England, including the Darcys, the Scropes of Bolton Castle, the Nevilles (the 'Kingmaker' and Edward IV's relatives), the Bellasis family of Newburgh and the Osbornes (dukes of Leeds). In fact it was at the end of the eighteenth century that the sixth Duke made Hornby his permanent residence as did his successors until the tenth Duke's death in 1927, when at last Hornby Castle was put on the market for the first time in its long life. The manors of Holtby, Hackforth and Ainderby – one by one, as I have indicated – had by the Georgian era also fallen into private ownership. The eighteenth century had arrived. The old ways were gone . . . . forever.

With the Georgian age came Georgian style, hand in hand with Georgian elegance. Together the Georgians finally eradicated the remaining scars of the Civil Wars. Encouraged by a new and affluent society, the grand and imposing facades of the Georgian country houses spoke volumes for those who occupied them, whilst row upon row of Georgian terraces were born to house traders and commercially successful businessmen in towns all over England. Towns favoured for their industry, towns favoured for their close proximity to the ports, even towns favoured for that new innovation, the holiday by the sea, were all bedecked in Georgian architecture and still are today. However, since the Georgians and, indeed, the Victorians had little impact on Ainderby or its surroundings and there is no evidence to prove otherwise, I have left any further comment on these particular ages until my final chapter on York, since their impact on that city did have a lasting effect.

As for Ainderby Myers, the last record of a servant here was towards the end of the eighteenth century. Approximately 150 years later it was to become the property of the Andersons (and still is) and through them I am proud to say that the Watts family, although unrecorded until now, have also left their firm and affectionate imprint on Ainderby's long history. To testify to its remarkable age, 3 ft-thick stone walls still clad the original manorial block house – now the east wing – and just after you enter the wing you come face to face with an ancient stone archway, which still retains some evidence of extremely strong iron door hinges. Just inside the arch the roof is beamed with gnarled oak, which would indicate that this was a main-porch door with probably one or two steps leading down into the room – i.e. the floor level was once much lower than it is today. This ground-floor room once served as the chapel, with a dairy adjacent, and the archway once had a heavy oaken door attached to those hinges I mentioned. There was also a side entrance to this room when the monks were here. It always amuses me how short people must have been in bygone days, since most old doorways only seem to cope with people of 5 ft or so in height; the rest of us have to bow to the fact or take the consequences and many's the time my head has nearly come to grief against this door arch when I have been wearing high-heeled shoes!

Outside, between the east and west wings of this old house, is a small courtyard (now reduced by 8 ft or so in depth, due to modernisation in the twentieth century) reached via the old preserved archway I mentioned earlier. Val always jokes the date of 16— is probably the last time the house was modernised. (She could well be right – externally anyway.) However, I hasten to add that Val does not cook over an open fire, nor does she draw water from the beck or a well and we do not have to sleep on pallets scattered about the solar or great hall, as they did in medieval times. Oh, and there are flushing loos now! Regarding the solar – every self-respecting medieval house had one – if you stand in the little courtyard and look up towards the east wing there is a doorway which has been sealed, the top half of which now forms a window. It is at first-floor level and was reached by an outside staircase. This doorway was the old entrance to the solar, now our bedroom, which no longer occupies the entire first floor of the east wing. The solar has been conveniently divided into smaller rooms. Goodness knows what the de Endrebis or the Covells would make of it all.

Sometimes I find myself imagining how it would have been. The cold stone, the incessant aromas of an age when cleanliness was not considered a main ingredient of Godliness. The poor visibility even in daylight. Mind you, that probably didn't worry anyone by nightfall, bearing in mind that water at this time was considered unfit to drink so the poor lived on ale, whilst the better-off lived on wine. Everyone was too drunk to see straight anyway. As for visitors to these remote parts, no wonder they stayed overnight. Imagine arriving and leaving your horse in the courtyard with a waiting servant on hand to take the animal off to the stable. Then, having ascended the outside stone staircase to the solar, the lord of the manor bids you welcome with a goblet of wine or jug of ale for your efforts. After a chat and, probably, another few glasses of wine, imagine having to negotiate your way back down that now moving staircase and onto the back of your animal, hoping he knows the way because you've totally lost the ability to even negotiate your feet back into the stirrups.

As well as the manor house, there would have been stone ancillary buildings, such as a brewery for ale making, a meat store, stables and a mill. The original kitchens appear to have been behind the dairy in the east wing, which would be appropriate. This is roughly where Val's son, David, and his wife have theirs now, since they live in part of the wing which has been sealed off from the rest of the house and so provides them with a self-contained home of their own. Outside their kitchen door, in the yard is the site of one of the old wells that supplied earlier occupants with water. The attic of this east wing is also of interest. It does contain fireplaces, which implies that at some stage it was used as quarters, probably for servants, as was the custom in the late Georgian and Victorian eras. There is little of the west wing left to speculate on, the major part of it having been rebuilt and altered considerably. Bearing in mind its age and the fact that the original manor (the east wing) has survived a thousand years of history virtually intact, it is not surprising that the house has had to be remodelled from time to time to accommodate a more modern way of life, particularly since, except for a few years, it has always been occupied. As I said at the beginning, few of our old houses could have survived the medieval age down to the new Elizabethan era without having added a few mod cons and becoming a little bit more with it (as opposed to without it).

Ainderby Myers was a hive of industry, agriculturally speaking, between the twelfth and sixteenth centuries and the beautiful far-flung countryside that surrounds it with its rich fertile land is probably farmed in much the same way as it was through all those centuries. Of course, the methods have changed. Here at Ainderby, as elsewhere, teams of oxen were once the mainstay of ploughing. A carucate was the old measure for an area of land that could be worked by any one team in any one year and this varied between 120 and 180 acres. It is interesting to note from old records that these carucates were subject to a tax even back in Norman times. Apart from the luxury of an oxen-driven plough, most of the work in the fields was carried out manually by the local village workers, as already described. With only a few simple tools to assist them, the work was hard, the days long and they were little rewarded for their efforts. Slowly, through the generations, more efficient tools were introduced to help ease the burden for the farm workers, although most of these are now no more than exhibits in farming museums up and down the country. Even the old and trusted heavy farm horses have virtually gone forever. Gradually the heavy machinery has moved in to take their place on the land and the modern-day farmer is grateful. Although expensive, the demands on today's farmers are such that they could not survive without assistance. Despite the automated help, they are still a special breed of men. Their work is still hard. Their days are still long. Their reward is very meagre at times, but they survive just as their forebears did, except now it is they that mostly reap the benefit of what they sow and not a lord of the manor – thank goodness.

Thus you will find no servants to assist with the daily labours at Ainderby Myers. Val and Graham, with Val's three sons, manage the farm and obviously work very hard to maintain it. Not only are there 423 acres of land with the annual crops of barley, wheat and corn to sow, cultivate and harvest, but there is, in addition, an abundance of livestock too. Of course, there are the sheep who need tending to. Tupping time starts in November when the rams are put in with the ewes. This hopefully results in a good lambing season, which may start any time from February onwards. All farmers value a good lambing. A good ewe can lamb every year for six or seven years, producing for the farmer on average nine or ten lambs in its lifetime. Of course, these figures can only be taken as a guide as they depend on a number of factors, including the breed of sheep. In any case, it's a very special time of year but it can bring its own set of problems for man and beast alike. The winters up here in North Yorkshire can be very harsh and February may bring no relief. My heart goes out to those poor farmers who are called from their beds on bitterly cold nights to tend a distressed ewe in a bitter north-easterly wind, up on an exposed part of a pasture. However, here at Ainderby the sheep are usually brought into the large barns that are penned, and with the golden hay spread deep over the barn floors they have a comfortable place to rest and have their lambs out of the chill of the late-winter weather. It was in here that I held my first newborn lamb many years ago and it was a marvellous experience as it nestled into me. With the lighting causing the hay to take on a warm tinge of gold as it gently rustled under the movement of the ewes nursing their young, and the wind outside only emphasising just how warm and snug it was inside, I remembered those monks of long ago. Little has changed. This would be a scene familiar to them. How like a manger this place is, I thought, and wondered if the monks would have thought so too.

As well as sheep there have been pigs and heifers from time to time and there are always the chickens, in their hundreds, kept for their eggs, which are sold under contract. Val's special favourites are her flock of geese which, although noisy at times, act as brilliant guard dogs, especially when they have goslings to watch over. Some time ago four little goslings were abandoned by their mother. Val had been worrying over them but soon discovered her intervention was not needed. There happened to be a very broody hen around at the time and before long everywhere the hen went the goslings were sure to go. Soon she was rounding them up and looking after their every need and they obviously worshipped the ground she pecked at. Unfortunately for the hen, the goslings grew very quickly and towered over her ever-watchful, loving eyes. It was an amusing sight, this little brown hen being followed by the four fluffy, long-necked goslings. However, it was obvious they had no intention of leaving her and so it was up to her to make the decision. Being a wise old bird she decided that if they were not going to fly the nest then it was she who would go. There were no tears. It was all done painlessly and very quickly. One minute she was there and the next she was back at the hen house with her old pals who looked her up and down with a peculiar knowing look in their eyes. Goodness knows what they made of it all – although it didn't seem to effect their laying performance. As for the four goslings, they rejoined the flock and are all grown up now. Dogs and cats complete the picture of the farm that is being worked by the Andersons at the beginning of Ainderby Myers' second millennium in the second Elizabethan age of its history. It is undoubtedly as unmoved by time as it was 1,000 years ago at the dawn of its first millennium.

In truth I have often thought that the clock has no place here – sun-up and sun-down seem to suffice as markers for the days, which, left to

ABOVE: Ainderby Myers – the East Wing (left) – this was the original stone manor house. (Chapter 1)

BELOW: Hornby Castle – once the home of the Conyers. (Chapter 1)

ABOVE: The cart track at Ainderby on a frosty morning. (Chapter 1)

INSET: Bedale's old Market Cross. (Chapter 1)

BELOW: The arduous, perilous roads of Norman and Medieval England. (Chapter 1)

ABOVE: There have always been sheep at Ainderby. (Chapter 1)

INSET: Thirsk's market square with its Victorian clock tower. (Chapter 2)

BELOW: Home of the Wren. (Chapter 2)

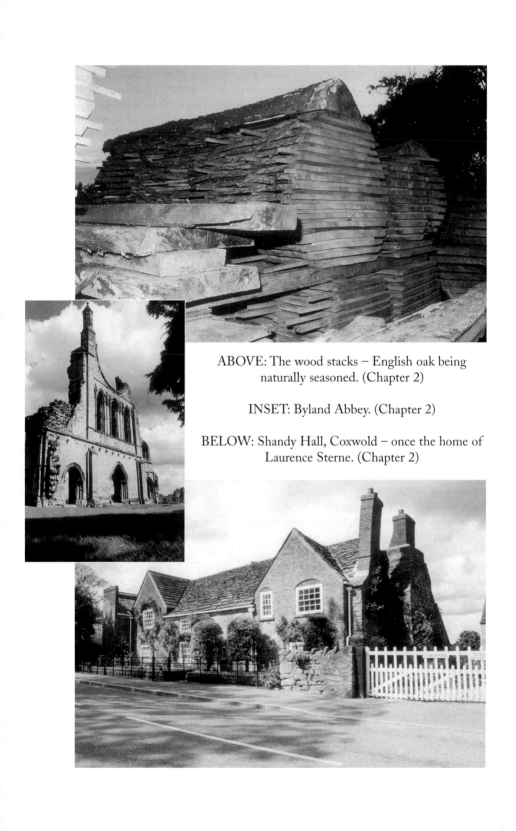

ABOVE: The wood stacks – English oak being naturally seasoned. (Chapter 2)

INSET: Byland Abbey. (Chapter 2)

BELOW: Shandy Hall, Coxwold – once the home of Laurence Sterne. (Chapter 2)

ABOVE: Alas, no more. The 'golf balls' of Fylingdales. (Chapter 3)

INSET: Helmsley. (Chapter 3)

BELOW: The remains of Rievaulx Abbey. (Chapter 3)

ABOVE: The road to Grosmont. (Chapter 3)

INSET: Lastingham church – the crypt. (Chapter 3)

BELOW: 'Tuesday' – the day her life was saved. (Chapter 4)

ABOVE: The Northern headland of Sandsend takes the full force of the autumn tide. (Chapter 4)

BELOW: Whitby – the 'pincer' piers from the '199 steps'. (Chapter 4)

ABOVE LEFT: Whitby – St Mary's churchyard
– 'beware prince of darkness'. (Chapter 4)

ABOVE RIGHT: Robin Hood's Bay – a huddled street. (Chapter 4)

BELOW: Anne Brontë's grave overlooking her beloved Scarborough.
(Chapter 4)

themselves, roll along at their own pace. As in olden times the individual hours seem superfluous. It is purely the seasons that count. Perhaps this is partly influenced by the fact that farmers seem much more attuned to nature's way than the mechanics of life, but I cannot help feeling it may also have something to do with the fact that, for the most part, throughout Ainderby's long life its days have solely been etched by the shadows of the sun without the aid of any other timepiece and she doesn't see the need to change. (Who can blame her?) In the summer, except for that sun glinting off the moving traffic on the far distant A1, there is no reminder of the hustle and bustle of an outside world beyond this peaceful self-contained haven. There is no hurry here, although everybody goes about their work as they must. The silence too fascinates me and it is just there for the taking if you really listen: a beautiful quiet, broken only by a light breeze rustling the leaves of the horse chestnuts and oaks that edge the fields or the gentle hum of a tractor at work in one of the distant fields.

Once a year sheep shearing time comes round, usually in June, and then the farm is anything but silent! The first major task is to part the lambs from their mothers, since the lambs are obviously not for clipping. All the sheep are rounded up with the help of the sheepdogs and Oscar, the Labrador (who thinks he's a sheepdog!), and shepherded slowly down towards the shearing pens, the idea being that the ewes are steered into the pens, whilst the lambs are diverted into the field to await their mums' return. Sounds simple in theory. Every available able-bodied man and woman is roped in to help, standing at strategic points along the route the flock are to take. However, although sheep are not known for their terrific brain power, it soon becomes obvious to them what is happening and it only takes one ewe to stubbornly refuse to be guided into the pen and a chain reaction is set up through the ranks. Total confusion then breaks out and the orderly procession becomes a raging stampede of panicking beasts and the noise of these normally peace-loving creatures is deafening – bleating, kicking, leaping over one another in desperation to escape. Mind you, the ewes are very protective over their young and it is the lambs that they fear for, not themselves. Eventually, puffing and panting with the physical effort of it all – that's the humans, not the sheep – we accomplish the object of the exercise and the ewes are finally penned up, ready for shearing, whilst the lambs bleat plaintively for their mothers in the opposite field. You feel so helplessly sorry for them since they sound so pitiful – that is until you go to bed, when you have to bury your head under the pillows to try and get some relief from the constant noise of bleating sheep that manages to penetrate 3 ft-thick walls!

The following morning the noise is still being kept up by the ewes and lambs alike, but shearing has begun and, by the time we have breakfasted, there is a large pile of rolled fleeces to indicate that good progress has been made. Once the shearers have the ewes backed up between their legs, the animals seem reconciled to their fate and don't put up a struggle. However, when I visit the pens I am tempted to be armed with one or two loo rolls because, like my dad when he got near a razor, not many sheep get away without a nip or two! My dad used small pieces of loo paper to absorb his bloody efforts and he would sit at the breakfast table with them stuck at random over chin, lip and ear, causing you to think the wretched razor had had a mind of its own. Often the red stained pieces ended up in his cornflakes! But the process did seem very effective for stemming the leaks – thus my thoughts for the sheep. Can you imagine a whole flock of sheep covered in pretty pink daubs of tissue to ease their wounds? Hmm. . . Although they wouldn't have the problem with the cornflakes, perhaps it is as well I resist the temptation for the sake of their dignity.

Seriously, though, the whole process of shearing is over very quickly and it's fascinating to watch as each fleece is removed in one piece. The poor ewes look more like mountain goats than sheep after their ordeal. Remarkably, however, when they rejoin the lambs their offspring have no problem recognising their own mothers and show their joy by starting to feed immediately.

And so I have ended my chapter on Ainderby Myers where I started – with the sheep and their young. They are a constant part of the Ainderby story; they graze in the same rich green pastures as all the generations before them and the same may be said for all the sheep scattered throughout the bounds of the Yorkshire landscape. They too are an integral part of the whole.

As for the Yorkshire people themselves, they have suffered much in their long history, their lands having borne the brunt of so many of England's worst troubles. But despite wars and political unrest, religious conflicts, industrial change and social change, they go on, generation upon generation, never wishing to be anywhere else. Justly proud of their heritage, they will never betray the land their forefathers worked so hard for.

As I said at the beginning of my chapter, the story of Ainderby Myers and its people is very much the story of how this great county itself evolved and became what it is today. You don't have to resurrect Yorkshire's past as it is all around you, from the Pennines to the sea. Many an evening I have strolled back up the old cart track to the lane which is lined with hedgerows leading back onto the old Roman road whence I came, and thought . . .

. . . it is 'passing strange' (as they used to say), that right at its beginnings weary travellers often sought sanctuary here, hoping to find food and shelter before continuing with their arduous journeys to the north or south, and 1,000 years later, thanks to Val's small facility for bed and breakfast, travellers are still stopping to rest awhile at the old Manor House of Ainderby Myers in the ancient parish of Hornby, North Yorkshire.

⧉ TWO ⧉

Towards the Hambletons

The Vale of Mowbray in North Yorkshire, sometimes referred to as the Great Plain of York, took its name from a Lord Robert de Mowbray who held lands here some 900 years ago, in the eleventh century. This vast expanse of fertile land reclines at the feet of the western buttresses of the Hambleton Hills and at its heart lies the market town of Northallerton, North Yorkshire's administrative capital. A popular residential area, as a town the variety of shops that line either side of the main street may fall a little short of some of the more familiar high-street names, but every week on Wednesday and Saturday the street is positively bustling with local folk and visitors alike as they cluster around the many market stalls packed onto the cobbles either side of the road. The market cross at its centre dates from 1777.

Northallerton is surrounded by farmland and beautiful countryside, but just north of the town, on the side of the A167 towards Darlington, almost obscured by the hedgerows, is a timely reminder that at least once this land knew terrible bloodshed. It is a very plain obelisk that was placed on the site in 1913 and, as the inscription describes, it commemorates the famous Battle of the Standard which took place here in August 1138. King Stephen of England was well out of harm's way in the West Country at the time and King David of Scotland seized his opportunity. His plan was to infiltrate the north of England

and take a large chunk of it for himself – or rather Scotland. Unfortunately for him, Stephen might have been away but his wife was not. Having already been alerted to the possibility of an invasion in the north by a substantial army of Scots, she took the appropriate action. Whilst King David and his army were crossing the Tees, Stephen's loyal followers had formed a formidable force led by Archbishop Thurstan of York and were already in position two miles north of Northallerton, around the Standard – a ship's mast mounted on a wagon. As the Scots advanced they were showered with a hail of arrows, broke ranks in panic and were chased by the English right back to the Tees. It is said that 10,000 Scots died that day. If they were not killed then they met their end in the river trying to escape. English losses were apparently minimal. Perhaps we shouldn't be too surprised that it took the Scots another 160 years or so to come back (although not to Northallerton).

Another popular market town in the Vale of Mowbray is Thirsk. A regular market has been held here since 1145, although it would not have been known as Thirsk back then. It might have been called Thrysk, Treussig or even Tresche, as it appears in the Domesday Book. Thankfully, Thirsk has lasted, which is easier for us to pronounce. Despite the change in name, the regular market day has remained the same since 1293 and takes place on a Monday, although today there is also a smaller market on a Saturday. Robert de Mowbray became the Lord of Thirsk after the Norman Conquest, probably as a direct result of his assistance to William in conquering England, and subsequently erected a castle on what is now known as Castle Garth. The castle attracted craftsmen and merchants who settled around its walls and those stallholders of that long-ago age would have been obliged to pay a toll on their stalls to their presiding lord of the manor. Thus the origins of today's market were born.

The de Mowbrays, who were from Normandy, were highly thought of and known for their generosity and chivalry. These qualities were inherited by their son Roger, who fought in the Crusades and was also the founder of Byland Abbey and Newburgh Priory. We will visit them later. Subsequent descendants of the de Mowbrays' faired less well. When Robert de Mowbray revolted against Henry II, he was taken prisoner and his lands around Thirsk were confiscated. Despite the King's anger, however, it seems he did not wish to be rid of the de

Mowbray name, since when the new incumbent of the de Mowbray lands, a Nigel de Albina, married and his wife, who was later to be known as the Great Lady of Thirsk, gave birth to their son, the King requested that he be surnamed Mowbray.

Unfortunately de Albina was later killed in Rouen where he was buried, but his wife spent the remainder of her life in Thirsk doing good works and raising their only son, Robert. As he grew up he proved worthy of the name and, like his namesakes, showed his care and concern for the ordinary people. In fact he and his son William Mowbray were amongst the 25 barons who met at Runnymede on 15 June 1215 to ensure King John signed the famous Magna Carta, drawn up so that the English people could have more liberty.

As for the castle at Thirsk, only evidence of a moat remains, nothing is left of the actual building. It has subsequently been assumed that the castle was probably wooden, as was often the case in medieval England, and thus succumbed to the torch, possibly when another Mowbray revolted against his king. It is rather amusing to think all these centuries later that, despite causing the King so much grief, it was the King who ensured that the Mowbray name lived on, albeit maybe a little longer than he had anticipated. Reducing their stronghold to smouldering ash in the grasses where a home used to be could not erase their existence when the best monument to the Mowbrays lies in the huge plain that forever bears their name at the foot of the Hambleton Hills. That will not turn to dust but continue to bear the sweet smells of freshly turned earth, lush green and fragrant blossom until such time as everything is nothing any more.

And so from a time when daub-and-wattle huts first huddled together on the east bank of the little River Codbeck, which now divides New Thirsk in the west and Old Thirsk in the east, Thirsk has grown and flourished. Its wide cobbled market square is always the centre of much activity. Visitors and locals alike cannot resist the tempting shops that curtain the square on all sides. Then there are the inviting inns, one of them being the Golden Fleece, an early eighteenth century coaching inn that served travellers to York, Darlington, Newcastle, Leeds or even London. Here in the stables at any one time there would have been 50 horses or more and, as the square is hushed by the fall of darkness and the warm glow of the street lamps accentuates the old brickwork of some of the buildings, I can, without too much stretch of the imagination, almost hear the coaches draw up, their wheels rumbling over the cobbles that simultaneously echo the clip-clop of the horses' hooves. The voices of coachmen, grooms, and whoever can be heard issuing their various orders whilst the friendly innkeeper welcomes his travel-weary guests. The street is suddenly filled with bustling and banter whilst the clinking of halters signal the horses are to be relieved of their burdens and bedded for the night. They throw their heads up and down, snorting their breath into the cold night air and pawing the ground with their hooves in anxious anticipation of the well-earned rest they know is to come. The new teams, fed and watered, hastily trot from the shadows of their stalls, ready to be assigned to their positions at the head of the coach to do their faithful duty. When all is ready, the piercing notes of the coaching horn issue a warning to travellers to quicken their step if they are to catch the coach ere it leaves for its onward journey. Such times were they. The clock tower that dominates the square would not have too many memories of such goings on. It was erected in 1893 to commemorate the marriage of the Duke of York to Princess Mary of Teck – later King George V and Queen Mary (the present queen's grandparents).

The roads onto the square are narrow and equally of interest. They are lined with houses that open directly onto the pavement and vary much in size and use. One rather impressive house I know well. It is the old veterinary surgery in Kirkgate known as 'Skeldale House', now the Herriot Museum. Here the world's most celebrated vet used to practise his skills, literally on all creatures great and small. His son Jimmy followed in his father's footsteps, although the practice has of recent years moved to new premises, still in the confines of Thirsk. I first had the unplanned pleasure of meeting the late Alf Wight (or James Herriot, as the world knows him) many years ago.

Our friends Chris and Brian, who often accompany us to Yorkshire, had happened to be in Askrigg in Wensleydale where the Skeldale House used for the BBC series *All Creatures Great and Small* is situated and, purely by chance, filming was in progress. Seizing the opportunity, they purchased a couple of artist's drawings of the house from the local shop and actor Christopher Timothy, who played James Herriot in the series, kindly obliged by signing both copies. Knowing that the real James Herriot in Thirsk did regular signings at his surgery and, thinking it would be rather nice to have his autograph too, we decided to leave our pictures with the receptionist at his practice for him to sign in his own time. However, on our arrival the lady at the desk asked us to wait, even though we explained we could leave them. Whilst in the waiting room a slimly built man with a moustache appeared out of nowhere and asked if we were waiting for assistance. I think he meant 'in the animal way of things', bearing in mind it is a busy veterinary practice, but we blurted out why we were there, feeling a trifle embarrassed because we suddenly realised that we were addressing the Donald Sinclair (or Siegfried Farnon) half of the partnership. This was not Robert Hardy (who played him on TV), though, this was the real thing! Although Robert Hardy may have had the same effect on my knees, as I think he is great too. Anyway Siegfried, as he is known for the purposes of the stories, was marvellous, and put us all at ease immediately. Talking as if we had met before and naturally obliging when we asked him for his signature on each of our pictures, he also assured us that his semi-retired partner would be delighted to sign them. So, after promising to pop back in a few days, we left.

However, that is not the end of the tale. Prior to going up to Yorkshire, my old faithful black cat Bimbo had sadly died. Despite her age and the fact I knew the day would have to come, it hit me very badly, as I am sure any caring pet owner will understand. Well, whilst I was daydreaming in the waiting room at Skeldale House, the others had, unnoticed by me, been busy. On the surgery wall, apparently, had been a notice. 'Home wanted for one black kitten and one black and white kitten – apply [etc.]' The 'etc.' was the Gerald Green Foundation at Catton, about three miles away, a sanctuary for waifs and strays. Apparently these two kittens had been found abandoned under a hedgerow and someone had thought to bring them into the surgery at Thirsk so that they could be put out of their misery – literally. Anyway, in true James Herriot style the vets would have none of it. The kittens were healthy and could be found good homes with a little effort, so the surgery took them to the sanctuary. Needless to say, I was also taken there forthwith, although not to be re-homed. Regardless of my state of mind – should I or shouldn't I? – the sight of the little bundle of black fluff with a dot of white on his chest won my heart immediately. I don't even remember saying I would have him. Everybody, including Ruth at the sanctuary, could see we had taken to one another. It also went unsaid that should we come back and collect him and find his black and white sister still needed a home, we would take her too. After all, how could I possibly leave her on her own? So it was all agreed on one proviso, and that was I would have the kitten or kittens checked over by the vet to ensure good health before we took them all the way back to our home in Berkshire. Thus we came to make an appointment at the practice in Thirsk for the Friday before we travelled home. After all, it was the nearest practice to the sanctuary and we had to return to 'Skeldale' for our signed pictures.

When we returned to Catton that Friday we discovered the little black and white kitten had been found a good home, so we collected my adorable bundle of black fluff and left, but not before Ruth had presented him with a cuddly toy he'd rather taken to. Of course, back in Thirsk it took all five of us to take the little puss into the veterinary surgery and we seemed to take over the whole waiting room. Then the shock came. A head popped round the door and called my name. The others looked at me partly in amusement and partly with disbelief. There could be no mistaking that accent, nor that familiar face that we had all seen on the covers of his numerous books. This was the famous vet himself, James Herriot, and I was about to follow him down the corridor – without the kitten! I was in such a state, I had gone without him. When I turned back into the room to take him from David everyone, including the local folk, was grinning from ear to ear and my face was burning.

I then had to renegotiate the door in a hurry, because Mr Herriot was waiting and as I fumbled with the knob with kitten precariously balanced in my other hand I sensed the grins were about to explode into laughter, especially as my legs didn't seem to want to work either. When we had made the appointment we had never thought for a moment it would be Alf Wight examining our little moggy, since we knew he was semi-retired. However, this kindly, brilliant man put me at ease immediately with his soft, gentle voice and natural modesty. He just had no idea how stunned I might be feeling at the sight of him. He asked me some questions and seemed pleased I should be concerned that the kitten be in good health for his long journey back to Berkshire. I, for my part, made no mention of his fame, just concentrated on the job in hand. He also asked me about other pets and, of course, I started talking about Bimbo and how she had recently died but then my eyes filled and he was quick to detect the huge lump in my throat that I was trying so desperately to suppress. His look of immediate concern touched me, especially when continuing his examination of the kitten he quietly remarked, 'I think this little chap has found a very good home. He's very lucky.' I, like so many others, had admired this man from afar, not purely for his dedication as a vet and the genuine concern he had for his patients' well-being but for his undoubted affiliation with his patients' owners too. Whether they be the stubborn and frustrating Mr Billings or the extremely wealthy but lonely Mrs Pumphrey with her pampered little dog, Tricki-Woo, he knew how to treat them and they held him in the highest regard. Now it was my turn and I was sharing a touching moment with Mr Herriot, who knew exactly how I felt and what I needed. Before we left he gave me some worming tablets – not for me but for my new charge – and despite an arthritic hand, wrote the label of instructions himself. I have treasured the bottle ever since. Thus, armed with kitten, bottle, lots of good wishes, and not forgetting the signed pictures, we left 'Skeldale House'.

As for our new kitten, well, we just had to call him Moses after the stray cat in Mr Herriot's much-loved book *Moses the Kitten* and he grew from strength to strength until he was enormous – not fat, just bigger than the average moggy – and, yes, the bond between us was very special. I never went anywhere about the house without him there with me and he was never happier than when I sat down of an evening and he would lie splayed out on me with his two front paws around my neck. Great in winter but a bit much in the warmer months! Once, when I was ill for quite a long time and had to be at home, he became my nurse and gave me his undivided attention the entire time the rest of the family were out. We were truly inseparable and I loved him for it. He loved people, but he loved me best. He was so intelligent and so powerful and yet so gentle. Sadly, at the young age of six years he suddenly became very ill. It broke my heart and I still cry for him, but those years we were together were amongst the happiest of my life and I would not have missed having him for the world. In fact this book is partly dedicated to his memory.

As a footnote to the above tale, within two years of my sad loss, both Alf Wight and Donald Sinclair had also died, within a few months of one another. It was the end of an era. A friendship and partnership that had spanned nearly 60 years was over. The name of James Herriot, however, will never be forgotten. His stories of his life in the county he adopted as his own will continue to inspire and capture the imagination of people from all over the world and they will still want to come and explore 'Herriot's Yorkshire' for themselves, just as he did when he arrived as a young vet in the town of Thirsk. Only then it was simply Thirsk in the heart of the Vale of Mowbray and it was the Mowbray name that had survived for 900 years. It still is Thirsk in the heart of the Vale of Mowbray but now it is also simply referred to as 'Herriot Country' in affectionate recognition of the man who inadvertently touched the hearts and lives of so many people and gave so much of himself to the Yorkshire he came to love. He gave me something too: the much treasured memories of my very special encounters with Mr Herriot and Mr Farnon and through them the best-loved encounter of them all – a Yorkshire cat named Moses.

Taking the Scarborough Road out of Thirsk, and making a left turn just before the village of Sutton-under-Whitestonecliffe brings us into the quiet, unassuming village of Thirlby, which nestles in the Hambleton foothills far from the reaches of normal tourist traffic. Thank goodness, you might say, since the lane twists and turns with blind bends and is positively dangerous. There is no shop in Thirlby, nor inn, not even a church. No one comes here without purpose. There is little point: the village is poised at the tail end of a country lane that fades just the other side of the bridge. Just before the bridge, set back to the right, lies Pear Tree House, thoughtfully arranged so that it veers off at an angle to expose the beck as it appears from the shadows of the bridge to trundle over the cobblestone floor of the ford – obviously a byway of bygone days.

Pear Tree House itself, with its red brick and white paintwork, is the home of the Hunters and we can always expect a warm welcome. We first met them many years ago in our quest for new dining-room furniture. Sounds odd? Not if you know that the Vale of Mowbray is home to some of the most skilled craftsmen in the country, who all specialise in the one craft: they are cabinet makers, using that most beautiful of woods, solid English oak. At the time we had visited many workshops in the area and been impressed with them all. The choice had become very difficult. Then, on a cool, bright October day at Ainderby Myers, a wren flew into the lounge through an open door, panicked and stunned itself on the window. I was upstairs at the time and a concerned David came into the bedroom holding the tiny thing very gently in the palm of his hand. I immediately took charge of the little darling – the wren I mean, not David! I put a droplet of water on the top of my finger, the idea being that it would run down to the beak of the limp body in my hand. The response was marvellous and shortly our little 'Jenny Wren' was indicating that she was feeling better. Taking her to the front door, I uncupped my hand and we all wished her well as she flew off towards the fields, just a tiny dot in the sky.

Later that same day, I was looking through a local brochure when I spotted an advertisement with a tiny wren imprinted. It was too much of a coincidence. Reading the advertisement, I discovered it was for a Bob Hunter, Cabinet Maker, Wood Carver, Pear Tree House, Thirlby, Home of the Wren. Here it would probably be advisable for me to explain that each of the cabinet makers in the area sign their work much as an artist would sign his picture, except it is not their names that adorn their work but a carved emblem. It may be a mouse, a beaver, a fox, or even an oak leaf, but in the case of Bob Hunter it is a wren. I showed David and Amanda the advertisement but I had already decided. We headed straight for Thirlby the next day and as soon as we entered Bob's showroom at Pear Tree House we knew we had found exactly what we were looking for. We did not hesitate, but ordered our table and chairs directly. Thus we met the Hunter family for the first time.

Since then we have become regular visitors to Pear Tree House. From the ford, a trickling beck wends its way round two sides of their enchanting garden, whilst on top of the steep bank opposite stands a formidable clue to Bob's trade. Etched against the sky, well open to the elements, are the stacks of aged English oak being naturally seasoned. The trunks of these mighty trees have been sliced by the saw to appropriate-width planks, which are then lain one atop the other with spacers between each one. It is only the uppermost plank of each stack that will not be used. For those planks of under two inches in width the whole process of natural seasoning will take approximately three years, whilst those of over two inches and under five inches will take up to five years. Obviously this is not a speedy process, but to a craftsman such as Bob Hunter it is considered of the utmost importance to ensure that the quality of the wood matches up to the quality of the workmanship it will undergo once it reaches his bench. Here, quality control is the craftsman's eye as he becomes familiar with the material, ensuring there is no flaw which will impede the work. With his hands-on experience, Bob Hunter knows what he is looking for in the wood he uses and he also knows what he expects of himself in progressing the wood into some of the finest pieces of furniture in England, if not the world. Therefore, the oak stacks are the essential beginnings of what he expects of himself; the beginnings of each piece of work he needs to be proud of because nothing less will do. If I exude enthusiasm for this man's work I make no apology. English craftsmanship of his high standard is something of a rarity these days.

It was approximately 55 years ago in 1948, whilst England was still in the process of recovering from the scars of the Second World War, that in this quiet unspoilt corner of Yorkshire a young lad, armed with high hopes and confident in the knowledge he could wood carve, first entered the workshops of the world-renowned cabinet maker, Robert Thompson, in the village of Kilburn, approximately eight miles from Bob Hunter's home in Thirlby. Bob was to be eternally grateful to his grandfather, a stonemason by trade, for it was through him and his friendship with Robert Thompson that Bob secured his apprenticeship at Thompson's.

Robert Thompson was born in 1878, the son of a carpenter and wheelwright, and lived in the half-timbered cottage adjacent to the inn in Kilburn. At the age of 20 he determined to become a carpenter and asked his father to teach him the trade. He also became very interested in medieval craftsmanship, practising carvings using English oak. He made a chair for the abbot of the nearby, comparatively modern Ampleforth Abbey, which can still be seen there today, and his first commission was a large wooden cross which now stands in the churchyard of Our Lady and St Benedict's Church at Ampleforth. Thus, his company was born. It was not long before Robert Thompson adopted the emblem of a tiny hand-carved mouse to adorn each piece of fine handcrafted oak furniture that left his workshop and he soon became affectionately known as the 'Mouseman of Kilburn' or 'Mousey' Thompson.

There was one person already working at Thompson's that Bob knew well – his uncle, who was to remain with the company for 53 years. Robert Thompson treated Bob as part of the family and Bob proved himself a good student, since he put his whole heart into learning the trade he loved under the watchful, trained eye of his mentor, whom he held in such esteem. Robert Thompson sadly died in 1955 at the age of 79, but the Cartwrights, the old man's grandsons, carried on the family business and the tiny hand-carved mouse still adorns each piece of furniture that leaves the workshop today. As for Bob, he remained at Thompson's until 1963.

When talking with Bob Hunter about the late Robert Thompson there is a note of sudden enthusiasm and obvious unfailing devotion in this usually quiet, modest and always deep-thinking man. He freely admits that the years he spent at Thompson's were amongst the happiest of his life. He does not speak of his own obvious talents and progress whilst under Thompson's roof: only of the 'old man's' kindness to him. There is no doubt in my mind that Bob regarded the 'Mouseman of Kilburn' as not just a great craftsman, but a great character too. One of the many stories Bob tells of those far-off days is the one about Robert Thompson apparently having a preference for lighting his fire with kindling as opposed to newspaper. He kept a log box by his back door, opposite the workshop, and every night it was the apprentice's job to chop his kindling for him, using only the off-cuts resulting from the construction of the table tops. Then they had to be deposited in the log box. However, Robert Thompson didn't like to hear you put them in, not whilst he was drinking his tea. If you did it right he showed you in and had a few words for you. Apparently he used to say, 'If lads can do kindling right then they'll make good apprentices.' There was obviously a lot more to that kindling than the old man's preference for lighting his fire with it. Bob also tells of how back in those days there were a fair few tramps in the area and if one happened to call at the lovely old cottage of Robert Thompson they struck lucky. Not only would a tray of food be brought out for him, but should the visitor request a pipe of tobacco, Robert Thompson would put his hand in his pocket and take out his own two-ounce tin of Balkan Subrani, a very expensive brand of superior tobacco which he always carried, and give the fortunate tramp not just sufficient for filling his pipe, but the whole tin.

Today the tramps, together with the log box, are long gone but Robert Thompson's is still a thriving family business and attracts visitors from all over the world into the showroom at Kilburn. In the shadow of the White Horse, which adorns the face of Roulston Scar above the village (it was cut there in 1857 by the village schoolmaster and 30 helpers), the oak stacks still stand open to the elements, seasoned in the same traditional way as they were all those years ago when Robert Thompson started his company.

It must have been difficult for Bob, leaving Thompson's behind him with so many happy memories of his time there and yet knowing that he had to now begin carving out the future he wanted for himself. There were no great ambitions. He had no thought then, or indeed now, of competing with Robert Thompson's or anyone else. That is not at all how the woodcarvers and cabinet makers of the Vale of Mowbray work. They are craftsmen offering their talents with pride, not with the competitiveness that one may well find in mass production. The end result Bob wanted for himself was to be able to use his skill to produce the finest-quality workmanship in the wood he loved that would give lasting pleasure and complete satisfaction to all of his customers, no matter what the job. All he wanted in return was enough money to be able to support his family, give them a decent home in his beloved Thirlby and be in a position to be self supporting as far as his business was concerned. A tall order some might say. However, everything did not happen at once. Bob had to work hard and used several opportunities to prove his talents. At one time he spent two years at York University – no, not taking a degree in cabinet making but doing joinery work.

Returning to the garden of Pear Tree House at Thirlby, if you let your eye wander along the bank from the oak stacks I mentioned earlier, there is another splendid reminder of Bob and Isabel's hard work: a bungalow. They built it between 1973 and 1979, and whilst doing so they dug into what appeared to be an old pottery kiln with a mass of compressed unglazed pottery which later turned out to be thirteenth-century unglazed urns. Amazing what people leave lying around, isn't it, albeit 700 years ago. I wonder why they weren't finished? Glazed, I mean. Perhaps there was a potter's strike and everybody downed tools. Must have been the longest strike in history if they did. In any case, some of the urns are now in the Folk Museum at Hutton-le-Hole, whilst a couple were donated to the William Lord Museum in Thirsk, once the home of Thomas Lord, founder of Lord's Cricket Ground.

The bungalow was not to be the Hunter's home for long. Below them, Pear Tree House at that time was occupied by a lady who proved to be very stubborn as far as the local council was concerned. They wanted her to install a proper loo in the house. She apparently still had an earth toilet, the last one in the village, and the council were very definite that either she arranged for the installation of proper facilities, or it would get the work done and present her with the bill. However, she was in no doubt that this was just not on. Bob was fully aware of the situation and, having a genuine liking for the property as well as a growing family to think of, he one day flippantly suggested, 'We'll do you a swap.' He was a little taken aback when she replied instantly that she would accept his offer but after talking it over with Isabel he decided to make it a definite proposition and the wheels were set in motion.

Thus in 1979 Pear Tree House had new occupants – the Hunters – but what of the elderly lady? She was quite happy with her side of the arrangement: one new bungalow with all mod cons, including a flushing loo. She must have liked it as she is still there to this day! However, for Bob and Isabel the hard work started all over again. A flushing loo was not the only item on their list of priorities. When they moved in and took full note of what was to be done it was obvious that once again they were going to have to start from scratch, although this time the bricks and mortar were in place at least! For example, there were only two 13-amp sockets in the house – one in the lounge and one in the kitchen – but what the new home lacked in the way of electricity and mod cons, it made up for in insulation. There were ten layers of lino in the lounge and no less than fourteen layers of wallpaper. As for the Hunters, they only had £90 to their name, because they had just finished the bungalow.

Adjacent to the house were a cowshed, goose house, meal house and calf house. In 1980 Bob converted them to his workshop and showroom. Fortunately, work was not in short supply and for two years he was fully occupied without going out of the parish, making windows, gates, doors, etc. Thus his reputation spread by word of mouth. Even Mr Herriot became a valued customer. At one point there was an exhibition in Thirsk Church. Bob took a stand demonstrating woodcarving and put on display a dresser and some small examples of his work. He explains that this contributed much towards his business growing in the early days, but knowing Bob as I do now I would say that it was as much the man as his woodcarving that drew people to him.

Today Pear Tree House is a picture inside and out and all their hard work has been well worth it. Under its roof they raised their daughter Jackie and three sons – David, Gary and Robert – all of whom have spread their own wings and fled the nest. Not the Wren's nest, however. Under Dad's careful guidance they have all become skilled cabinet makers and woodcarvers in their own right. Yes, all, including Jackie, who is one of the few lady woodcarvers in the trade. She, just like her brothers, can often be found working away with her own set of chisels, at a bench alongside her dad in the workshop adjacent to Pear Tree House. There is no mass production here. You will find only a few basic machines. Most of the work they do is carried out in the traditional way, by hand, and each completed article carries a tiny hand-carved wren. Bob says it was Jackie who decided on the Wren as their emblem. Apparently the farm buildings attached to the house used to be used as a furniture store and the wrens used to perch on the furniture and on the beams across the roof. Later, when the workshop was up and running, the wrens still came and went, watching over the Hunters, willing them on in their work – one even made her nest behind a saw blade on the wall and reared two babies. Needless to say, they were not disturbed but made to feel right at home – at the Home of the Wren.

One of the traditional tools used by Bob and other woodcarvers in the Vale of Mowbray to create the special finish on their furniture, is called an adze. It has a long handle, at the head of which there is a curved steel head with a very sharp flat blade at one end, and the skill required to use it properly is an art in itself. Firstly, the craftsman will look at the grain of the wood because this will affect where to start adzing. Then the adze has to be held in such a way that it can be swung relatively freely over the surface, just enough to glance the wood at a certain angle to make a very slight square-shaped indentation before leaving the wood again. Keeping up a rhythm, the whole area is gradually worked over in this way, leaving a fine traditional, slightly undulating surface. After being waxed, this finish, in certain lights, always reminds me of calm water shimmering in the sunlight of a warm summer's day. Once Bob offered us the opportunity to try it for ourselves. David went first but didn't find it easy. Bob explained that the secret lies in the angle at which the blade meets the wood since the adze mustn't be allowed to chop the wood, just shave it slightly. Then I decided to accept the challenge and have a go. After striking the wood a couple of times I remarked on how sharp the blade must be, but Bob assured me: 'I've never known anyone to cut themselves on it yet . . .' The blade swung. Too late. The wood went red and my heel (I was wearing sandals) was looking distinctly unhealthy. It didn't hurt but I managed to drop blood everywhere. Out came the first aid box and a good laugh was had by all at my expense. As for Bob, he'll never be able to utter those immortal words again, will he? I cannot help thinking Robert Thompson wouldn't have let me near his kindling, but I have a sneaking suspicion that if he was looking down on us at that moment he would have had a good laugh too. As for Bob and Isabel, they still chuckle about my experience to this day and I still have the scar to prove it!

Two miles from Thirlby in the village of Felixkirk there is a favourite retreat of the Hunters – appropriately named the Carpenter's Arms. This public house, full of character and old-world charm, contains a fair sampling of Bob's handiwork. There are many such examples of this man's versatility all over the area. He has helped to restore old houses to their former glory, whether it be a magnificent staircase or general furnishings; he has used his skills to renovate church screens; and he is often asked to produce a special piece of work for someone. Even the Golden Fleece that hangs outside the inn of the same name in Thirsk is his handiwork. He was asked to renovate it a few years ago. This is all besides working within the confines of the normal family business, which all the while continues to produce beautiful furniture to customer order.

In 1989 he was assigned to make the plaque for the opening of the sports complex at the Doncaster School for the Deaf. The Princess Royal did the honours on the great day and naturally Bob was present. When she came to shake hands with him she remarked, 'How nice to see a lovely plaque carved from oak rather than the usual brass ones.' I know that Bob must have felt justly proud of this royal approval but he doesn't readily mention it. He wouldn't. Perhaps he just leaves the little wren to say it all – for there is no doubt that Bob has put an enormous amount of effort into designing and developing his own style of traditional, hand-made English oak furniture, but whether it be letter rack or dresser, table or whatever, only when it has been passed by his expert eye will it be considered worthy of his personal signature. The perfect replica of our little 'Jenny Wren', who I held in my hand all those years ago and who led us not only to the Home of the Wren and the Hunters, but also into the fascinating world of the Vale of Mowbray's woodcarvers who mostly reside 'towards the Hambletons'. I am very glad she did.

The attractive village of Sutton-under-Whitestonecliffe is very near to Thirlby and is apparently so named to distinguish it from the many other Suttons in the area. Glancing towards the Hambleton Hills you will have no difficulty in spotting the white stone cliff from which it so appropriately takes its name, since it is visible for miles around. In 1755 there was a horrific landslip when tons of rock on the face of this part of the escarpment gave way to leave a gigantic white scar; the rest, as they say, is history. Apparently John Wesley, who was touring the country preaching, was staying in Sutton at the time and is said to have remarked he thought the world was coming to an end!

'Shandy Hall' lies approximately two miles south-east of Kilburn on the outskirts of Coxwold and was the home of the celebrated, if somewhat eccentric, writer Laurence Sterne between 1760 and 1768. He may have been Sterne by name but certainly not by nature, since it is said he possessed a rather astute sense of humour. He was born in Ireland in 1713 but had a sad and lonely young life. His father was in the army and the family moved around quite a bit. His father, who he loved dearly, was killed in action abroad when Laurence was only 18 but he found comfort living with a wealthy cousin near York. The cousin sent Laurence to Jesus College, Cambridge, where he fared well and achieved a BA degree. However, that same year he developed the dreaded incurable tuberculosis which was rife in those days. Notwithstanding his weak health he became an Anglican clergyman and eventually married Elizabeth in York Minster in 1741. They had many children, but only one daughter survived infancy.

His parishes were Sutton-on-the-Forest, where he lived for 21 years, and Stillington, just next door, but he also occasionally preached in York Minster, much to the congregation's displeasure. In fact, it is said that so many would leave before he was halfway through that he virtually ended up preaching to himself. Apparently he had a 'disagreeable voice', which, whilst possibly acceptable in the smaller confines of the parish churches, I imagine was magnified to unbearable proportions by the acoustics of a huge cavernous building such as the magnificent Minster.

Laurence Sterne was an intelligent man who loved good company and exhilarating conversation. He also enjoyed society, such as could often be found at nearby Lord Fauconberg's residence, Newburgh Priory, where he was a frequent visitor to social gatherings. However, he unfortunately had a reputation for not being trusted where women were concerned. Is there no hope? And a parson too! His wife, apparently, was prone to bouts of bad temper and had a mental disorder. Is that surprising, with a husband who spent much of his time away from home, was rarely discreet about seeking other company in such places as York and then boasted about his conquests? It's a wonder she didn't throttle him with his dog collar and be done with it. Maybe she tried and that is why he had such a disagreeable voice!

In 1759 Laurence Sterne wrote the first two volumes of his *Tristram Shandy*, which were published in York. His novel was an instant literary success and it was also at this time that he was offered a third parish, that of Coxwold, with the help of his friend Lord Fauconberg and so, now separated from his wife, he moved into 'Shandy Hall'. The house is obviously so named after his books and it was here he wrote the remaining seven volumes. However, this very attractive fifteenth-century house has more the appearance of an extended cottage than the expected grand residence the description 'Hall' evokes. On reflection, however, perhaps that is the impression Laurence Sterne wanted to give to those who might never visit, since on his own admission he sought fame not money. Whatever else the man may or may not have been he had proved he could write and *Tristram Shandy* certainly brought him the recognition he wanted. He openly admitted much of it was based on the people and events from his own life. He even portrayed himself as Parson Yorick and the work is still available in print today, over 200 years after he wrote it.

He avidly continued writing until, on a visit to London in March 1768 he contracted flu and died of pleurisy. He was buried in the Bayswater Road (no, not literally). But that wasn't the end of him. Two days later his body had disappeared. It had been dug up by what they used to call 'the resurrection men', who were offered good money for bodies for research purposes. Ironically, Sterne ended up virtually where he had started, at Cambridge University. Only this time he was on the dissecting table under the poised knife of a professor. Fortunately, he was recognised in time and discreetly returned whence he'd come. But matters didn't rest there, or rather he didn't. Approximately 200 years later, in 1969, the burial ground was set for redevelopment and Sterne's remains were respectfully retrieved and reburied in the churchyard at Coxwold, virtually in sight of his beloved home, 'Shandy Hall'. And he would not be disappointed. After falling into a very poor state of dereliction, the Laurence Sterne Trust rescued it and faithfully restored it to its former glory just as it was when Laurence Sterne lived there. Only now it is a museum relating to the life and times of the country parson and famous author who put it firmly on the visitors' map.

As a footnote, Laurence Sterne may have found some amusement in the fact that some 170 years after his demise, another author could frequently be found at Shandy Hall supping tea in the kitchen after his work was done. Only he didn't come here to write his books. He came as the country vet and his name was Alf Wight. His name as an author was James Herriot! Shandy Hall, at that time, was a farmhouse and many a time the vet was called to assist a difficult lambing or attend a sick animal. However, he too was very pleased to see the house back the way it was when its most acclaimed tenant lived there.

The attractive village of Coxwold is part of the Newburgh Priory estate. An old Augustinian priory, it was given to the order by Roger de Mowbray in 1145, shortly before he left to fight in the Crusades. He had inherited the Newburgh lands from his father, Robert de Mowbray, who had in his turn been granted them by William the Conqueror.

To put this period into historical perspective, King Stephen had sat precariously on the English throne for some ten years. His uncle Henry had tried, without success, to persuade his barons to accept his daughter Matilda as queen since his son and heir William had been drowned at sea on the 'White Ship', but when Henry died his nephew Stephen was offered the crown. Generally well-liked, Stephen seemed to show promise of being worthy of kingship, but gradually he gained a reputation for being unreliable and lacked a natural instinct for action. Coupled to this, Matilda was not content to let matters rest. She had married the count of Anjou and borne him sons. Now she was back in England challenging Stephen for his crown. She got support too, since Stephen's barons were rising against him and Matilda seemed a better option. However, by this year of 1145 it was obvious Stephen was at last getting the upper hand and she eventually returned to France. But she didn't give up, because a few years later, when Stephen's son died at Bury St Edmunds in Suffolk, she sent her son Henry over to form an agreement with Stephen that when he died, Henry would inherit the crown. Stephen agreed and in so doing pacified his rebellious barons, kept Matilda at bay and ensured England's future was secure after his death in 1154, when Henry II not only inherited the crown but the loyal following of his relieved people.

There is very little recorded evidence of life at Newburgh Priory at this time, or indeed until the dissolution of the monasteries by King Henry VIII in 1538. Henry's chaplain at the time was Anthony de Bellasis who was responsible for the dissolution of Newburgh together with other monasteries in the area. After the dissolution, the King sold de Bellasis the Priory for the princely sum of £1,062. It was Anthony's nephew William who turned the Priory into a private residence and it has remained in the same family ever since. However, in 1627 Sir Bellasis was promoted to baron and became Lord Fauconberg, the title by which Laurence Sterne knew the family. With no male heir, the title became extinct in 1802.

Newburgh is set in the most picturesque of landscapes and the groundsmen keep the gardens and surrounding parkland immaculate. When we drove through the impressive wrought-iron gates, despite the visitors' notice, I couldn't help thinking to myself, 'I hope we're not trespassing.' There were no obvious signs of anyone else about the place and it was so quiet I felt I was intruding, but a gardener put my mind at rest and told us where to leave the car. After that we were free to wander until it was time for the next tour of the house to start. It was so peaceful it almost felt like those Augustinian monks were still there but, from across the lake came reassurance that time had in fact moved on – the White Horse at Kilburn dominated the landscape.

Although during its lifetime the house has undergone substantial changes, particularly in the Georgian era, it is still essentially Tudor. However, the tour we were given begins in what is known as the Black Gallery, which probably dates back to the original building of 1145. The name apparently refers to the fact that this was the outer waiting room to the inner Justice Room, where you came before the local court to hear your punishment for whatever crime you had committed. Doesn't sound very promising with that title, does it?

It was the Unfinished Room that fascinated me most. Apparently this room dates back to 1758 when Lord Fauconberg was transforming Newburgh into a Georgian home. There was a fire before the room was finished and a maid was trapped here. Despite her screams for help, Lord Fauconberg's son could only think of himself and left her to die, but before she did she cursed the room, proclaiming that if anyone should ever try to finish it their eldest son and heir would die an untimely death. I wonder who stayed behind to hear her say it? Certainly not the son, by all accounts.

Anyway, apparently Lord Fauconberg took the warning seriously and, although he went on to complete his rebuilding of this part of the house, he never touched the room. And nor did anyone else until 1889 when Sir George Orby Wombwell decided the whole story was 'pog-wash' – or was it 'hog-wash'? – and ordered that the room be finished. Oh dear . . . A few days later poor Sir George's eldest son died in India. Work on the room was stopped immediately but it was too late. A few years later his second son died in South Africa. He must have been devastated. Since Sir George's efforts, no one has touched the room. Maybe they should have asked the local parson, Laurence Sterne, to say a few words over it in 1760 or so. His voice alone might have deterred the curse. What do you think?

The other fascinating feature in the house is in the attic, or rather what was the attic. A huge wood and stone arrangement, rather like an old coal bunker, is set under a small window with the death mask of Oliver Cromwell on the top of it. It is claimed to be the tomb of Oliver Cromwell, Lord Protector of England 1649–58. His last resting place, after his daughter Mary, who had married the foresighted and ambitious Thomas, Lord Fauconberg, had rescued her father's body from obscurity after it had been dug up in Westminster Abbey. Don't ask, because I don't know. But it seems even the dead were not safe during these uncertain times; remember Laurence Sterne was still roaming the countryside after his demise. Poor Mary used her husband's influence, so they say, to retrieve her father and here he lies . . . or does he? No one knows for sure since no one has ever looked. Permission was even withheld from the Prince of Wales – later Edward VII – who visited the house and tried to bribe an estate mason to open the tomb. Personally I think the family are right to leave well alone – especially as Cromwell's 'tomb' is in close proximity to the unfinished room. Who knows what would happen if he and the maid were to join forces. One thing's for sure, you wouldn't find me in that part of the house after dark. And goodness knows what the monks would have thought of it all. There is no doubt, however, that Newburgh Priory is a great place to visit and it does have a fascinating story to tell its many visitors. I was very sorry to leave, but then the sun was still shining!

Newburgh Priory was firmly established when approximately 30 years later, one and a half miles north-west of Coxwold near the village of Wass, another monastic house arose from the flattened plain in the southern reaches of the Hambletons. After many difficulties finding the right place for their home, the Cistercian monks eventually settled here and began building their magnificent abbey in 1177. It seems to me that the majority of abbeys I have come across are always so beautifully situated, almost as if there was purposefully a space for them already set so that these elaborate buildings, hand carved out of quarried stone, as large and ornate as they may be, would appear to have arisen naturally out of the landscape and blend with it perfectly. Byland Abbey is no exception. Although now merely a ruin thanks to the dissolution, it still maintains an eerie dignity and portrays enough of its former self for the onlooker to know it was once a magnificent building achievement.

A substantial part of the west front remains, giving us a clue as to just how spectacular the abbey must have looked in its heyday. It includes a huge half circle of its 7.8 m-diameter rose window, which for nearly 500 years, it would appear, has partly relied on just one turret adjoining one side of it to help keep it in place. The monks would be justly proud that what little of their beloved abbey is left is still held in awe by all those who visit it, nearly 900 years after they built it with their own hands.

Retracing our steps nearly, but not quite back, to Sutton-under-Whitestonecliffe via Kilburn we make a right turn onto the main road out of the village towards the face of those formidable Hambleton Hills that beckon the traveller out of the Vale of Mowbray and on to their summit. However, this can only be accomplished by first addressing the steep climb up the notorious Sutton Bank, which alternates between a one-in-four and one-in-five gradient that twists and turns to the top. Not for fun is the warning made to test your brakes, neither is the request for you to engage a low gear. This incline can be treacherous in bad weather and totally deceiving in good conditions. Even locals treat it with the respect it deserves and it is worthy of note that in pre-war days people would judge the car you owned by asking the question: 'Will she go up Sutton Bank?' However, once at the top all can be forgiven, and your efforts are well rewarded.

Rarely have we resisted the temptation to park the car for a few minutes in the convenient car park at the top of the climb and wander over to take full advantage of the view. Here at your feet lies the Vale of Mowbray, resplendent in its carpet of many colours, whatever the season. Here lies a kingdom in miniature and over in the distance on a fine clear day can be seen the arched backbone of England, the Pennines, etched in pastel, blending with the skyline. To the north lies Cleveland and County Durham and to the south that great city of medieval rivalry: York. So much of England's great history has been played out in these now calm lands. To me it is the finest view in all England and so many legends are stored below us.

From this vantage point high up amidst the gorse bushes, long grasses and heather there is a grand view of Hood Hill situated to the right of the road as it starts the climb. It was here that those troubled monks of Byland first tried to settle after leaving their sanctuary at Thirsk Castle. Up here it takes on the appearance of a flattened green pyramid, but in fact it has a tale all its own. Apparently, a local hermit upset the Devil in some way, who forthwith took him one night from

Roulston Scar and carried him to the top of Hood Hill where he transformed him into a rock. Bearing in mind that the hill is 800 ft high, I cannot help thinking the Devil must have been very wise not to turn the poor offender to stone before reaching the top! To this day nobody knows who the hermit was or in what way he upset the Devil, but one thing is for sure and that is there was a huge stone on the top of Hood Hill and nobody knows why, although it was also said to be used by the Druids as a sacrificial stone. I say 'was' because one night in 1954 an aircraft crashed, sadly killing the pilot. The aircraft struck Hood Hill and hit the stone, which subsequently tumbled down the Hill and broke into tiny fragments. Some say the stone weighed 20 tons, although locals believe that to be a very conservative estimate. Not a very pleasant end to the tantalising legend.

A host of legends also surround Gormire Lake, situated towards the foot of Whitestonecliffe. Its azure blue waters apparently hide many a dark secret. Some say it is bottomless, whilst others tell of how a village is lost beneath its surface. They say if you are brave enough to take a boat out onto the lake and peer down into the watery depths, you will see the spire of the church. Yet another tale suggests that a girl leapt to her death over the cliff astride her white horse and that both fell into the lake. Neither body was ever recovered. I don't suppose they would have been if the lake is bottomless. However, do not mistake me – there can be much truth hidden in these ancient stories and I am the first to admit there are many things we know nothing about and would do better not to question.

There is no doubt about the truth of one relatively recent tale concerning this magnificent view of the Vale of Mowbray – the fact that on a clear day you used to be able to see the old trains get up steam in York and follow them all the way to Darlington. That indeed would have been a sight to witness. They say you can do the same today, but I haven't tried since I feel without the head of steam to guide the eye, the practice would not be quite so easy or so much fun. However, one game we have played out many times is seeing how many familiar landmarks we can recognise. It is only when you have made a reasonable mental list that you can truly appreciate the mockery this view makes of distance and how trivial and insignificant a mile can be.

I have been up and down Sutton Bank in all seasons and all weathers, but on a blacker than black night, with the winds hurling up the autumnal fall of leaves on top of the Hambletons and the rain thrashing almost horizontally at the side of your vehicle as you make your way back whence you came, knowing that the descent of Sutton Bank lies ahead of you, anyone, including me, may be forgiven for feeling a little bit apprehensive about what lies ahead. However, on one such terrible night my fears were proved unnecessary. As soon as we started to wend our way down the bank the wind strangely dropped and the rain no longer sounded like a thousand spears pranging our car. At the time the sudden silence was eerie, although also a great relief, but as soon as we were off the bank the rain and wind were back and I remember thinking afterwards, perhaps Sutton Bank looks after her own and is mistress of her own moods. A romantic thought – surrounded by so many legends – is it?

Anyway, the most exhilarating view from the bank for me is watching the sun go down over the Vale of Mowbray on a fine summer's evening. A sight sadly missed by the majority of tourists to the area, but one that is well worth waiting for if the night is right. The vermilion red of the sun's fire turns the sky into a spectacular array of vibrant colour as it begins its descent through the all-absorbing earth, waiting silently as if in awe. Slowly it slips from view, leaving in its wake the hushed glow of orange soon also to be soaked up by the dark violet silhouette of the earth below. All the while the scene completely captivates me every time I see it. In fact it makes me feel I am in the front row of an audience, completely spellbound by the performance being played out before me on centre stage. Not until the final curtain do I release my gaze and quietly take my leave, returning whence I came, back down Sutton Bank, into the Vale of Mowbray that lies towards the Hambletons . . .

❧ THREE ☙

Onto the Moor

As the evening shadows lengthen and the moon bids welcome to the night and whilst the Vale of Mowbray sleeps, it is time for the moors to awake. In the haunting darkness the moon heralds their dawn . . . but first . . .

The North York Moors from their western boundary of the Hambleton and Cleveland hills across to the North Yorkshire and Cleveland Heritage Coast cover some 553 square miles and embrace the largest expanse of heather-clad moorland in England. It is indeed a fascinating land and I love every inch of it. Especially up on the high moors where there appears to be no beginning and no end – a wilderness, that responds only to the voice of its ever-present mistress, Mother Nature, obeying her every command, reflecting her every mood. Whether cloaked in the rich vibrant mauve of the heather in high summer or drenched in the golden hues of late autumn, thickly coated in a fresh fall of snow or damp with early morning dew on a fresh spring morning, there is always an awesome beauty present that cannot be denied.

Make no mistake, though, these moors can be harsh and show little mercy. Their mood can change with little warning. Sudden violent storms or driving rain are no strangers here. Nor are the notorious heavy mists or thick fogs that can shroud the moors in moments. Then travellers would have to be very brave to venture far without sound knowledge of their direction, for there is little to guide them and the silence will overpower their very sense of judgement. A potential wrong turn or over-steer in a vehicle could be into a ditch or worse. To walk would be utter madness, and in the days before the motorcar many a poor soul became the victim of the waiting moor on a foggy night and was never seen again. Although I have travelled these moors many times and know them well enough, I still respect them and for more than just their mood of the moment, according to Mother Nature.

Despite initial impressions of a sparsely populated area, the moors include in their landscape a fine assortment of interesting sights, towns and villages to visit. Individual in character, most have a story to tell that will capture the imagination – and so we will go on a journey . . .

Taking the A170 Scarborough road from the top of Sutton Bank gives fine uninterrupted views over Ryedale with its gently undulating plateaus of cultivated farmland. It was here, in the twelfth century, deep in the valley of the River Rye and away from the commotion of town or busy byway, that the Cistercian monks built their first monastery in the north, Rievaulx Abbey. They could not have chosen a more idyllic place. On this large plateau, overlooking the river and surrounded by woodland, they could live in their community without interruption from the outside world. It took years of hard labour both by the monks and their lay brothers to complete their fine work, but what a credit to them it is. Although today the abbey is but a skeleton of its former self, it is not difficult to imagine what a magnificent building it must have been before it met its downfall alongside its sisters throughout England, during the dissolution of the monasteries in the late 1530s.

These impressive, extensive remains give a good insight into the layout of the abbey and how the monks lived and worked within their community. Depriving themselves of all worldly goods or pleasures, the order led a very simple life based on prayer and hard work. They needed to be self-sufficient in their seclusion from the outside world and they were very successful, since they were brilliant farmers and their crops, together with the wool from their sheep, provided them with their basic necessities of food and clothing. It appears they were very resourceful too, since they sold any surplus farm produce to pay for the continued building of their beloved abbey. They were given their land by Baron

L'Espec, a powerful lord who lived at Helmsley, now a popular market town situated two miles from the abbey, on the edge of the North York Moors.

At various times in its history, Helmsley has withstood much change, for it would appear that for approximately 3,000 years someone has lived here. In the beginning just a small area of the intruding forests that edged the huge swamp areas of the Vale of Pickering was cleared to allow man the hunter to come down off the high limestone moorland and settle to a new life of farming. Apparently, proof of early man's existence here is still regularly being dug up by unsuspecting farmers and the like today, according to the locals, and there are indeed quite a few exhibits in the nearby Folk Museum at Hutton-le-Hole to illustrate their tales. Anyway, despite this new settlement increasing in population, there is little doubt that the actual way of life in and around Helmsley was not to alter for many hundreds of years, and even when the Romans and subsequently the Anglo-Saxons arrived, these events had little effect on this small community, although surrounding Ryedale thrived. However, with the migration of new settlers from the continent, the first important historic change to the settlement did finally happen. They gave it the name of Helmsley which means 'Helm's forest clearing', and thus this rather small, insignificant hamlet had an identity at last.

From then on Helmsley was destined for a very different way of life, for other events were about to unfold which would ensure that its days of being a quiet, unassuming, farming hamlet were well and truly numbered, and indeed in the late twelfth century it was to become dominated by a new and very formidable feature on its landscape – a castle. After the Conquest there was much trouble in northern England with the Scots. One of the victors of a battle with the Scots was the Baron L'Espec and he chose to settle himself and his family at Helmsley. This, naturally, of necessity brought many changes all at once to this peaceful settlement. They now found themselves the very centre of attention, having to supply their new lord with all the requirements both he and his large household required to sustain themselves, plus coping with a huge influx of new neighbours who would be serving the castle too, such as guards, craftsmen, attendants and so on, and that was not the end of it. As I said earlier, this powerful baron gave land for the new Rievaulx Abbey to be built. Within a short time it was home to some 600 or 700 monks and lay brothers and fast became the leading Cistercian monastery in England. It therefore played a great part in yet a further population explosion in the area at the end of the twelfth century and again it fell to the local people of Helmsley to take the strain. However, their reward was to come eventually, and indeed came directly from the Cistercian monks. It was the monks who first introduced sheep to the moors, and the wool from the sheep was to provide the peasants of Helmsley with a new-found industry: weaving. Thus, Helmsley reaped the benefit of all its hard work throughout its years of change and now it had a new and significantly prosperous trade to call its own by way of a thriving textile industry. Notwithstanding the enforced closure of Rievaulx Abbey, nor the changes of ownership of land and castle, Helmsley continued to flourish. That is, until the Industrial Revolution of the 1800s when, like so many other weaving communities, it became the casualty of one change too many.

However Helmsley again survived and, personally, I'm very glad it did. Yes, recent generations have, again, had to adapt to change, this time to accommodate the town's comparatively new industry of the tourist trade, but the changes are merely cosmetic. The Helmsley of today has returned to the quiet dignity of a rural market town with a comparatively small population, although there are still many reminders of its long history for all to enjoy.

While taking a stroll through its narrow streets and byways it is interesting to note that many of the town's shops have obviously not been purpose-built, but are dwelling houses adapted to serve the purpose. As with the majority of market towns in North Yorkshire, there are few familiar high-street names, but who needs them when there is enough variety of charming little shops of character and interest to suit most people's tastes? In Helmsley's case, these include tantalising clothing shops, which, according to the town's long tradition, only sell articles made from the finest cloth (or wool, of course).

As well as the shops, a weekly market occupies the square on a Friday. Although Helmsley has hosted a regular market since 1285, the square was not used for this purpose until the mid-1400s. Apparently the markets were previously staged in the churchyard where the Market Cross also stood. However, once they were re-sited, the cross had to be moved too. Not an easy job, I would have thought, and it has often occurred to me that maybe in that great effort lies the reason for the shaft of the cross being the original but the cross itself being of later date. It's only a humorous notion of mine, but I just have a mental picture of these powerfully built men moving the cross, and by the time they reached the market square, finding it headless (if you know what I mean). No disrespect intended.

The modern day Helmsley is still dominated by the crumbling remains of its castle. No longer the grand fortification it was, it has, however, become a shrine to which many an inquisitive visitor will willingly go to pay his or her respects to what was once, without doubt, Helmsley's way of life, and it still makes for an awesome sight. It was in the 1600s that the Duncombe family bought the castle but later, in 1713, they moved to a much more comfortable residence which they had built in Duncombe Park, just across the way. The castle was forsaken but its stout walls were put to good use, since much of the stone was then used by the villagers in the construction of their own houses. I wonder if that is why we have that saying, 'Every man's home is his castle'? Sorry, just a thought.

Duncombe Park's splendid grounds are open to the public for much of the year. However, in the 1760s this rather palatial house and its titled residents were very closely linked to a man who in future generations would become the subject of a popular nursery rhyme sung by millions of children. In fact it would surprise many to know the lad really did exist. He was born near Spennymoor in County Durham in 1732 and was the son of wealthy parents. His name was Robert Shafto and the song, for the uninitiated, went as follows:

Bobby Shafto's gone to sea, Silver buckles on his knee,
He'll come back and marry me, Bonny Bobby Shafto.

His family were ship owners and Bobby did go off to sea in his father's ships occasionally. The sad story is, however, that he had met and fallen in love with the heiress of a wealthy family. Her name was Eliza and he fully intended to marry her. Unfortunately, whilst he was away on another sea voyage, Eliza contracted consumption and died. Thus, although he had a reputation with the ladies and as the lyric suggests may well have broken many hearts, it seems a cruel jibe in view of Eliza's illness and subsequent demise. However, obviously Robert Shafto did not take it too much to heart, as within a short time he found himself another wealthy heiress. This time he did marry her. She was Catherine Duncombe, daughter of the Earl of Feversham, who lived at Duncombe Park in Helmsley. Shafto never returned to sea but instead took up politics. He was elected Member of Parliament for Durham in 1760 and thus began a new and successful career, but despite his wife bearing him many children he never ceased to be a 'ladies' man' and young girls can still be heard singing his song today in school playgrounds up and down the country.

Off the A170, approximately halfway between Helmsley and Pickering, is the picturesque village of Hutton-le-Hole and the site of the Ryedale Folk Museum, which I mentioned earlier. The brainchild of Bertram Frank, the open-air museum first opened its doors, or rather its gates, in 1964, but over the years has been extended considerably to take on the appearance at first glance of a village within a village. There is a chemist and village shop, a blacksmith's forge and shoemaker, charming thatched-roof cottages with neat gardens and water pumps. Then there is the old Cruck House which was built over 500 years ago in Danby on the North York Moors. It was brought here piece by piece like a huge kit and accurately resurrected to its former glory. Nearby stands the Elizabethan Manor House from the village of Harome. There is even an Edwardian photographic studio, as well as a charming Victorian cottage. It soon becomes obvious this is no ordinary village. Here the visitor is invited to time travel and gain a fascinating insight into how people lived in this area of Yorkshire down through the centuries.

There is nothing extraordinary about Hutton-le-Hole itself but it can easily be described as a 'picture postcard' village nonetheless. It comes complete with all the essential ingredients that add up to most people's expectations of an idyllic English village. There are comfortable little tea shops that overlook the wide stretch of green which divides the village in two, where sheep graze and a narrow beck flows between the banks. Shady trees and a mixture of variously styled dwellings and village shops line the two sides of the green. Altogether it is a vision of peace and tranquillity that appears to have let time go by without hurry or interruption . . . but appearances can be deceiving and nothing could have been further from the truth in the nineteenth century.

Climbing up and over the north road out of Hutton-le-Hole with its breathtaking views and eventually taking the steep descent into Rosedale Abbey, past Chimney Bank, it is hard to imagine that anything ever happened here. But it did. Oh great, wild, beautiful land, how well you conceal your wounds. Only the scars are left to bear witness to a time when man battered your very heart in his quest to bring forth the wealth that was yours . . .

Yes, once there were many areas in this largely uncultivated and extraordinary part of Yorkshire that were a source of much industrial interest, and Rosedale was one of them. This beautiful dale, which is surrounded by hills and extends well into the moors, together with its main village of Rosedale Abbey, once harnessed the very soul of industrial mayhem. Here, as far back in time as the Iron Age, man had plundered the sod for its rich ironstone deposits. Even the monks from Byland Abbey in the 1200s reportedly mined here. However, nothing prepared the valley for the onslaught that was to come in the mid 1800s. The first commercial mine was opened in 1851 and Rosedale became host to a new industrial community. At its peak 5,000 men worked here from dawn to dusk, and when darkness fell the valley echoed with the sound of drunken men's voices as they washed away the dust and grit with ale and revelry until their eyelids closed in stupor and all was quiet – just for a while.

Naturally, the local villages suffered a population explosion and could hardly cope. Rosedale Abbey and Rosedale East were most affected, but Hutton-le-Hole is said to have possibly doubled its population. It wasn't purely the influx of so many miners that caused problems for these small villages, it was the animals too. In Hutton-le-Hole there were already sheep on the village green, just as there are today, plus the villagers' donkeys and horses, ducks and geese, but then the miners brought in their own animals. Their donkeys, ponies and horses and carts were their only source of transport to get them up and over the moors to the pit in time for the early morning shift, which started at 5 a.m. regardless of weather or anything else. If the miners were late they risked being fired, so their animals were necessary. Whether the villagers agreed is debatable, since the village streets became positively inundated with manure. It must have been 'refreshing' on a warm day! Nevertheless, perhaps the local traders didn't object too much, since from existing records they appear to have grown in number at this time, obviously to meet the demand for their services, from which undoubtedly they profited well. At a guess, the local innkeepers too were probably also prepared to overlook some 'miner' inconveniences – one of them being to literally do the deed when it came to 'chucking out' time, since there are many old stories of men lying about the streets during the night, 'sleeping it off'. Ah, well. The manure was probably a soft option.

Soon a railway too came to Rosedale to transport the fruits of the miners' labours. This was no mean feat. The track laying had to be a precise act of physical engineering in itself, since to avoid the steep-sided valley, it had to have numerous curves incorporated, and then there was the problem of sharp gradients and the vision of heavily loaded wagons being in danger of toppling over the side. However, the rail link was successfully completed and an engine shed was also erected to cater for engine maintenance. Thus Rosedale became a self-sufficient mining centre and this was to be the way of things for many years. Although the mines had reached their peak by the 1880s and were on the decline, they did not finally close until 1926 in the wake of the General Strike. In 1929 the railway too was removed, as it had been built, sleeper by sleeper. Only a huge chimney remained up on Chimney Bank beside the old rail bed, but that too has now been demolished for safety reasons.

As I indicated earlier, Rosedale is by no means the only area on these moors to have succumbed to man's need to harvest its treasures for his own use, as I will explain in a later chapter. I have simply used it here as an illustration to show how so much of this picturesque landscape has at some stage during its yesterdays been ransacked for its natural resources such as iron ore, alum and jet, exhausted of its wealth and then left alone to heal itself, with Mother Nature's help. And help she has, for as the seasons have rolled over into years, past industrial areas such as Rosedale are now purely visions of peace and tranquillity to the roving eye. Havens for ramblers and sightseers alike, who can enjoy their beauty without even knowing their history. Many a voice has described the high moors as barren land. How little they know. As I have said previously, how well this land conceals its wounds. How well Mother Nature takes care of her own.

Within easy reach of Hutton-le-Hole is the quiet, attractive moorland village of Lastingham. I use the word 'quiet' because that seems to best describe it. Although on my first visit that initial impression was, for a few seconds, completely shattered, but more of that later. It was a warm day in high summer when we – i.e. myself, husband David, daughter Amanda, and friends Chris and Brian stopped in Lastingham, potentially for some light refreshment. Instead we ended up in the church. It was my fault because I wanted to find out more about the village and churches are always a good place to start. Lastingham Church is a little formidable from its outward appearance, with its unusual accentuated bowed eastern wall. It possesses no elegant spire stretching skywards as would seem fitting to dominate the traditional village scene surrounding it, but instead a classic Norman square clock-tower, which is partially hidden by trees. Once inside the building, however, I had to admit to being impressed, and we were soon to find out just how important this Norman church was in the history of religion in these parts. Apparently it was here on this site that Christianity first established itself in the north with the founding of a monastery by St Cedd in the year 654. Sadly, he did not live to see his work completed. This task fell to his brother, St Chad, who succeeded him as abbot, and was later to become Bishop of York. The Danes came and destroyed the monastery some 200 years later, but in 1078 Abbot Stephen of Whitby wanted to rebuild the abbey at Lastingham. Permission was granted and the work started with the crypt, but fate was to strike another blow when, after the completion of the crypt, the abbot was sent away to St Mary's at York. Thus the abbey was never finished.

That was over 900 years ago, but, as we discovered, the crypt which he built is still here and can be seen by descending the steps in the aisle. I have to admit that my passion for seeking out the past ebbed a little when my foot left the last step and my eyes glanced around the cave-like, rather claustrophobic room before me. The numerous low-arched supports for its roof, and subsequently for the foundations of the church above, for me only added to the eerie atmosphere of the crypt. Natural light can only enter by a single narrow arrow-slit window behind the stone altar and I tried to imagine how dark it really would be down here without the subtle glow of strategically placed lamps. The thought sent shivers down my spine. The Norman church above has been used as the parish church since 1228, but down here is another world. A church in its own right, this type of crypt is one of the very few in this country that have survived and is truly a remarkable testament to those faithful pilgrims who built it all those hundreds of years ago. Simple, almost humble, in appearance, no elaborate decoration to detract from its sincere purpose, but at the same time you sense that within these walls you are indeed on very sacred ground. I began to forget my initial wariness. It was replaced by fascination and awe. Unscathed by time, for time I well believe stood still for this holy place the day the last stone was sealed, it holds no hint of the 900 years of history that have taken place since its conception. Unblemished by the hands of reckless men or their messengers, who have constantly through those years plundered and destroyed our houses of religious connection, using either the power of the sword or the power of the Throne, it still remains untouched, unsoiled, almost unique. It is said that St Cedd is buried to the right of the altar and that this crypt is his shrine. I can believe it, and I can believe that this man was indeed remarkable, and indeed still is.

I decided it would not be too disrespectful to try for some photographs, and the others seemed to be doing likewise. However, I can become more than a little carried away when using my camera and unfortunately completely oblivious of what is happening around me. Consequently I did not notice when they left. Nor that I was alone. Nor how silent and empty the crypt had become. By the time I did, panic set in and my imagination ran riot. Suddenly I was aware of the dark corners behind the dumpy pillars of the low arches. I didn't want to be there (all due respect to St Cedd). I turned and noticed the iron gate at the foot of the ascending steps. I froze. Someone must have caught it on the way up; it was half way to closing. 'Please – oh, please – don't shut!' I thought. My feet thawed and I made for the gate. Of course it didn't shut, it couldn't . . . could it? I rushed up the steps back into the church without a glance behind. Then I had another shock. It was empty! The rotten lot had left me completely and the church door WAS shut. I yanked it and, oh, such relief, it opened easily.

Dazzled by the sunlight, I found the others in the porch and gave them a good piece of my mind, I can tell you. I was still trembling and they were more than amused, which only added to my wrath. However, more was to come. As Chris and I followed the men and Amanda down the path away from the church my still slightly shocked nerves were shattered again, and so was the peaceful solitude of the churchyard. The crack was deafening, followed by a thunderous roar and it was coming straight for us. It passed just over our heads, piercing our eardrums. Chris and I whirled and ducked as a reflex action. The men and Amanda turned, looking a little alarmed, but then they laughed. Of course, they wouldn't admit they too had been startled. I had been sure we were being attacked. So was Chris. Then the silence returned. You can't imagine my feeling of relief when we discovered it was a couple of Harrier jets practising manoeuvres. I have to admit just for a second, the briefest of moments, I wondered if this man St Cedd was more in touch with the outside world than anybody realised and was punishing me for what I was now beginning to admit was a little bit of an overreaction in his holy place. Chris and I laughed too in the end, although my nerves were a little the worse for wear and the others were more than a little amused when I related my experience in the crypt after I had discovered they were gone. Although I still suspect they did it on purpose, I also feel that someone up there had a great sense of humour (and I don't mean the pilots). All in all, my first visit to Lastingham Church had been very eventful and I knew I would never forget it. I haven't!

Despite this fascinating detour, we are still within easy reach of the A170 Scarborough Road which we rejoin as far as the busy market town of Pickering. As a matter of interest, according to local history, the section of this main road from Helmsley up to Scarborough is an ancient byway. How ancient I don't know. However, it has been modernised to include double yellow lines, traffic lights, crossings and, of course, the statutory signposts hidden behind foliage!

Pickering itself is also ancient and goes back to 270 BC when a King Peredus is said to have lost his ring in a local stream and found it again in the stomach of a pike he was eating. I wonder if that is how 'Pick-a-ring' got its name? Hmm . . . However, it was the Normans that gave the town its castle, the remains of which can still be seen today, overlooking the town. It was mainly used as a hunting lodge since many of our monarchs from the eleventh century onwards used to enjoy hunting in the Royal Forest of Pickering. Part of that great forest still stands today and remains in royal ownership. It is situated to the north of the town. The marketplace itself is uphill all the way and attractively lined with shops, the modern frontages of many totally belying the true age of the buildings themselves, which are far more ancient than they first appear. At the top of the marketplace is the church of St Peter and St Paul that dates from the twelfth century. It was in the mid-1800s that fifteenth-century murals were discovered on the inside walls, under layers of whitewash, depicting such scenes as the murder of Thomas Becket. Many churches in England have been known to harbour such secrets and it may be that with so much religious unrest in the country in the sixteenth and seventeenth centuries it was felt prudent to not be so demonstrative in religious houses for political reasons.

Pickering has always held one great fascination for my husband David. It is the southern terminus of the North York Moors Railway. He has been a lifelong lover of steam trains and, as any wife in a similar position would doubtless sympathise, you as an individual just do not stand a chance where several tons of steaming locomotive are concerned. You either have to grit your teeth, smile sweetly and bear it or seek a divorce on the grounds of infidelity and duck when the court clerk reads out the details of your husband's other women. Especially when the clerk gets to the part which reads 4–6–0, or something similar. Just imagine the judge's eyebrows going up when he or she tries to picture this midget with a 4 cm bust and no bottom. (For the uninitiated, a 4–6–0 refers to the arrangement of wheels on the locomotive, not its boiler measurements.)

Anyway, I think it's true to say that we know Pickering Station rather well and I have enjoyed many a cup of coffee on the platform whilst David has run up and down with his camera looking rather like a demented journalist looking for a scoop. However, I cannot mock too much for I must admit that the sight of a steaming locomotive is an impressive one and I, too, love the sight and smell of them, although not the soot! Pickering being in the far south of the moors, boarding the train here you would travel north through some of the most spectacular scenery up to Grosmont at the other end of the line, a distance of some 18 miles. For the time being, however, we will return to the road. More on the trains later.

Heading north out of Pickering on the A169 towards Whitby, another ancient byway apparently, the passion of the moors begins to unfold. Here the sheep alone keep the verges trim and there are no walls or fences to restrict their wanderings. They are an integral part of the landscape, out and about in all weathers, seemingly belonging to no one. In fact, they belong to the local moorland farmers who all have their own way of marking them, which serves two main purposes. It identifies their own animals from those of their neighbours and also hopefully deters sheep thieves, who can be a major problem. The sheep also, apparently, possess a remarkable homing instinct. Although they are known to wander a fair distance, even venturing into local villages, they will eventually return to their own area of moorland and the instinct is inborn, since the lambs too have little difficulty in finding their way home to Mum (I'm very relieved to say). Perhaps they are not quite so woolly headed as we humans imagine. They do, sadly, have one distinct disadvantage to contend with, however. The lambs did not follow us to school, as the nursery rhyme suggests. Nor did they learn the Green Cross Code. Their biggest problem is the increase in traffic over the years, mainly due to the popularity of such areas with tourists. Unfortunately, many sheep are killed or maimed by vehicles and it is not always their own fault. Accidents happen, regretfully, but I do feel very strongly that those of us who are road users should have a little more common sense and remember when travelling through sheep territory that it is the sheep who have the right of way and not us. It is tragic that a farmer can lose a valuable animal in this way, and sheep are not only valuable to their owners, they also play a very important part in the perpetual life cycle of the moors.

For most of us to see the sheep casually grazing by a roadside is very much a part of the pleasure we derive from the scenery around us. However, up on these moors, where the folds of the dramatic landscape are alive with heather and bracken, the sheep have a far more important role to play in the way of things then at first glance you may imagine. They help spread the all-important heather, by first of all eating it and then letting nature take its course. The seed is then expelled with the rest of the sheep's waste as they roam the moor and this in turn germinates to form healthy new heather bushes in the soft peat.

The sheep are not the only ones who find the heather a tasty morsel.

The red grouse, which is unique to our island, feeds solely on it and therefore also plays a very important role in the process of dispersing the seed. Unfortunately, despite their good work, the poor grouse do have one failing. There are just too many of them and this is not good news for the heather or the grouse. Too many grouse would soon eat themselves out of house and home, as it were. Thus the birds could face probable starvation and, possibly worse, complete extinction. Man's answer is to cull them, and so ensure the continued abundance of heather on the moor and grouse in the heather. On 12 August every year grouse shooting begins and continues until the 10 December. I have never advocated the deliberate destruction of any creature and, until I knew the ways of these moors, strongly opposed the annual grouse shoot. Now I have to admit there is no other kinder or quicker way of protecting the species from outrunning itself. I would never raise the barrel of a gun against them. I couldn't. But at least now I do understand why others are allowed to. The money brought in by allowing the shoot to take place provides valuable funds to help maintain the heather in first-class condition, which in turn provides the remaining grouse with a good home and larder.

Having explained a little of how the heather and sheep, not to mention the grouse, support one another, it seems appropriate that I should also mention that they all have one common enemy. It has been here as long as they have and they have learnt to live with it: the bracken. Despite its remarkable ability to transform the moors into a sea of gold after the heather has paled, it is invasive. Once it grew mainly around the lower reaches of the moors, but now it has found its way onto the high moors too, and where bracken grows no heather will follow. Plus, it is poisonous to animals and therefore well avoided by the sheep and the grouse who know instinctively it's not for them. Talk about unloved.

Unloved is not the way I would by any means describe our next port of call on the road to Whitby. As the road climbs and skirts round the rim of the famous Hole of Horcum, or Devil's Punchbowl as it is sometimes referred to, there is a fabulous view of the deep valley below. I always look to see whether an engine is steaming its way along the valley floor, because himself would not be happy if I missed it. Yes, it is a continuation of the North York Moors Railway from Pickering and I must admit a give-away blast of white steam way below us only enhances the spectacular view over this great hollow, which is said to have been carved out by the bare hands of the Devil himself. Apparently he threw the earth over the moor to form nearby Blakey Topping. True or not, these legends have lived a long time and are all part of the scenery.

The Devil must have had rather a large hand, because as well as the railway track the hollow is also home to a couple of farms with beautiful backdrops of much heather and other shrubbery. The road that saunters around the Hole of Horcum is known as Saltersgate Bank and as the road descends around a bend there is a sight that has been welcome to travellers for the past three centuries: the Saltersgate Inn.

However, that was not always its title. Long ago it was a coaching halt called the Wagon and Horses, but it has to be said by the very nature of its situation, isolated on this moor with no village or town in sight and only high open moorland between it and the sea, it does conjure up a much more intriguing picture – that of an old smuggler's inn.

Sign board creaking on a dark moonlit night, with horses tied up in the yard and men's voices raised in argument over ownership of some booty. Three-cornered hats filed on pegs on the timber and stone walls. Pewter drinking vessels reflecting the light of the scanty candle lanterns and the air filled with the smoke from the long-stemmed pipes of those enjoying the scene. An occasional hound enjoying a lap of ale that has spilled from a carelessly emptied keg. The smell of peat as the fire burns a warm glow in the wide hearth. Ah, the fire. Maybe that is the secret of the atmosphere within these stout old walls that have borne witness to so much.

It is no well-kept secret nowadays to those that know the inn well, that in the year 1796 a man fell victim to murder here when he disturbed a group of smugglers who undoubtedly were up to no good. To cover their crime it is said the guilty buried the evidence under the hearth of the turf fire and that from that day the fire has never been allowed to go out. The reason is, it appears that the murder was so brutal that the men feared the victim's ghost would take revenge and their only hope was that he would not stir whilst the fire burned. And so it has, for over 200 years as far as anybody knows. Nobody has ever proved or disproved the story, but for some reason everybody subsequently has gone along with it, despite the fact that the perpetrators of the crime have obviously long since joined their victim. No, not under the hearth! There wouldn't be room! Although maybe they were destined for a hot place, bearing in mind their criminal tendencies.

By the way, the smugglers had every reason to be fearsome – the poor soul beneath the hearth is said to have been an officer of the dreaded customs and excise who disturbed them whilst they were about their business. A small detail that immediately raises the suspicion that the tale of the man's ghost taking revenge was purely a 'smokescreen' – I know, I'm sorry, I couldn't resist it. After all, if the man was a customs officer then those responsible for his demise would certainly have cause to fear him even from the grave, for there would be no sanctuary for the guilty if his mutilated body was found by the authorities. More likely, an informal trial and instant dismissal to the same place they sent their victim, and I don't mean under the hearth. This is further substantiated by the fact the 'customers' of the inn at the time seem to have taken out double insurance by making it known that the Devil supposedly rushed in on them one night and threatened all present with damnation. To quieten him, they offered a seat by the fire. As soon as he was seated, they pushed him into the flames where he is supposed to still reside. If the fire goes out, he will escape into the neighbourhood. What better way in those days of yore, when superstition was rife, to keep anyone from investigating the hearth beneath!

Anyway, although much smoke has gone up the chimney, so to speak, since then, still the fire burns and no wonder, since some would also tell how, despite the fire being kept in, glasses have danced from shelves and smashed to the floor, whilst others report just the weirdest of feelings that they are not alone.

To substantiate the story of smugglers you only have to look to the right of the fire with its splendid 200-year-old range. High up in the alcove, there is a tiny window. This window was used for a very important purpose – not so much to let light in, but more to let light out. It was here that a lighted lantern would be placed – whenever necessary – to act as a beacon to warn all those approaching the inn that the customs men were nigh. If no good was afoot I presume the warning was not only welcome, but heeded immediately, and many grateful souls had second thoughts about proceeding with their journey. It seems, however, on one night at least there was no warning of an unwanted intruder; then again but for him there would be no fire.

Once upon a time, not that many years ago, climbing over Fylingdales Moor from the Saltersgate Inn, there would always be good views of the three huge white 'golf balls' or radomes of Fylingdales Ballistic Missile Early Warning Station rising up out of the moor like three great gods. Strangely, to me, they never seemed out of place. Perhaps it is because they were a familiar landmark for so many years – even a popular one to many, being much photographed for magazines, local postcards and visitors' photograph albums. They even appeared on television occasionally. All in all they were celebrities in their own right.

Regrettably they too passed their sell-by date and disappeared into oblivion. Their replacement is an odd-shaped pyramid that has no character or charm and can only be described as a concrete blot on an otherwise scenic landscape. The first time I came this way after the golf balls' demise, as I glanced across the moor, I noticed three unmistakable huge round, yellow blemishes on the earth and I couldn't help feeling a little sad that these beautiful moors had yet another scar for Mother Nature to heal.

Within easy reach of Fylingdales is Goathland. This small, usually peaceful, moorland village found stardom overnight when Yorkshire Television decided to use it as the backdrop to their drama series *Heartbeat*, based on the *Constable* books by Nicholas Rhea. Of course, the village is the perfect setting for the show, and I am an ardent fan, but personally we avoid Goathland when filming is taking place because it becomes just too crowded for comfort. One of the things I love most about these moors and their villages is that they appear to be locked into a time all their own, perfect in every way and untouched by the mayhem of present-day life. I suppose logically this is why Goathland was chosen for *Heartbeat*. The village only requires a few basic alterations to recapture the 1960s era of the series.

One warm summer's day a few years ago, with Brian and Chris, we decided to walk down the road from Goathland's car park into Beckhole. When I say down, I mean down; it gets quite steep near the end but is well worth the one-and-a-half mile effort. The tiny hamlet is a garden of fine trees and shrubs and very popular with our feathered friends, who were out in abundance. Peeping out from the close foliage of the hedgerows or bobbing from bough to bough in the bountiful green mantles of the various trees, they seemed so happy that I wondered if this wasn't perhaps their sanctuary from the stark vulnerability of the open moorland close by that would not suit some of them at all. A sort of oasis in a desert.

The road down into Beckhole actually continues over a bridge covering a stony beck, which being in a deep hollow probably gives the place its name, and the road rises sharply again on the other side. I definitely felt here all was at peace with the world, for who in the world would come here unless they lived here or knew it well. Luckily, we discovered it by venturing off the beaten track. Still, I decided we must have chosen a quiet time for there didn't appear to be another soul around. If you blinked on passing through this village you'd miss it. However, I liked it. We all did. Just over the bridge, away from the road, is the hilly path up to Thomason Foss, a rather spectacular waterfall by all accounts. It turned out to be a dodgy climb out of Beckhole to see it, so I chickened out, I'm ashamed to say. I'm not very good on narrow ascending paths with not a lot to hold onto. David tried to persuade me, using the usual encouraging tones and tact that men seem to have on these occasions when they wish to do something and you don't. (Apologies to any male readers, but I am sure my female readers know exactly what I mean.) Telling me it would be all right and there was nothing to worry about, then with more impatience telling me to get on with it and finally calling me a 'spoilsport', among other things, when I just would not be coaxed, but instead stretched myself out on the mossy grass to soak up the midday sun, feeling not the least bit guilty. As it turned out I made the right choice. Amanda and our friend Chris soon returned and Amanda admitted the climb was very difficult and slippy, so they had backtracked. David and Brian had gone on with their adventure and been very impressed with the result. Apparently it really is beautiful up there, as their photographs were later to prove, although they did have the grace to admit it was stiff going and you had to be very careful. After their efforts we were all glad to take some light refreshment in the gardens of the inn with the birds serenading us, before our climb out of Beckhole and back to Goathland.

You might have thought everybody would have had enough of waterfalls that day, but you would be wrong. On the other side of Goathland village there is another, more accessible one, known as Malayan Spout, adjacent to a hotel of the same name. The path here leads straight down and we decided to tackle it. Even me, as it did not seem as daunting as the upward climb of Thomason Foss. Downhill we went for approximately one mile and Amanda and I were in the lead. Then we had to clamber over some rocks and I was still in the lead. Surprisingly I can be very sure-footed when I have something fairly substantial to tread on. I was enjoying the view to my right as the water rippled in the sunlight over and around the stones in the rushing beck. The path was getting a little bit hit and miss with the rocks and a trifle narrow.

As I rounded a large protruding rock on the bend of the path, Amanda close to my heels and Chris too, we were suddenly stopped in our tracks by a heavy thud from behind. David had slipped and fallen. It all flashes through the mind at once, doesn't it, as you rush back to the scene? How hurt is he? Where can we get help quickly? What if there is something broken? However, I needn't have worried. We found him still smiling, with his arm held at an angle as he had tried to avoid hitting his camera on the rocks. My relief was instant. It was obvious he had fallen quite hard, but although shaken and a little pale he did not seem much the worse for wear, putting his fall down to the soles of his boots being worn and not good for grip on the wet rocks. Something, however, was broken: sadly, the lens filter of his camera had shattered and he was far more concerned about that than anything. Brian helped him up and we sat him on a convenient rock, Chris administered the necessary health checks whilst I shook the broken glass from the lens and made sure there was no glass on the path for other people to encounter. All the while I had to smother a rather smug grin. All the ear bending I had received for not going up Thomason Foss and here was my 'mountain goat' of a few hours earlier looking more like a scolded kid, cleaning his poor camera with his hanky, on a rock in the middle of nowhere.

After a while the injured party decided he was recovered enough to go on and so we continued our clamber over the rocky path to our goal – the beautiful Malayan Spout, the highest waterfall in the North York

Moors. I remember first noticing the rainbow as we rounded the curve in the path and got our first sight of the column of water issuing from somewhere above the leafy bank. It was like another world. The path disappeared completely here and we had to stop anyway, but the view was perfectly magical and with the sun highlighting or throwing into shade the various green, yellow and gold hues, it seemed the whole scene was floodlit somehow. David had decided that, apart from the filter glass, his camera should be undamaged so he was going to try it out, but not from where we were standing. No, that wouldn't be a good enough shot. Brian agreed. So they did nothing more than start playing stepping stones across the water to some rather large rocks. I just closed my eyes. Knowing the stones would be slippy and that he had gone down once, I just couldn't watch, especially bearing in mind he was holding the camera, which wouldn't take kindly to a ducking.

Brian, who was wearing more reliable footwear, saw him over the dodgy bits, although that didn't prevent him from missing a footing again. This time, though, he didn't fall but just managed to wash his foot in his shoe and sock. They made it to the large rocks. Next minute there is David laying full stretch on a large slab without an inch to spare either side, pointing the camera upwards to take what turned out to be a very good picture of the spout and the rainbow. The fact that Brian did as well, standing upright, is nothing to do with it. At last they had finished and safely retraced their steps back to us. The five of us then returned back up the path to the top in good spirits, even though one of us had gained a soggy foot, a couple of bruises and lost a filter lens. It was definitely time for dinner back at the Saltersgate Inn, where David could dry his foot out by the famous fire, which, despite the hot day, would most certainly be burning.

Goathland holds another fascination for David, other than its surrounding waterfalls. It has a very attractive railway station that is now part of the North York Moors Railway. Of course, since the *Heartbeat* series is set in the '60s, the steam engines are definitely an on-site advantage for the film crew. No mock ups are needed. No cheating by using another preserved railway. No, it's all here with the availability of rolling stock and atmosphere packaged in the authentic setting of the North York Moors.

Esk Dale is but a short distance north of Goathland on the northern extremities of the North York Moors, and was once the home of Nicholas Rhea, the author of the *Constable* books on which *Heartbeat* is based. He was born in Glaisdale and, typical of so many of the moors villages, it too has a history of once being a mining community. In the mid-1800s it is said that there were two blast furnaces here which undoubtedly did nothing to enhance the scenery. However, today the scenery is just perfect and so is the river – for its salmon fishing. Glaisdale is also known for its legendary seventeenth-century Beggar's Bridge, which spans the river amidst shady woodland. A perfect spot for lovers, so the story goes. Apparently, Tom Ferris was a penniless young man who had fallen in love with Agnes, the daughter of the rich local squire. If this wasn't problem enough for the lovers, Agnes lived in Glaisdale, whilst Tom lived on the other side of the river. Consequently, every time they met, since there was no bridge, Tom had to get his feet wet. Of course, the squire did not approve of young Tom as a suitor for his daughter. Tom was not one to be put off, however, and asked the squire whether, if he too became wealthy, he would grant them permission to marry. The squire said he would, obviously confident it would never happen. He didn't know Tom very well. The young man went off to sea and apparently fought the Spanish Armada with Sir Francis Drake before embarking on a career as a pirate and, indeed, eventually making his fortune.

Well, his Agnes had been loyal and, forsaking all others, waited for her lover. The squire had to be seen as a man of his word and the couple were married. In fact, Tom did so well he established a shipping company in Hull and in 1614 became mayor. Sadly, only four years later his beloved Agnes died. The devastated Tom had never forgotten his early courting days and how faithful his wife had been to him and so he returned to Glaisdale to build Beggar's Bridge in memory of her, no doubt to ensure that future lovers in a similar predicament to Agnes and Tom could meet without getting their feet wet. His initials are carved on the bridge simply as 'TF 1619'. Tom outlived his wife by 13 years, dying in 1631, but his legacy to the romantic amongst us still stands.

Having virtually followed the path of the railway from Pickering up as far as Goathland, it is only fitting we should finish our journey over the moors with Grosmont. Approximately four miles east of Glaisdale, Grosmont too was once an industrial town in the Esk Valley, now it is the northern terminus of the North York Moors Steam Railway. The railway mostly employs the helping hands of enthusiastic volunteers, many of whom are experienced ex-railwaymen – drivers, firemen and the like – responsible for ensuring that the engines, rolling stock and track are well cared for and maintained to the highest possible standards. No risk is ever taken. The sound reliability of the engine and safety and comfort of the passengers is paramount. As well as the more professional staff, there are numerous people who give their services willingly to the line. Indulging their love of the golden age of steam, they too play a very important part in keeping the railway up and running and must not be excluded from praise for their efforts. Their responsibilities are great and I soon learnt this was not a case of little boys playing trains, as is so often mistakenly presumed. This is a professionally run railway, carefully regulated so that each member of the team has a part to play. A rota is posted regularly so that everyone knows their duties.

These beasts of the track need much tender loving care to coax them into life. Apparently, if an engine has been used the previous day then the water in the boiler should retain a good deal of its heat overnight. This means it should only take approximately four hours the following morning to lay the fire, light it and then get the water in the boiler up to temperature. The latter is essential to avoid any unnecessary excessive stresses being put on the boiler, according to my sources. The waiting time is put to good use, maintenance checks are made and the oil can is employed for an 'oil round' to ensure the locomotive's moving parts are kept well lubricated. All these preparations are carried out by the capable hands of the experts, under the watchful eye of the experienced, so that when the regulator is opened and that first rush of steam is heard as it passes into the cylinders, all is perfectly attuned to the knowing ear of the driver and he is confident it will run well and to time.

Although the means to an end seems to take an awfully long time to the uninitiated and requires very early risers to clock on long before the first locomotive leaves Grosmont shed, I have been assured that four hours is nothing compared to the possible twelve hours it can take for an engine to be ready to roll, when starting from scratch, with a stone-cold boiler. I have to say, to me it's all grit, coal, oil and hard work, but to those that work on the North York Moors Railway I am absolutely sure it is complete dedication, a way of life. Obviously, they do thoroughly enjoy their work and why not, since they pass so much pleasure on to approximately a quarter of a million tourists each year, who combine a trip behind a steam locomotive with a trip through some of the most fantastic scenery in England.

Despite my hesitations concerning the muckier side of a well-oiled and 'in-steam' locomotive, I have been known to mount the footplate of one of these incredible machines, whilst it was standing in the station, and take more than a passing interest in its more intricate parts, much to the utter disgust of the male spectators also on board. The fun really started, though, when I was allowed to take the hallowed shovel, fetch a few lumps of coal from the tender and throw it into the fire bed. That was just too much for the men to bear and they immediately disembarked, strutting off like injured peacocks. Mind you, not so the driver and fireman who were well amused and continued to give me their undivided attention. Before I left the footplate I couldn't resist the offer to give a blast on the whistle. That was the final straw, since when I nimbly descended the precarious steps to the platform below there was more than a note of disapproval in the air. Not to be intimidated in any way I quickly wiped my blackened hands on my hanky, waved goodbye to the driver and fireman, laughing all over their faces on the footplate, and smiled sweetly to my huffing and puffing audience as I left the scene; prudently, the engine too took its leave.

Although I have called Grosmont a terminus, that strictly only applies to the Moors Railway, since it is also the junction with the Esk Valley line, still part of the national network, which runs from industrial Teeside to Whitby. I cannot help feeling that it would definitely enhance the NYMR if it too were able to extend its route so that once again there would be steam trains rolling into Whitby. Maybe that is food for thought for the future.

Despite the varying pulses of life on these moors, many of which I have written about here, for me nothing dominates them more than the incredible blackness of the night. Ghastly in its entirety, shameless in its deception of what lies beyond, it submits to nothing but the moonlight of a cloudless sky. But on such an evening, before darkness descends, the flattened moor does not hinder the panoramic views of the heavens where the gold of a spectacular sunset seems to stand aloof over the sunken blackness of the earth. Soon the swirling colour will be gone and in its place the moon, guardian of the night sky, will reign supreme.

Many a fascinating story has been cast about the happenings on these moors after dark. Eerie tales, which mainly involve smugglers, and other dubious characters of dubious means, not to mention the ghosts who frequent the area whenever the mood takes them. From first-hand experience I wholeheartedly admit these stories are certainly spooky enough to make even the most sceptical amongst us feel a shiver down the spine or a sudden rush of adrenaline if they happen to come to mind when you are driving over the moors roads at night. With hardly another car in sight and just your headlights to guide your path they do not make for good companions, particularly when you come to notice how your lights only seem to enhance the blackness, and therefore the unknown, on either side of you, and the occasional glint of a pair of eyes of some wandering beast glancing your way does not help matters either. Naturally, the moors are the perfect setting for suspicious goings-on and I can well believe that in years gone by there were many characters who prowled around this area under the cover of darkness, definitely up to no good. After all, the previously mentioned Saltersgate Inn could well testify to that fact with its need to display a lantern to warn certain of its customers away when the customs men were around, not to mention the poor soul laid to rest under the hearth. As for the more legendary tales of ghosts wandering the moors and terrifying the unsuspecting, the blackness of the night certainly can evoke the belief that there is some truth in what has been told.

One fact is indisputable, witch posts in the sixteenth and seventeenth centuries were an integral part of most houses in the area and presumably still exist in some older houses on the moors today. They were unique to the North York Moors and the very fact they were considered an essential integral part of the house illustrates just how superstitious people of those days really were. They sincerely believed in the power of witches or demons to cast mischievous or evil spells. In fact, most often they blamed anything from the slightest mishap such as a cow not producing her quota of milk to a child becoming sick with fever on a witch's curse. Thus the witch post, they firmly believed, kept the evil at bay, and it was strategically placed to one side of the hearth away from the wall, usually acting as a support for the chimney hood of the fire. Many of these solid posts, which were made of oak or rowan, bore peculiar markings that we would have difficulty understanding, but it is said they may have been the work of priests who, in blessing the posts, added insurance that they would be effective.

As a matter of interest there is a fine example of a witch post in one of the houses at the Ryedale Folk Museum. No witches, though. I cannot find any firm evidence as to how witch posts originated, but I do wonder whether the combination of the post and the power of the fire to eradicate evil provided the basis for burning at the stake all those suspected of witchcraft or heresy in the fearful days of the witch finder. However, whatever lurks about the moors at night, and whether those people of yesteryear had good cause or not to live in fear, I would not know, for one very good reason: I have never stayed around long enough to find out – and that is no accident!

One thing I am positive about, however, is that, as sure as the sun rises each morning, I will always return to these glorious moors that I have come to love, and, who knows . . . perhaps on the morrow, if the sun is shining, I'll venture farther.

❧ FOUR ☙

. . . And So to the Sea

Time was when a trip to the seaside was a special treat that the majority of people could not afford very often. Poor wages, large families and the cost of travelling did not help. However, children growing up in the years that followed the devastation of the Second World War were more fortunate and it became, for most, an annual tradition to be taken to the seaside for a week or two during the long summer breaks from the routine of school.

I was one such child and it often occurs to me nowadays how truly hot and sunny those summer days at the seaside always seemed to be. Cloudless skies, the sun glinting off the water and people enjoying a paddle or even a swim, whilst little ones clutched their buckets and wandered along the shore looking for shells or maybe a crab or two. Then there were the jubilant cries of the children as they wielded the metal blades of their spades into the sumptuously obliging soft sand as another array of castles was about to be born. Standing by were always the traditional bunches of paper flags, awaiting their turn to be placed by sandy hands on the tops of the battlements to flutter in the breeze when the works of art were complete. Of course, there were always the tears too, as a careless foot in its excitement trampled a castle wall, or worse, caused an unstoppable avalanche as the sand cascaded back whence it came. As the little engineer looked on, the end of the world seemed nigh and he would become inconsolable until Dad appeared with that most acceptable of bribes, the ice-cream cornet, and the castle would be forgotten and left to be reclaimed by the sea as the relentless tide turned and edged its way up the beach to wipe the slate clean for the new day, tomorrow.

Apart from the sun, sea and sand, my memories of the seaside always conjure up one particular picture: that of the beaches being covered by hundreds of deckchairs with hardly any space of sand in between. There they all were, like row upon row of alerted grasshoppers (so many of them were covered in green canvas and their erect frames were just like the long jointed legs of those creatures when poised to jump). An army that still invades many of our beaches today. Regardless of all the progress we have made over the years, and our technical prowess, we have still not mastered an improved version of this ever-vigilant enemy of man. Man, whose only desire is to use it as a means for lazing in the sun and reclining his body in the fully fashioned wide canvas strap that is slung between those ever-waiting lethal wooden jaws. However, first it has to be put up, and it is going to protest, for the gentle art of erecting a deckchair is one of the most difficult tasks known to the human race. No one escapes. And the enemy is never satisfied until it has protested wildly by pinching a finger here, catching a toe there or even whacking a chin occasionally as it spins around the canvas, perplexing the innocent completely as to which way the one end should be placed on the other one with the notches in. And then, how many times has the victim thought he's actually got it right at last, sat on it with a real sense of achievement, only to suddenly be sprawled on his posterior in the most undignified of poses with the thing as flat as a pancake once more?

This would be the appropriate time for Mum to produce the sandwiches from the bag of goodies she always brought down to the beach with her. Do you remember those 'sandwiches', reader? It didn't matter what she put in them or how well wrapped they were, they always tasted the same. Gritty! It was sand, of course, and although you tried to persist and hope the next bite would be better, it never was – and your poor teeth!

It was the same with the towel. After playing happily in the water, you would run back up the beach, teeth chattering and body shivering uncontrollably. Mum would be waiting with towel at the ready, which she would lovingly drape around you to help keep you warm. At first you would be grateful, but alas, then it came. The rub down. Oh dear, how it scratched and clawed at your delicate skin. You then knew what a plank of wood felt like when it was being sanded, except wood doesn't get red blotches. Mum would notice the red blotches and say you'd been out in the sun too long. You would protest, but she would insist that she knew best and reach for your T-shirt to cover you up. Then came the final straw, the T-shirt would be stretched over your head and it would rain sand all over you. It would be in your hair, in your eyes, on your lips, and didn't it stick? Trying to brush it off was like stroking yourself with a razor blade. Funny how that awful stuff could give you so much pleasure under foot and so much pain and discomfort when it got anywhere else. I wonder if it was in league with the deckchairs – probably!

These are just a few of my observations from a notebook of childhood memories associated with the seaside. However, I have never lost my fascination for the sea and still feel that same surge of excitement whenever we head east to Yorkshire's coast. The Heritage Coast, as it is referred to, is the 35-mile stretch of dramatic and fascinating coastline between Saltburn in the north and Scarborough in the south, and has been given the title because it is considered worthy of special protection. Apart from the first few miles, which are now part of the Cleveland coastline – i.e. from Saltburn down as far as Boulby – the Heritage Coast forms an integral part of the North York Moors National Park and in its entirety encompasses a fine assortment of towns and villages that is well worth exploring.

It is very hard to imagine today that Saltburn could ever have been involved in the risky but profitable business of smuggling. Its elegant Victorian houses that line the cliff top and overlook the bay seem hardly in keeping with smugglers or anybody who would contravene the laws of the land. However, Saltburn was not always a prim and proper Victorian coastal town. It only became one after the arrival of the Stockton and Darlington Railway in 1861 when it was decided to develop the area as a seaside resort. Prior to that time it was a small hamlet consisting of a few houses and the Ship Inn, which nestles into the bay at the base of the cliffs. It was in the 1770s that the inn's new

proprietors, a Scotsman by the name of John Andrew and his wife
Anne, took up residence, and from then on smuggling became big
business in Saltburn. John and Anne profited so well that eventually
they moved to the White House. No, not the one in Washington – just
to the top of Saltburn Gill overlooking the bay.

Smuggling was rife in many of England's coastal areas between the
late 1600s and the mid-1800s and Saltburn was certainly not alone on
the Heritage Coast. In fact, it seems that everybody who was anybody
at the time was somehow involved in smuggling. It was an age of heavy
taxes here in England (so what has changed!), which meant that goods
such as tobacco, snuff, linen, brandy, gin and even tea were welcomed
on the black market. The smugglers had no problem finding traders
willing to take the contraband off their hands and they were kept very
busy meeting the heavy demand.

It was, therefore, necessary to be well organised. The majority of
landings took place under the cover of darkness and there were always
plenty of armed men keeping watch just in case the customs men were
about. If they appeared, a warning was sent out to the vessels waiting at
sea and the off-loading would be postponed. If the coast was clear then
the locals would be sent out in their boats to fetch the cargo off the
waiting vessels. As soon as their precious cargo was landed, it was
disposed of with the greatest expediency and efficiency. It disappeared
into caves, secret hideaways, underground passages and the like. Later,
the smugglers would transfer their precious haul onto the backs of
ponies so it could be carried over the moors to a pre-arranged venue,
such as the Saltersgate Inn, mentioned in my previous chapter, or some
other safe-house where it would then be distributed to those awaiting
their share.

Although the smugglers were well organised and quite ingenious in
carrying out their side of the operation, sadly the same cannot be said
for the poor Customs Preventive Officers. Oh, they tried, of course they
did. But their success rate was not very impressive. It was not all their
fault. They were an underpaid, understaffed and very disorganised body
of men, whose skill on shore was only marginally better than their skill
out at sea in their rowing boats and later their few revenue cutters.
Their efforts on the open sea were no match for the experienced,
hardened seamen they were trying to catch and mostly they returned

empty-handed. Naturally, with the law of averages, they had to make a few arrests occasionally, but these often came as a result of tip-offs and the informants then expected to be paid out of the prize money that was awarded for the successful apprehension of offenders. Thus the customs men lost out again.

Of course, the smugglers were fully aware that if they were caught the penalty for smuggling was by no means light and it could mean a term of imprisonment, enforced service in the army or navy, deportation or, worse, the hangman's noose. However, they must also have held the opinion that the rewards from their illegal but profitable trade far outweighed the risks and, bearing in mind they undoubtedly knew how inefficient the customs men were at that time in their history, the majority continued to prosper and escape capture well into the 1830s. It was around that time that things began to change, and with tighter government controls and a more efficiently organised customs service, time began to run out for these diligent rogues. The strong arm of the law forced the majority of smugglers to think again and decide to come down on the side of caution. Enough was enough and the nets were definitely closing in. Their heyday was over and the tables were now being turned in favour of the customs men at last.

However, I am not convinced this is the whole story. As much as I would like to believe that law and order prevailed, I am not sure that it was the only reason for many of the more professional smuggling rings to suddenly decide to call it a day. After all, they had proved themselves to be very adept at what they did best, overcoming all the obstacles of officialdom and earning a pretty penny for their efforts. I cannot help feeling there was a little more to it and that maybe it was not so surprising that the sudden decline in smuggling activities along this once quiet and sparsely populated stretch of coastline very much coincided with the arrival and establishment of the mining industry.

Just imagine it. The great population explosion that was created by the mines would have been a very real threat to the smugglers' ability to carry out any secret rendezvous with a ship off-shore. The risks of being discovered would have increased greatly, and even if they had managed to get their precious bounty to shore, with so much activity at the cliff face, where could they be sure it would remain undiscovered until they had time to move it on to its destination? And even if they did find a safe hidey-hole, with so many new workings being exploded every day, how could they ensure their haul would not be blown up or, worse, showered around the shoreline for all the world to see? Then they may just as well have done their deeds by daylight with a sign displaying their intent. No. If the new customs controls did not wholly convince the more hardened smugglers, I think the unsuspecting mining community clinched the deal!

As for Saltburn, the smugglers would probably have appreciated the helping hand one Victorian innovation could have provided. In 1870, a vertical hoist was constructed to carry passengers the 50 metres from the cliff top to the beach below. Unfortunately, being wooden and only secured by guy ropes, its days were numbered and within 13 years it was to be dismantled and subsequently replaced by the present, much more sturdy, structure. The inclined tramway has remained in place since June 1884 and has required little attention. Although it receives regular maintenance checks for safety, it is virtually as built and holds the title of the world's oldest water-balanced cliff lift.

By the way, if you are wondering what happened to Black John Andrew, his smuggling exploits finally caught up with him at the great age of 70 when he was arrested unloading a cargo at Hornsea. He was imprisoned in York Castle. However, during his long and fruitful career he had made many influential friends who had also no doubt profited from the proceeds of John's activities from time to time. These friends were now anxious to secure John's release. One cannot help wondering whether it was more for their benefit than the prisoner's, i.e. to ensure the authorities never discovered their relationship with the smuggler. Or perhaps the crafty old man actually blackmailed them? Who knows? John gained his freedom after serving just two years in prison and returned to Saltburn in 1829, but, by this time age and prison had taken their toll and he never returned to smuggling. He died in November 1835 and is buried in the graveyard of All Saints Church, Skelton.

The Ship Inn still dominates the bay at the foot of the cliffs. It has undergone some modernisation since John and Anne were there, but you can still find them next door in the old cottages, which have been transformed into a Smugglers Heritage Centre, where you can take a step back in time and enter the world of the smugglers – if you dare. One more fact may be of interest: John Andrew's booty was never found. Was it eradicated by the blasting of the mines or is it still hidden in a secret place somewhere in Saltburn, where John left it all those years ago?

The majority of villages on North Yorkshire's Heritage Coast cling precariously to the cliff face and it is easy to understand why they are prone to being cut off in the bleakness of winter when the snow and ice compact themselves in layers on the steep inclines of their access roads. Staithes, reputedly the most northerly village in North Yorkshire, is no different and visitors are politely asked to leave their cars in the car park at the top of the cliffs annexed to the more modern Staithes housing estate, before making their way down into the older part of the village. It must be remembered that the fishing villages around our coasts were purpose-built for easy access from the sea and in the days when they evolved it was the pack horse or cart that mainly took priority as far as traffic was concerned, usually carrying provisions to the local people or transporting the fish from the quaysides. The streets were cobbled to lower the risk of the horses' hooves slipping on the steep hills and, give better grip to the cart wheels too.

I have never forgotten my first visit to Staithes, or 'Steers' as it is known locally. It was a grim, overcast day. One of those days when a low canopy of thick, grey cloud, throws the earth below it into half light tinged with an eerie, almost yellowish hue. Having left the car, we followed the road down into the village and as we walked were amused to find ourselves eye to eye with several seagulls perched on the various chimney pots of the houses that tumbled down the cliff to our left. Maybe it was the weather that day and the peculiar stillness that hung on the air, or perhaps it was the increasing awareness that the village was completely devoid of any signs of life, but I at once took the view that Staithes had been lost in some sort of time warp – a time somewhere in the distant past when it had just stopped and nothing had moved from that day to this. It couldn't go back but it hadn't wanted to come forward into the future either.

Amongst the small houses that opened directly onto the cobbled main street that led directly down to the waterfront, there were a few shops which appeared to be open for business but, apart from one elderly lady who was seated just outside her front door, there was nobody about. The lady did not even look up as we passed her by, but she did appear to be waiting, for what I don't know. A couple of stray cats joined us as we walked and showed their approval of our company by continually rubbing themselves against us in the hope of some fuss. They were not disappointed as we stopped to stroke them. Afterwards they made no attempt to follow but just stood and watched as we continued our walk. It was no surprise to find the waterfront also deserted, except for an array of lobster pots. As we looked out on the dismal, yet calm, grey-green sea merging with the angry, swirling grey sky above, I recalled that age-old saying 'the lull before the storm'. Apart from the rhythmic lapping of the water over the rocks there was no other sound and the eeriness of it all was very unsettling. Even the gulls were unusually silent and still, visible as a mass of white dots against the dark, sombre background of the foreboding headland. Just like the old lady, they too seemed to be waiting.

It was growing darker and the weather was rapidly closing in. Our mood for exploring had been dampened and we decided to retrace our steps back to the car. We never saw the cats again and the old lady had gone indoors. The shops, too, were now closed and shuttered but we had neither seen nor heard anyone. What is more, as we made the climb back up the steep incline out of the village, we noticed the gulls had left the chimney pots too. We didn't have time to think about it. Suddenly, abruptly, violently, the deathly silence was shattered. From directly above us it came, that first tremendous clap of thunder. Our pace automatically quickened. It was still rumbling and echoing around the bay behind us as we reached our car. I'd never heard anything like it. It was just so fearfully penetrating. The second clap was even more fearful than the first, accompanied by a blinding flash of lightning and then the heavens well and truly opened. As we drove out of the car park, we took a last look back at old Staithes, now in the darkened clutches of the raging storm. It was then I realised the waiting was over!

As I said, this was my first encounter with Staithes and after reading this you may, with good reason, believe I had no inclination to return to the village. You would be wrong! I did go back, and more surprisingly, David and Amanda came back with me, even though they thought Staithes had little to offer, based on first impressions. They were wrong too. The day we returned was a very different story. It was very warm and the sky was a clear azure blue. The sun burned into our skins as we again let our legs take the strain on the now familiar descent into the sun-drenched village below. The white-painted cottages reflected the sun's powerful rays and dazzled our eyes, whilst the parched, burnished grasses of the cliffs rustled in a light summer breeze and bowed longingly towards the sea. The gulls were once again in residence on the chimney pots, and the houses on the main street threw sharp shadows across the sunlit cobbles. Windows were open and curtains were blowing gently in a light refreshing breeze. People chatted with their neighbours in doorways, oblivious to our presence, and we could hear the excited voices of children playing somewhere out of sight, but close by.

This was Staithes, and regardless of my initial, rather hasty impressions of this village only a few months ago, I was delighted to be back. Yes, of course, the buildings were of a bygone age and nothing could change that. Long ago they had been built to house a community which derived its livelihood from the sea – shipbuilders, fishermen – and later the miners. Today they continue to serve the same purpose, providing homes for the people who live and work here, tolerant of all weathers and adding their own character and charm to the older part of the village. This was certainly not a village locked firmly in the past, as I had first thought. This was a village that was proud of its past and had ensured it survived alongside its present. How quickly I had prejudged Staithes on a mood of the moment that day. The buildings, empty streets, sullen sea, all drenched in that dreadful heaviness before the storm had influenced me too much, but at least they had aroused my curiosity too, which was why I had had to come back. Of course, a place needs people to bring it to life, give it some sense of time and place in the order of things. Now all around me the local people had brought Staithes to life for me and I was not disappointed.

I also realised that this community, who have the sea as their perpetual neighbour, well understand the unpredictability of the elements, and in particular how quickly the weather can turn. A storm had been brewing and they knew it would be a bad one, so where else would they be but safely out of reach behind closed doors, out of sight. I could see the funny side now, of them observing us from behind their curtains and thinking, 'Look at those daft outsiders', for no locals in their right mind would be wandering the streets near the waterfront on such a day with such a storm in the offing.

On exploring the village further it soon became obvious that Staithes is a fascinating maze of little nooks and alleyways, yards and byways where houses and other buildings jostle for space. There is no room for a garden here. One of these alleyways led us behind the main street onto a narrow metal bridge which spans what remains of Roxby Beck after it leaves the moor and before it meets the sea.

Standing in the middle of the bridge looking out to sea, this is obviously the vantage point from which the most popular picture of Staithes is always taken. It often appears in tour guides, on postcards and has even been painted. It definitely is a picturesque view, with the high rugged headland to the left, or north, overshadowing a row of delightful cottages on the quay below, of which not one is the same as the next. They are in Cleveland, apparently, whilst to the right, or south, the old houses sited right atop the wall are officially in North Yorkshire, as is the remainder of the village. Mind you, the houses on the right are so precariously perched they give the impression they could topple into the sea at any moment – when the tide is in that is – and end up in Cleveland too! This particular day, however, the tide was out, and there was only a narrow ribbon of water running under the bridge. Either side, on the banks, there were a few colourful rowing boats, some having been left upside down, perhaps to dry in the afternoon sun. The whole spectacle was indeed quite beautiful.

Back down in the harbour the sea was calm and very blue. Children were hunting for crabs under the rocks and it was tempting to join them, but I had decided to accept the invitation of the local Captain Cook and Staithes Heritage Centre and take a look inside. I had done some homework on the village before coming back and it was time to get it marked. The centre is housed in the former Primitive Methodist Chapel, which is over a century old. Once inside, I was greeted by a very helpful gentleman who was only too pleased to answer my many questions on Staithes and its surrounding area. The museum was fascinating, and the tales it tells through exhibits and newspaper cuttings kept me enthralled for a long time – a very long time, according to David and Amanda. By the time I rejoined them, the sun was beginning to throw evening shadows over the peaceful bay, which is protected either side by two huge headlands, the same headlands that once stood witness to the real story behind Staithes.

ABOVE LEFT: Hornby church, where many of the Conyers family have been laid to rest. (Chapter 1)

ABOVE RIGHT: Ainderby Myers – in the shadows of the Vikings. (Chapter 1)

BELOW: Spring lambing, Ainderby Myers. (Chapter 1)

ABOVE: Towards the Hambletons . . . the White Horse at Kilburn. (Chapter 2)

INSET: The original vets' surgery in Kirkgate, Thirsk. Now the James Herriot museum. (Chapter 2)

BELOW: Gormire Lake from Sutton Bank. (Chapter 2)

ABOVE: 'The largest expanse of heatherclad moorland in England' – the North York Moors. (Chapter 3)

BELOW: The famous fire at Saltersgate Inn. (Chapter 3)

ABOVE: Goathland garage – 'Mostyn's garage and funeral parlour' for TV's *Heartbeat*. (Chapter 3)

INSET: The haunting silhouette of Whitby Abbey. (Chapter 4)

BELOW: 'Head to head' at Grosmont. (Chapter 3)

ABOVE: A view over Whitby harbour with St Mary's church prominent on the headland. (Chapter 4)

BELOW LEFT: One of Whitby's atmospheric back streets. (Chapter 4)

BELOW RIGHT: 'In Search of the Brontës' – a byway in Haworth. (Chapter 5)

ABOVE: The steep incline of Haworth's main street. (Chapter 5)

INSET: Masham – an unusually empty market square in late Autumn. (Chapter 6)

BELOW: Haworth Parsonage – 'the snow is no stranger here'. (Chapter 5)

ABOVE: Aysgarth Falls – on an October day. (Chapter 6)

BELOW LEFT: Hawes – at the head of Wensleydale. (Chapter 6)

BELOW RIGHT: The warm and inviting West front of St Peters – or simply York Minster. (Chapter 7)

ABOVE: Approaching
Micklegate Bar, York,
along the wall.
(Chapter 7)

BELOW: One of the
butcher's shammels that
give the Shambles its
name. (Chapter 7)

⁂ . . . And So to the Sea ⁂

Once upon a time Staithes contributed much to a thriving fishing industry that had become well-established along this stretch of Yorkshire coastline. The villagers were justifiably proud of their reasonably large fleet of cobles, a sturdy type of in-shore fishing vessel, said to have evolved from the old Viking longboat and capable of withstanding the roughest of seas. There were also a good number of larger ships that were able to cope with the more demanding work. It was just as well the fishermen were so well equipped, since they were expected to meet a heavy and ever-increasing demand for their harvests from all around the country – even as far afield as London. Thus the smell of fish was ever prevalent on the air, wafting up from the harbour into every crack and crevice of the village; as permanent a feature here in Staithes as the resident gulls, who waited noisily on the wing for their pickings when the opportunity arose.

Once the catch was in, the fish had to be transported to market and in the days before the railways 'horse power' was the only method available. For journeys of some distance, such as the market at York some 70 miles away, or even farther afield, a relay method was devised involving several teams of horses along the set route. It is indeed a credit to all concerned that the fish nearly always arrived not only on time but in the best of condition. Of course, with the advent of the railways, life became much easier and longer distances could be covered in a much shorter time, with far less risk to the delicate produce.

It might have been the men that went out in the boats to bring in the fish, but the women of Staithes also played an important role. It was often left to them to prepare the fishing lines, which they carried in coils on their heads down to the boats. They also mended nets and cured the fish. They were renowned for a special type of bonnet they wore, peculiar to this stretch of coastline. Made of a light material it had a wide pleated frill at the front and was tied at the back. Known as the 'Staithes Bonnet', it has been suggested that it had its origins in protecting the ladies' hair from the smell of the fish, although the tradition was continued well after the decline of the fishing industry towards the end of the 1800s.

Although business had been booming, the decline was inevitable. Over-fishing had taken its toll and the fishermen began to realise their livelihoods were now in jeopardy. Shipbuilding, which was also a major source of employment, ceased and the men of Staithes were soon to relinquish the call of the sea for a very different life, exchanging their fishing nets for the miners' pick. A new and growing industry had developed during the second half of the 1800s, providing a more reliable source of income for the men of the sea – the age of the ironstone mines had arrived and these were to change the lives of the families hereabouts forever.

There were three mines around the area: Staithes, Boulby and Grinkle. I am not sure that I would have coped well with the total transformation that must have virtually erased Staithes' identity as a lively but independent fishing community. As with Rosedale, which I mentioned in my previous chapter and many other areas of inland moorland, Staithes now joined the ranks as a mining community and had to suffer the consequences. It had to accommodate the tidal flow of miners that were drawn like a magnet to the area in the latter part of the 1800s from all over the country, including Wales and Cornwall. They needed work to support their families in the hard times of the mid-Victorian era and Staithes had to adapt. Of necessity, there followed the mass construction of additional housing, including a group of corrugated iron cottages, subsequently known as 'Tin City'. They were in close proximity to Boulby and remained for over 30 years. Hospitals and other essential buildings were also erected, all hugging the cliffs that surround the bay and dramatically changing the whole landscape into something resembling an industrial town. And beneath this town, men prised their way into the earth to collect the vital ironstone by the ton. Through the narrow passageways, with pillars to support the upper stratas, the men walked and sometimes crawled to their area of workings: sometimes a distance of some four miles. Forever watchful of water seepage, or worse. Forever aware of their vulnerability.

I have no doubt that the bravery of these men was indeed reflected in the number of incidents that were faithfully recorded by the local press at the time. Tragic accidents leading to the death or permanent injury of many stand as testimony to the dangers awaiting these men. One newspaper report caught my eye that did not involve men at all. One young boy, aged only ten, was trapped between the cage and the shaft wall of a mine, a gap of only six inches. He had been responsible for taking empty tubs from the cage for use in the mine. The other young lad at the top of the shaft was unaware of his workmate's dilemma down below. It was his job to signal to the engine man to raise the cage when it had been relieved of the empty tubs. Tragically, he did just that. The young lad was hauled up the shaft with the cage, a distance of some 30 feet. He was killed instantly. The judge at the inquest ruled that this should have been men's work and not left to inexperienced boys. However, in the days we are talking about, young lads were cheap labour and keen to work for a living and, since school was not a priority for the working classes, they were always available for work.

The miners' wages depended on the quantity of stone they managed to extract. The full tubs were measured by the weighman, who was especially employed by the mine owners for this important job. He was not a man to be envied for his responsible position, because he was constantly in danger of being accused of underestimating the true efforts of the poor miners and the sad truth is the miners often lost the argument, even though they were right. However, they dared not provoke the situation too much for fear of losing their jobs, as there were plenty who would fill the vacancies they left, so in the end they had to keep silent and accept the weighman's word.

For the people of Staithes, the mines certainly brought mixed blessings. Even their shoreline had rapidly been transformed with piers, docks, tramways and other paraphernalia, to not only cater for the constant turnaround of ships being loaded with the ironstone, but also to allow for the vessels delivering coal and other essential equipment for the mines. From Staithes down to Runswick Bay, inshore waters had been as much invaded by the mining industry as had the land itself. Now the smell of the fish no longer had precedence on the air, instead it was the tainted smell of the furnaces and earthworks, the smell of sweat and toil, the smell of oil and engine that was all-pervasive. Only a few men now fished, but all men worked until they could work no more. The mines continued to yield up their wealth of ironstone until they were closed in the 1930s, by which time the majority of mine owners had become rich, although the miners found themselves once again without work, and most packed their belongings, gathered up their families and returned inland in the hope of finding other employment. For many of them work would find them. The Second

World War loomed on the horizon. As for Staithes, when the mines grew silent it once again looked to the sea for survival and many of her men became fishermen once more, just like their forefathers.

It was from Staithes in 1745 that a certain Captain James Cook took his first long hard look at the sea and fell in love with it. Lucky for him his was an uninterrupted view, since the mining industry had not yet littered the scenery with its debris. At the time, he was working as apprentice to a grocer and haberdasher, William Saunderson, where he remained for some 18 months before moving on to Whitby. The shop where he lived and worked stood right on the edge of Staithes harbour and eventually succumbed to the constant pounding it received from the restless sea. Some materials from the original shop were salvaged and incorporated in the new premises at 12 Church Street in 1812, approximately 33 years after the death of its eminent employee. These premises are now known as Cook's Cottage and carry a plaque to advise visitors of their importance.

Despite Staithes' popularity with tourists, it has never allowed itself to succumb to commercialism but instead kept its natural charm and identity. (Which is why it could be mistaken for being caught in a time warp!) What is more, knowing its history, I hope it will always remain unspoilt for us to enjoy, but never on a grim overcast day . . . like the locals, we too have learnt to wait!

Just as in Staithes, the inhabitants of the villages and towns all along the Heritage Coast accept they have a temperamental neighbour. They are used to her moods but occasionally have to pay the price for residing in such close proximity to this unruly element of our earth. The persistent battering from tidal and stormy seas and the forces of so much water have gradually taken their toll and inevitably made for some dramatic changes to our coastal landscapes. Sometimes a landslide can be so slight it almost goes unnoticed as it slips obligingly into the mouth of the awaiting sea. On the other hand, as with Staithes, sometimes the sea's brutal bombardment takes a little more than a clump of disposable land and a few buildings are also sacrificed. However, Runswick Bay probably paid the highest price of all when, in 1682, the erosion was so great that the whole village was lost to a watery grave except for one house. Unbelievably, nobody was killed.

Of course it has been rebuilt and today this tiny fishing village still remains defiantly nestled into the broad and restless hand of the steep headland. Runswick Bay seems a village in miniature, where the houses clamber for space on the cliff face and are so tightly packed together in places that they give the appearance of a model village using life-size buildings. I have no doubt that with its attractive miniature gardens, houses of different shape and style and narrow corridors of walkways and steps and unsuspecting twists and turns down to the sea wall, it would take all the prizes for a particular character and charm not witnessed elsewhere. The occasional lamppost of character, the minute squares of grass and the ankle-high edgings to the neatly kept flowerbeds all contribute to the fascination of this once busy fishing village, now mostly made over to holiday homes. Within half an hour you have probably seen it all. There is no commercialism here. Just a café where you can enjoy a cup of tea and look out over the beautiful bay, the fishing boats and that ever-encroaching sea as the tide comes in yet again.

Since we are travelling from north to south along this coastline, we arrive at Sandsend before the sand has begun. The name actually refers to the two-and-a-half-mile stretch of sand between Whitby in the south and here. It has given children pleasure for generations and when Amanda was very young it was to this sandy stretch of shoreline that we used to come so that she could build her castles and give us an excuse to do the same. After all, mums and dads feel far more comfortable with a bucket and spade in their hands when there is a child around.

On one occasion in particular, Amanda had started to dig a hole and was making good progress. Of course, we couldn't resist the temptation to help. I went over to the shop and bought some more spades, since there were five of us, so that we could all dig at once. The hole naturally grew wider and deeper very quickly. You would have thought we had all 'lost it'. People were glancing over at us as we took turns standing in it to dig more and more sand out. Eventually, we were all in the hole – up to our necks, literally. By the time the five of us had been digging for a good couple of hours the hole was enormous, but there was one major flaw in our design. We had all been so busy digging that we had not realised how deep it had become. Height-wise there was not only the depth of the wall of the hole itself to be taken into account, but the huge heap of sand around the top of it too. It was so large and held us all so comfortably whilst we were digging, that we just hadn't thought about how we were going to get out of it – and you just cannot climb a wall of sand.

'A running jump should do it,' was David's bright suggestion.

I said, 'Go on then.'

There was one fault with his idea – no room to run before the jump. How funny we must have all looked stuck in that hole with just the tops of our heads bobbing about. Anyway, in the end the boys gave us girls a helping hand and with a bit of a struggle and a few abortive attempts we finally managed to scramble out, to the amusement of a good many onlookers. That left the men room for their 'running jumps'! We were all a little sad to leave the beach that day but whilst the tide would virtually eradicate our hole by morning it could never erode our happy memories of being children again!

Sandsend is certainly a beach for inspiring creativity, and not always in sand. For example, it was here, apparently, that the world-famous author of *Alice Through the Looking Glass*, Lewis Carroll, received inspiration for another of his tales, *The Walrus and the Carpenter*.

Then there was the exiled Maharajah of Duleep Singh from India who had rented nearby Mulgrave Castle in 1849. Up until this time, there had been no roadway between Sandsend and Whitby. The sand at low tide had served the purpose well. However, the Maharajah had brought with him his elephants, who did not like to walk on the sand. I suppose with their weight it was an almost impossible task. Anyway, he loved his animals and decided no expense should be spared to please them and so he had the roadway constructed at the top of the cliffs for their convenience. Naturally, his creation not only served his elephants but the locals too, who no longer had to rely on low tides. Lucky for them he hadn't thought to bring camels.

Not to be outdone, as old photographs of Sandsend will testify, shortly after the roadway, along came the coastal railway and for over a century it literally passed over the heads of all who lived, worked or played here. Erected on huge metal pillars, it ran its course to meet the steep incline out of the bay and certainly the engineers who created it were inspired with ingenuity. It was finally dismantled after the railway was closed in 1960. Of course, the Maharajah and his elephants have long gone, too, but there is still a coast road which has been thoughtfully redesigned to cater for both the modern-day traveller and elephants, if they happen to come this way again.

Around Britain's shoreline, elephants may not be the norm, but seagulls certainly are. They are as much a part of our seascapes as the cliffs, rocks, sea and sand and sadly, because of that simple fact, the majority of us take them too much for granted. We all know that piercing cry. It is always there, even dominating the sound of the roaring tide. No need to look. It is the sound of the seagulls, those scavengers of the skies, as they descend like a plague of locusts on the fishing boats still well out at sea, bringing in the hauls of fresh fish. When not on the wing they perch on cliff tops, roof tops or strut the quaysides, ever waiting, ever vigilant, ever there. However, what if they weren't? Imagine a fishing harbour without the gulls. How long would it take any of us to notice their absence. Not very long! I have already illustrated how I particularly noticed the gulls in Staithes because they were strangely silent on the day of the storm. I am sure they became more visible to me because they were so quiet. My point is that we should put aside our complacency, because more and more of these apparently robust and resilient birds are falling prey to man's thoughtlessness. Whether it be carelessly thrown litter, unwanted fishing twine or inconsiderate disposal of chemicals or other poisonous substances, they are all known by the experts to be contributory factors to the diminishing numbers of wildlife around our coasts. They can all cause excruciating pain and suffering and, ultimately, in the majority of cases, death. For the most part not many of us can put hand on heart and say we are not affected when we read of the illegal bludgeoning to death of seal pups who, whilst often having a final breath in their feeble bodies, feel the pain of the knife as they are skinned. On the other hand, how many of us are aware that by leaving our debris about a beach or in the sea, we too may be condemning a creature to a similar fate, albeit perhaps innocently, because we just didn't think?

Whilst walking along Sandsend's beach one day Amanda and I noticed a seagull bobbing about a few metres off shore. Although not an unusual sight in itself, we became concerned because it seemed unable to move, almost mesmerised, and after we had watched it for a while we decided it was in trouble. Luckily the tide was coming in and slowly buffeting the gull towards the beach, but something told us time was of an essence. Without thinking twice about the fact I was fully clothed, in I went and without any resistance it allowed me to handle it and steer it into shore, as if it knew I was trying to help. I knew then this bird was really sick and possibly dying. Once on the sand I looked for obvious signs – an open wound, a broken wing, leg problems – but could find nothing obviously wrong, although I am not an expert. Knowing sea birds can get wire or fishing line caught inside their beaks, I decided to take a look but I got a quick response. She (I decided 'it' was a girl because she had a pretty face) would have none of it and I got a nip on my finger for my trouble.

Amanda and I had been so busy examining the poor creature that we hadn't noticed the arrival of a lady and gentleman who had been swimming, apparently at the time we had brought the bird into shore. Smiling at my dripping wet clothes, they said they had seen her out at sea and wondered if she was in trouble but I had got to her first. They asked if they could help and whilst Amanda fetched a towel to keep the bird warm, we discussed what should be done. It turned out the couple were from Whitby and, what is more, they actually knew someone who ran a sanctuary and might be able to help our ailing friend.

Amanda was by this time draping the towel gently around the gull who, apart from a few pecks, was far too weak to protest. We were all fully aware that speed was imperative and the couple kindly offered to take the bird immediately to the sanctuary, if we could find something to put her in. A very strong carrier bag was all we could come up with but at last we managed to get her into it, taking care not to hurt her just in case we caused more damage. It was not the easiest of procedures, remembering that ever-nipping beak and just how enormous a gull is at first hand. She did look a pathetic sight, peeping out from the top of the bag, and we all had a lump in our throats as we wished her well. I even gave her a name: Tuesday – the day, we fervently hoped, her life had been saved.

Having exchanged telephone numbers with the couple, we were able to keep track of her progress. It seems that our friend, Tuesday, may well have been poisoned. There was no room at the sanctuary for her, unfortunately, but her new friends did not desert her. In fact, with considerable patience and lots of tender loving care, they nursed her back to reasonable health. Apparently she progressed so well that she loved to splash around in a bowl of water and exercise her wings. She even took to answering the calls of other gulls as they flew over her and a few weeks later, when she was taken down to the beach to see if she would like to join her friends again, she straddled around for quite a while as if she was trying to make her mind up, but at last made no attempt to fly and returned home with her foster parents. She is now happily settled in the sanctuary, which is better equipped to suit her needs. As to whether she will ever fly again, that is up to her. Meanwhile, she has a home for as long as she wants to stay, with people who care for her and new friends – and a name, Tuesday, the day her life was saved.

However, the fact remains Tuesday's suffering was undoubtedly the result of a harmful toxin inconsiderately disposed of by man. Without help she would have perished, and no one would have missed her. Are we going to wait until our coasts are silent and littered with 'Tuesdays' before we take responsibility for our actions? Some things are beyond our control, but perhaps if we as individuals become more aware of the consequences of what we are doing then we can all help to preserve the gulls and the other creatures we take so much for granted – whatever day of the week it is.

In complete contrast to the Sandsend of high summer, on a late autumn evening, with the moon high in a black sky, the noise of the roaring incoming tide is almost deafening. The rollers devour the beach without mercy. In the eerie gloom, just visible to the naked eye, the bulky silhouette of the northern headland of the bay juts out into the encroaching sea, defiant but powerless to stop the constant thrashing of those ceaseless waves on the ever-tolerant rocks at its feet. Looking down over Sandsend beach on such a night, from the edge of the grassy bank, with the strong sea breeze carrying the salt air into my face, I am always captivated by the Sandsend few but the locals ever see. Farther along the bay, the sea wall does not escape the onslaught of the tide as, without any regard for the limit of height determined by the wall, the water cascades over the top in a foamy spray, leaving the roadway temporarily flooded. The force of so much water, although almost terrifying to watch, hypnotises the eye. How mighty this vital element of our earth is, that knows no bounds and will never be completely tamed either by boundary of land or hand of man. Despite the unpredictability of this Great Lady's moods, despite her uncompromising power over all within her grasp, there is no doubt that since the beginning of time men have always been ready to take up her challenge and to put themselves in her hands for one reason or another – not least the fishermen.

Many people have heard of Whitby even if they haven't been there. Famous for its cod and bulging with fish and chip cafés and restaurants to prove it, the sprawling harbour is littered with a dazzling array of fishing boats of every shape, size and colour. Every one of them has a name, some are straightforward and some are tinged with humour, while all are well chosen. Along with their name they also bear their own registration number, with the prefix WY for Whitby so they can easily be identified. The smell of fish wafts on the air from the well-used decks of these vessels. Not really surprising, since it has been washed and baked into every grain of wood throughout many years of faithful service and no amount of diligent scrubbing will remove it completely. The scene would not be quite complete without the ever-present seagulls piercing the ear with their shrill cries as they swoop down onto the harbour wall in the hope of finding a small morsel left over from the morning's haul.

Whitby is a town divided in two. The River Esk runs between, via the marina and upper harbour, onward towards the sea where two piers extend outward like two massive pincers to emphasise the mouth of the lower harbour. The original Whitby piers, which dated from the early 1500s, were wooden and nowhere near the length of today's impressive projections. At that time Henry VIII owned most of the town and therefore the royal coffers paid for their upkeep. It was approximately 100 years later that they were rebuilt in stone, which must have been a formidable task by anyone's standards, especially in the seventeenth century. But matters did not rest there. Eventually, in the early twentieth century, the town became responsible for the piers and harbour and subsequently decided the piers should be lengthened by 150 metres. We can only imagine the huge intakes of breath at the local meeting when this announcement was made. After seven years of hard labour the work was completed just before the outbreak of the Great War in 1914. The town must have been horrified that all its efforts might prove worthless when the conflict came to its shores. Germany, having observed our fishing boats off the east coast, thought the boats might well have spies on board or be out laying mines rather than filling nets. In actual fact, the innocent fishermen were in the main going about their normal business of bringing in the fish, but the Germans weren't taking any chances. Just in case they were all undercover agents working for our government they decided to attack our fishing ports along the east coast and that is how Whitby came to be fired upon by German battle cruisers. Thankfully, the new piers did survive, but sadly the abbey was less fortunate and received further damage. Although Whitby is on the eastern coastline of Britain, the town faces directly north and it is an interesting fact that the two piers are in complete alignment with the North Pole. This means that from a vantage point on the cliff tops in midsummer it is possible to enjoy the rare sight of the sun rising out of the sea in early morning, or setting into it at dusk (for those of us who aren't early risers).

It is because the town faces north and is divided by the River Esk that the definitions east and west are used for ease of identification. West Whitby is of more recent date, whilst east Whitby is often referred to as Old Whitby, being essentially much older. Between the upper and lower harbours there is an attractive and convenient swing bridge to enable pedestrians and traffic alike to cross from one side of town to the other, as well as allowing the easy passage of ships with taller masts to access the upper harbour, marina or up river. The present bridge is only 100 years old, but there has been a bridge on this site since the fourteenth century, according to local records.

On the waterfront of the lower harbour stands the lifeboat station manned by another fine body of men who, whenever the call arises, willingly risk their lives in the hope of saving others in trouble out at sea. Thankfully, these days the lifeboats used around our coasts are sturdy, powerful craft, well-equipped and reliable, but the lifeboats of our forefathers were a different story. They were merely rowing boats and it was in fact here at Whitby that the last rowing lifeboat used in Britain was finally withdrawn from service in 1957, having spent its last ten years as the second boat to Whitby's motor lifeboat. Rowing boats they may have been, but, regardless of weather conditions or the mood of the sea, they still went out and did a magnificent job whenever they were needed.

Tragically, on Saturday, 9 February 1861, one such lifeboat met a terrible end in cruel seas. The heroic crew had already achieved five successful rescues that dreadful day. Storms ravaged the coast and snow and sleet made conditions almost intolerable. Their sixth call out was to assist the schooner, *Merchant*, which had run aground. Despite suffering from exhaustion as a result of their previous efforts of the day, they gallantly once more took to their boat in horrendous seas to do what they could for the stricken vessel. However, having reached the *Merchant* they were to be cruelly robbed of a sixth successful mission. They took the full force of a gigantic wave that capsized their lifeboat. The men did not stand a chance. All but one perished. The sea showed no compassion. It was a terrible blow, not only to the bereaved families, for whom a disaster fund was set up, but also to the town of Whitby itself. I cannot help thinking how dreadful it must have been for the poor survivor, a Mr Henry Freeman, who had to learn to live with his memories of that fateful day. It is said that he was the only crew member to be wearing the new cork lifejacket, which probably saved his life. There is a memorial to the disaster in St Mary's Church, but to me the most poignant reminders of that awful tragedy are the relevant tombstones in the churchyard overlooking the sea.

Before this tragic year of 1861 drew to a close there was another terrible loss that was to have repercussions on Whitby, only this time it was to Whitby's good. The town was acclaimed for its jet – no, I do not mean engines, I mean the hard, black mineral which could easily be polished and formed into luxurious pieces of jewellery fit for a queen (and queen she was – Victoria by name). In December of 1861 her beloved husband, Prince Albert, died. Her Majesty chose to wear jet jewellery whilst in mourning, since being black it was more than appropriate. By doing so she set a precedent for others to follow that was to last several years, as did her mourning. It was a boom time for the industry, despite the sad circumstances, since the demand for jet jewellery soared. Jet has been used in the making of adornments for thousands of years, but the best-quality jet comes from the coast in and around Whitby and many people wanted the best. At first it could be picked off the beaches or out of the cliffs, but soon supplies were becoming harder to find and it became apparent that mines would have to be opened up, employing many extra men in order to meet the heavy demand. Jet is found in thin small seams and, consequently, sometimes the miners worked for days without a find. By 1870 it is reported that over 1,500 people were skilfully employed in the area making jewellery and other ornaments. It wasn't to last. When Queen Victoria came out of mourning she stopped wearing jet. Many others followed, and the industry rapidly declined.

It was in the mid-eighteenth century that Whitby, by that time one of the leading seaports of England, became the setting for a young man to realise his dreams. The man was blissfully unaware in his early years in Whitby just where destiny would take him. All he knew was that he had an indisputable fascination for ships and a craving for adventure on the high seas. His hopes led him to serve an apprenticeship under John Walker, a master mariner and wealthy ship owner in Whitby engaged in the business of shipping coal. He was given accommodation in the attic of that gentleman's house in Grape Lane and for ten years enjoyed gaining knowledge and experience of these fine locally built collier ships. He then took his leave of Whitby and, after 'signing on' in London with the Royal Navy, joined in the war that was erupting with France that was to last approximately seven years. After the war he remained with the Royal Navy and was so highly regarded that he was selected to undertake various important missions. During his time away he had never relinquished his confidence in and affection for those sturdy flat-bottomed Whitby vessels, as he proved when he chose to use them, and only them, on his three great voyages. The names of those ships are as famous today as they were then, when they were first entered into the history books: *Endeavour*, *Resolution*, *Adventure* and *Discovery*. The man's name was also entered: Captain James Cook, R.N., F.R.S.

Overlooking the old town of Whitby and his beloved sea, on West Cliff there stands a bronzed statue of Captain Cook. It pays tribute to the men who built those famous four Whitby ships and the men who sailed with him into the unknown. On the large pedestal beneath him, engraved in stone, is the Whitby ship *Resolution* which took the brave captain out on his final voyage from which he never returned. Sadly, this great Yorkshireman of the seas was slain on a Hawaiian beach by the knife of a native during a dispute on the 14 February 1779. He was 50. However, his ship and her brave crew continued with the expedition

and were not to return to English waters until November of the
following year. There is one inscription on this statue which always
manages to raise a lump to my throat: 'To strive, to seek, to find and not
to yield'.

Resolution certainly did not yield and nor did her crew. They went on
to strive, to seek, to find, as their captain would have wanted, and when
their job was done they came home, as he would have hoped. Looking
up at the statue of the man with his compass in one hand and charts in
the other, I can well appreciate Whitby's obvious pride in its ships, the
men who built them and sailed in them and, of course, its young
apprentice, Captain James Cook R.N., F.R.S.

Although James Cook would probably still recognise much of
Whitby and, in particular, his old friend's house in Grape Lane, which
is now open to the public as The Captain Cook Memorial Museum, he
would find it much harder to relate to the comparative sedateness of
today's harbour when compared to the one he would remember. The
trading ships with their huge masts and rigging intertwining against
the sky obliterating the view are gone. No longer are the quaysides
bulging with the clutter and chaos of cargo being loaded or off-loaded
whilst the vessels' hulls constantly clonk against each other, moved by
the permanent motion of the water somewhere below. No more do the
yards resound with the shipbuilders' hammers, for no longer are ships
being built here in Whitby . . . but there are still the fish and the
fishermen, as there have always been, and he would remember them.

Apart from the harbour, Whitby is all hills, and standing proud
against the skyline on East Cliff there is still a great landmark which
has presided over Whitby for centuries, defying all the elements: the
austere remains of Whitby Abbey. It was the Venerable Bede (673–735)
who, through his brilliant books, such as *The Church History of the
English People*, bequeathed so much information concerning early
Christianity in England. Although as a young lad he never ventured far
from his monastery at Jarrow on Tyneside, he was an ardent scholar and
he never wrote anything that could not be fully authenticated, either by
written evidence or reliable sources of his time. Thus he enlightens us
on the founding of Whitby Abbey by St Hilda in 657. In his last book
he also describes how Easter is calculated each year. Up until 664,
apparently two methods had been used, the one known as the Celtic

method and the other used by all those who followed the Church of Rome (i.e. the Pope's method). Inevitably it was the subject of constant speculation as to which one was correct. Finally, at the Synod of Whitby held within the confines of St Hilda's Abbey in the year 664, a historic decision was reached that the Pope's method should be universally adopted. This meant that in future Easter would be calculated to fall on the first Sunday after the first full moon that occurs on or after the spring equinox. This method, which is still used today, explains why the date for Easter varies from year to year, although it will always fall between 22 March and 25 April.

At the time of the great debate on Easter, St Hilda's Abbey was little more than a small wooden church and had little in common with the grand stone structure that was eventually to stand on the site. The humble church was replaced by a stone monastery in the seventh century, but this was demolished by the Vikings in the ninth century and it was not until after the Norman Conquest in 1066 that the foundations were laid for the new stone abbey in 1078. Sadly, however, this prestigious new structure was beset with problems. By virtue of its vulnerable position it was regularly the victim of excessive storm damage and, consequently, various parts of it were constantly having to be rebuilt. Then, in December 1539, it was cruelly destroyed by Henry VIII's men during the dissolution of the monasteries. Much of what remained, such as the nave, the west front and the central tower, gradually collapsed during the eighteenth and nineteenth centuries and if that wasn't enough, as I have already mentioned, it was fired upon by the Germans in December 1914. Today, despite its ruinous state, it still makes for a distinctive and impressive sight, especially at night when its skeletal silhouette hauntingly dominates the landscape on East Cliff.

The parish church of St Mary also has pride of place on this headland and has been here nearly as long as the abbey, having been built by Abbot de Percy around 1110. It seems odd; comparing the two holy buildings to their counterparts throughout all England, there cannot be many that have been erected on such high and vulnerable ground as these. The monks nearly always chose sites on even ground for their sanctuaries, with lush surroundings for grazing and raising their crops, usually a reasonable distance from the thoroughfares of everyday life, whilst the majority of churches were situated within easy reach of the local people, since they played such an important role in the everyday life of their communities. Why St Hilda chose to found her abbey, originally a seat of learning, high on this headland is a mystery in itself, and the Venerable Bede does not enlighten us, but since the landscape of Whitby would have been very different in 657 perhaps a prominent place was required away from the enchroaching unpredictable sea and rough terrain of rocky hills, and the flat cliff top was probably the best option. By the time the present structure was built in 1078, undoubtedly the headland atop and beneath had become the centre of a bustling community and it would have probably seemed logical to rebuild on the site of the original monastic building. Despite its position seeming a little unusual, it can well be imagined that, back through the centuries, it would have probably served as a formidable warning to all those of ill intent, as well as a welcome sight to the ships' crews coming home from the sea. As for the church, no doubt it too served the growing community at Whitby and supported the teachings of its neighbouring religious house. By the way, if any of you reading this have heard of Bing Crosby and his world-famous song 'The Bells of St Mary's', then I have just introduced you to the church that inspired that hit!

In the beginning, to reach the abbey or the church must have been quite a climb, but at some point somebody, thankfully, had a brainwave and erected a grand staircase for our convenience. The legendary 199 steps run alongside the less comfortable cobbled 'donkey road', which is so narrow it's a wonder any donkey could get over it. The steps are known as the Church Stairs and I will never forget the first time I was invited to climb them. It was many years ago and we were with some friends. Of course, I knew the steps were there. I had been to Whitby hundreds of times. I had just never been up them before and for reasons of my own I wasn't very keen then, especially as it was getting late.

However, pride won and I couldn't let the others see I was nervous, so up we went, slowly because they all wanted to enjoy the magnificent views as we climbed. The steps are wide and made for relatively easy going but, oh dear, I just didn't want to be there and desperately tried to ignore the benches which are spaced beside the path as I had no desire to be reminded that these are not really seats at all (although nowadays people use them as such to rest their legs). They were originally put there for a much more sombre purpose. They were in fact coffin rests, which once provided the bearers with some momentary relief from their exhausting task of carrying the deceased to his or her final resting place in the graveyard above. The views from the steps over the harbour and out to sea were indeed fascinating the higher we climbed and I began to forget my initial apprehension and enjoy the experience with the others, shrugging off any negative thoughts. That is, until St Mary's Church loomed into view, and I realised the path at the top of the steps actually went straight through the graveyard.

I had hoped it would skirt the perimeter of the church grounds. Fear struck. 'I'll have to tell them,' I thought, but I didn't. Although I did get a funny look when I suddenly stepped up my pace and strode well ahead of the others through the graveyard without a second glance and out onto the headland where the abbey stood. This was my first real close-up view of the abbey I knew so much about but I was quite relieved it was closed. Our stay would be that much shorter. I moved over to the far side of the headland whilst the others took a few pictures of the views over the North Sea and, of course, of the abbey. Stripped of its former glory, just like its brothers, in such close proximity it made for an almost ghastly spectacle against the fading blue sky. It didn't help. Night was fast approaching and I had a pressing desire to leave! The others were naturally in no hurry at all and I did attempt to appear normal. As we returned along the path between the abbey and St Mary's I spotted a skull and crossbones on two headstones. They obviously marked the graves of two pirates, but I was in no mood to point them out to my companions. Instead, globules of sweat started breaking out on my forehead as I quickened my pace through the graveyard and back to the top of the steps. I was aware the others had lingered somewhere behind me to take a closer look at the church, which was thankfully locked. I didn't wait. I headed straight down those 199 steps without looking back and without stopping until I reached the bottom.

To this day I have never told the others what I foolishly feared about our excursion up to Whitby Abbey that very first time, and they've never asked me. Perhaps they didn't even notice. They will know now, however, because it will be written here. I had heard tell that Count Dracula, that legendary lord of the undead, apparently survived a shipwreck hereabouts, came ashore at Whitby's Tate Hill pier as a large dog, ran up the famous steps and, in his more recognisable form, took his customary nourishment from a young girl before taking up residence in the grave of a suicide in the churchyard of St Mary's. Yes, I know, once again I let my imagination run riot. I just cannot help it!

I suppose, just as a footnote, I had better confess the rest. Some time later I found out this story had actually originated from Bram Stoker's novel *Dracula*, part of which he wrote whilst staying in Whitby towards the end of the nineteenth century (i.e. it wasn't real). I know, but it was a long time ago! Since then, when we have visited Whitby I have often climbed those 199 steps leading into the old churchyard and feel far more confident now I know the truth: Dracula is purely confined to the pages of a book. He is, isn't he? Yes, of course he is. When you've finished laughing we will go on . . .

Despite the unique appeal I mentioned of Runswick, I cannot help but couple it to the ever-popular and more commercialised village of Robin Hood's Bay, which lies south of Whitby. The connection is simple. Although the latter is larger and more populated, it too is smothered in a picturesque charm that cannot be ignored. It is full of narrow byways and stepped alleyways too, which glide any which way between the various buildings, the steps helping to even out the climb. Old-world charm is in abundance here and this, together with the traditional atmosphere of a fishing village, make Robin Hood's Bay an ideal centre for tourists.

However, in days of old the village was frequented by a very different kind of visitor. It was very popular with the smuggling fraternity and beneath the innocent exterior of a thriving fishing industry, the more dubious trade of smuggling was rife. When I say beneath, that is literally what I mean. Apparently under the cottages and various other buildings around the bay there existed a warren of tunnelling any self-respecting bunny would have been well proud of. The story goes that these tunnels were used to smuggle the booty directly from the waterfront through the village without it even seeing daylight, let alone a customs man. I can't help being doubtful about the whole village knowing the goings on beneath their feet, but I have to applaud the ingenuity of the smugglers. Where these tunnels emerged I am not at all sure, but if the customs men had any knowledge of them at all I reckon with their record in those days they would have been waiting at the wrong one! Although, having said that, the area surrounding Robin Hood's Bay is Fylingdales Moor, which extends well inland and includes in its landscape the Ballistic Missile Early Warning Station, which, as you may remember from the previous chapter, is very close to that one-time notorious smuggler's meeting place, the Saltersgate Inn. Maybe the customs man under the hearth at that establishment did get the right tunnel . . . for once! Pity he didn't live to tell the tale.

When I first visited Robin Hood's Bay, I was at once curious about the name of the village, and found that, although there have been many disputes about its origins, popular belief lies in the tale that Robin Hood used to seek sanctuary here when he'd come a little too close to being captured by King John's not-so-merry men. It is also said that he had a boat here for a quick escape should it ever be necessary and, because the villagers knew him and were so kind to him, he returned their kindness with money and assistance whenever they needed it. Whether the legend is true or not, I rather like it. However, if we are to believe the stories we have heard of Robin Hood, I can't help feeling King John's men were a little like the early customs men and would never quite have got their man anyway.

There is one niggling fact that does conflict this nice legend. The village was not called Robin Hood's Bay until the reign of Henry VIII, probably when he owned most of Whitby too and had a vested interest in this coastline. Robin Hood, however, occupied Sherwood Forest in Nottinghamshire during the reign of King John, three centuries earlier, so was it a coincidence from which the legend arose or was old Henry fully aware of the stories surrounding the outlaw Robin and his arch enemy King John, secretly admired him and decided to give him an appropriate epitaph? Just a thought.

The well-known spa town of Scarborough is situated at the southernmost point of Yorkshire's stretch of Heritage coastline and I have to say that if the Victorian gentry who once paraded its promenades in their finery for a breath of sea air to help ease their ailments and tone their complexions could see the town today, they would probably turn in their graves. I hasten to add that by saying that I do not mean it is any less a fine town. On the contrary, it still holds much of its elegance and charm that once could only be appreciated by the richer classes of a bygone age. Then they came and took the waters, enjoyed croquet on the lush lawns and stayed in luxurious boarding houses overlooking the magnificent beaches lined with changing huts and edged with elegant promenades. Of course, the fishing harbour was here then and would probably be instantly recognisable to them today, as would the ruins of Scarborough Castle high on the headland that separates north and south bays. But much else is changed. Alas, we live in a world of high commercial enterprise and Scarborough has its fair share. It has to in order to satisfy the appetite of the modern age.

Scarborough is noted as England's oldest holiday resort. Its popularity with visitors began in the 1620s, when the town's spring water was found to contain health-giving minerals. Down through the centuries, people came from far and wide to take their fill of this naturally produced possible cure to all their ills – real and imagined. I mention the latter because the Victorian era was well known for its fair share of hypochondriacs in the upper classes of society, as literary writers of the period well record. Unfortunately, the lower classes, who for the most part experienced the real suffering, were far less likely to experience the luxury of 'taking the waters' or taking anything else for that matter, as the doctors charged for their services in those days and medicine was just too expensive. However, in the mid-1800s the York to Scarborough Railway did help make the spa town more accessible to ordinary folk, and by this time Scarborough was known as England's foremost holiday resort. From the eighteenth century it had been necessary to build elegant boarding houses and hotels in the town to house the growing numbers of visitors, but by the time the railway had arrived, larger and much more extravagant accommodation had had to be supplied to suit the requirements of the even more discerning Victorian upper classes. Sadly, most of these buildings disappeared during the twentieth century.

Dominating the cliffs overlooking the bay is the Grand Hotel. Huge and magnificent it may be, but it would not be a familiar sight to the Victorians of the mid-1800s. Originally this site was occupied by luxurious lodgings, where wealthy Victorian families stayed during their annual holidays. It was in one of these very same lodging houses that Anne Brontë, one of the famous novelist sisters, first acquired her love of Scarborough when she accompanied the Robinson family here on holidays as governess to their children.

However, on 25 May 1849 she was to return to her beloved Scarborough for a very different reason – she was dying. Her sister, Charlotte Brontë, together with Charlotte's friend, Ellen Nussey, brought her here in the heartfelt hope that it would revive her spirits and subsequently her failing health. They had smaller but very comfortable accommodation almost next to the much more expensive lodgings that Anne had stayed in previously. The day after their arrival Anne wished to take a drive on the magnificent sands, but having always been concerned about the treatment of animals, she insisted on taking the reins herself to ensure the donkey had an easier time pulling the cart than perhaps the handler would allow. It said much about Anne, but must have taken colossal effort considering her ill health. Sadly it was only two days later – on 28 May – at 2 p.m., in the room at their lodging house overlooking the bay, that her beloved sister Charlotte and good friend Ellen watched tearfully as Anne peacefully passed from this world, where she had borne her illness so bravely, into the world she never showed any fear of.

Charlotte could not bear to accompany her sister home for burial in the family vault at Haworth. She was also, even in her hour of grief, concerned for her father who was still recovering from the recent deaths of her sister Emily and her brother Branwell. She therefore concluded that Anne should be buried in the graveyard of St Mary's Church, overlooking her beloved Scarborough – knowing that Anne would approve.

Today, below and above her, Scarborough continues to thrive, serving the needs of both its people and its many annual visitors, a different world to the one Anne knew, since life has had to move on. However, unlike many of her fellow Victorians, because of her very nature in life, I think Anne would be an exception and not 'turn in her grave' but simply accept. In fact I agree with Charlotte, and am sure Anne still does approve.

❧ FIVE ❧

In Search of the Brontës

Tucked away in the sprawling village of Haworth in West Yorkshire there is a house of particular note. It stands alone, away from the steep incline of the main street where the cobbles are especially designed to give the horses better grip on their slippery climb.

This house is approached by a dusty or muddy track, depending on the weather, and wends its way up past the church and graveyard on the left, and the Sexton's small house and the Sunday school hall on the right. Beyond the graveyard lies the lovingly tended front garden of the house, enclosed by a low wall which has two gateways: one to and from the pathway through the graveyard that leads to the church, and the other to the left of the ascending track previously described. This gate, creaking with age, is a welcome sight to the weary inhabitants of the house when they return from their various wanderings. Thus the scene is set for the benefit of the reader.

It has long been dark this night and there is the glow of burning wax in both the sitting-room windows to the left of the front porch and the study to the right. The dampness of an early autumn mist hangs on the air together with the wafting smell of the peat fires burning in the grates of some of the village houses, heralding the beginning of what may be a long, wet, cold winter – no stranger to these parts.

The man is pleased to be returning home from his evening at the

Black Bull Inn in the village. He feels unwell and even the cold stone slabs of the passage floor, which are kept scrupulously clean under the watchful eye of Tabitha, are a comfort to him. Echoing from a nook on the stairs the rhythmic ticking of the old grandfather clock fills the silence and he can see from a crack in the study door that the very short-sighted Rev. Patrick Brontë is totally absorbed in preparing his Sunday sermon, with glasses perched on the end of his nose, magnifying glass in his left hand and quill poised in his right. The man does not wish to interrupt his father at work. Instead he enters the sitting-room on his left where seated around the table are his three sisters: Charlotte, short-sighted like her father, has her head bowed low over her writing desk; Emily and Anne are both engrossed in their needlework. They all stop what they are doing to welcome their brother Branwell, with immediate expressions of concern for his health. His father, having been disturbed, comes to his son's aid and insists that Branwell sleep with him this night. This night is Friday. Branwell offers no resistance, but allows himself to be helped to his father's bed, where the reverend comforts and consoles his beloved son through the ensuing feverish and restless hours. Branwell never recovered. On the following Sunday, at 9 a.m., he was dead.

The month is September and the year is 1848. This house is home to the Brontë family and within nine months of the death of their brother, its walls will no longer echo with the voices of Emily or Anne either. They too will succumb to the dreaded consumption. Their relentless struggle to find a little happiness in their sadly short lives will be over, leaving behind them a grieving sister and an inconsolable father. Six children he had in all and a wife he cherished. Now only his daughter, Charlotte, remains and can be his only comfort. Not for long – after her marriage to the Rev. Arthur Bell Nicholls on the 29 June 1854, she has only nine short months of happiness before she too, three months pregnant with her first child, departs this earth where she has known so much torment and sadness, flecked only sparingly with moments of true joy and happiness. Her last words to her husband are: 'I'm not going to die, am I?' The date is 31 March 1855, just three weeks prior to what would have been her 39th birthday.

And so Patrick Brontë is left alone in his Parsonage, a sad and reflective old man with only his son-in-law, Arthur Bell Nicholls, for company in the remaining six years of his life. Doubtless this falls very short of the memories of the family life he had once known. Two sombre men mulling over the past night after night in the house that had once been a home, the atmosphere only uplifted by occasional smiles or laughter when they touch on happier times, before they again retire within themselves to remember how short-lived those happier times had actually been. For Patrick, relief comes at last when he is reunited with his family on 7 June 1861 at the age of 84 years. All are buried in the Brontë's family vault in Haworth Church, except for Anne, who rests in Scarborough.

And so the house fell silent, the candles flickered and dimmed and time would stand still forever for the Brontë children at the Parsonage. They had only known a brief moment of fame before their premature departing, but their beloved home would see to it that their story would be told.

The Rev. Patrick Brontë was born in County Down, Ireland, in 1777. In the following year, many miles away in the tiny village of Haworth, West Yorkshire the building work on the Parsonage was completed. Although it would take approximately 42 years for these two seemingly unrelated events to eventually come together, the coincidental timing of their conception has to occur to the observer. It is almost as if even back then what was to come had already been written down and that, when the time came, both the man and the house would be ready to play their essential supporting roles to one of the most famous and remarkable stories in the history of English literature. It would seem then that it was Patrick Brontë's destiny to become rector of Haworth Church and reside with his young family at the Parsonage. It was their home from February 1820 and still is to this day. It was bought from the church trustees by Sir James Roberts and presented to the Brontë Society in 1928, who opened its doors to the public in the same year. Since then, thousands of pairs of feet have walked over the Brontë's doorstep in the hope of catching a glimpse of their world and a taste of their story. A story beyond Charlotte's *Jane Eyre*, *Shirley*, *Villette* and *The Professor*, Emily's *Wuthering Heights* and Anne's *Agnes Grey* and *The Tenant of Wildfell Hall*. A true story – the story of the Brontë sisters themselves. A story I too, along with millions of others, continue to be fascinated by.

On approaching the village of Haworth, the wild and windswept moorland provides an indication of how hilly and rugged this part of West Yorkshire can be. It is not difficult to imagine how hard the winters are in such an exposed place and how snow-covered moors would only add to the chill of the air whistling its way through the numerous alleyways and gradually finding its way into the vulnerable houses huddled up the steep slope of the main street. At the top of the street, behind the church, the once 'muddy or dusty track' is now cobbled and known as Church Lane, but it still leads directly up to the Parsonage and beyond to the Brontë's beloved moors. On a fine spring or summer day the morning sun warms the grey stone of the old Parsonage walls and throws shadows across the lawn from the tall trees that punctuate the graveyard as a steady flow of daytrippers wander the modest grounds and soak up the atmosphere. The old gateway from the garden to the graveyard through which all the Brontës, save Anne, were carried to their final resting place in the Brontë vault, has long since gone, but there is a plaque on the wall to commemorate the place and just the other side of the wall are the graves of the Brontë's beloved servants: Tabitha Aykroyd, who died just six weeks prior to Charlotte, and Martha Brown, who died in 1880 – some 19 years after the Rev. Brontë's death and the dispersal of the household. It was Tabitha's nephew, William Wood (an appropriate name for Haworth's joiner), who not only made pieces of furniture for the Brontës but also did a last service by making their coffins.

Despite the high number of visitors who cross the Parsonage threshold daily, everything about the place is spotlessly clean and orderly. Tabitha and Martha would be well pleased. From the dove-coloured walls in the passageway to the arrangement of the furniture and pictures, all is much the same as it was *circa* 1850, after Charlotte had made some alterations to the house following her success as a writer. The gabled extension, however, was not her innovation. It was built between 1872 and 1878 by the Rev. Brontë's successor, the Rev. John Wade, and now houses the Exhibition Room on the upper floor.

On entering the Parsonage it is very obvious how well the Brontë Society have preserved this very special place. I feel it is very difficult to ignore a haunting presence, almost as if the Brontës are watching nervously from every quarter. This family who were shyly reticent with strangers and found the best company was their own, apart from a few precious close friends, who they loved dearly. This family who so quietly and unobtrusively went about their lives oblivious of the interest and genuine affection they would eventually stir in the hearts of so many people, not just from their own land but from every corner of the globe. How would the timid and quiet Anne, the reserved but independent Emily and the ambitious but nervous Charlotte have handled such a host of adulation? Personally, I don't think they would have coped very well at all. They so often walked hand in hand with grief and disappointment, heartbreak and dissolution, facing all with quiet dignity and courage, but fame was something else to them, something foreign to their lives that Emily and Anne did not really have a chance to know and Charlotte had for such a brief time.

Glancing in through the doors of their sitting room, with the window blinds low to protect the precious Brontë furniture, it is not difficult to visualise how cosy and special this, their sanctuary, was to them. Within the walls of this neat but unpretentious room, the Brontë children talked of their hopes and plans, read out their writings and criticised one another's work, laughed together over their experiences and, above all, formed such a close bond that even death could not completely separate them.

They knew so much heartache and trauma in their young lives. Their mother died of cancer only 18 months after they arrived at Haworth and subsequently the young children were brought up by their rather strict father and their mother's sister, the stern and often aloof Aunt Branwell. Then came the untimely deaths of Maria and Elizabeth, their elder sisters. The children naturally looked to one another for comfort and companionship and during the hours they were left to their own devices, when lessons were over and the daily chores were done, they began to realise and develop their natural talent for writing. Their father had always encouraged them to read as much as they could and doing so enhanced their ability to put their rich imaginations into the written word. From an early age they wrote miniature books in the tiniest of writing about a mythical country called Angria and an equally mythical island called Gondal. They created a world to escape to, full of high adventure, battles, heroes and love. A world in sharp contrast to their own rather shy and secluded existence at the Parsonage. As the events of their imaginary world unfolded between the pages of these little books, the sisters were blissfully unaware that they were indeed laying the foundations for their eventual recognition, individually, as highly accomplished novelists. The difference being that these literary masterpieces would be based on more underlying fact than fantasy and the sisters would purely draw on their own imagination, real-life observations and surroundings to further their initial inspirations.

Thus, they spent the evening hours working around the table in this sitting room at Haworth with hope and enthusiasm their constant companions. Here they were happy and content. It is little wonder that wherever their individual lives took them, in spite of months away – first at school and later working as governesses, in spite of Charlotte and Emily spending February to November 1842 in Brussels and Charlotte returning there alone for the whole of 1843, all three sisters could never suppress the desire to return to their home at the Parsonage – their sanctuary, their own world that they had come to cherish and where they felt free to be themselves.

It was Emily who suffered the worst homesickness of all when away. Her lifeblood was in the moors that surrounded her home. Out there she was at one with the world and nothing could take their place for her. It was a love affair she never grew tired of and the moors were the setting for *Wuthering Heights*. In this same sitting room where so much of that book was written, there is a poignant reminder of Emily – the couch over by the wall. It was lying here, on the cold afternoon of Tuesday, 19 December 1848, only three months after the death of her brother, Branwell, whose portrait in plaster still hangs above, that Emily drew her last painful breath. She was only 30 years of age and never had the satisfaction of knowing just how successful her single contribution to the literary world would eventually become.

As well as writing, Emily also had other artistic talents and enjoyed playing the fine cottage piano in her father's study on the other side of the entrance hall. It was in his study that the reverend spent hours alone with his work – and his thoughts. Sadly, by doing this, he would distance himself from his children. He even ate his meals alone in here. It was almost as though the passageway marked the boundary between his world and that of his children, although at times the distance could be described as far greater. Despite this, he was not unkindly towards his family, but he would leave Aunt Branwell and the loving Tabitha to provide the children with their more emotional needs in life whilst he purely looked after them spiritually.

Unfortunately, Aunt Branwell was also a little short on showing any emotional feelings towards the children, but constantly complained about the coldness of the place and how she longed for the warmer climate of her beloved Cornwall. She frequently took to her room and remained there, directing the household and the children from her refuge, away from the draughty stone-flagged floors of the downstairs. However, it has to be said the children learnt much from her and held her in great affection, for she was not completely unapproachable; it is said the quiet and gentle Anne was her favourite. She had a remarkable sense of duty and devoted her life to raising her sister's children as well as she could. She never returned to Cornwall, but died at the Parsonage on Saturday, 29 October 1842, whilst Emily and Charlotte were still away in Brussels. Although they hastened home on hearing of her illness, they did not arrive in time and could only mourn her passing. Her room now contains displays of the family possessions, including Charlotte's tiny gloves and boots. I don't think Aunt Branwell would approve at all! She most certainly would not have approved of Patrick Brontë's nightshirt being displayed on his bed for all the world to see, but she may secretly have been rather proud of the quilt underneath it, which was the work of the Brontë sisters, since she had directed the girls in sewing techniques at an early age.

There is so much within the confines of this house to stop and admire related to this talented and yet modest family. As you view one room after the other, each one portrays another aspect of their lives until gradually a picture unfolds that gives you a unique insight into the world of the Brontës themselves. In fact, as I said, it is more than an insight, it is almost as if their presence forever resides here. For them, time has stood still. In this house they are not dead, only sleeping. Tomorrow they will awake and their day will begin as usual, with the chores that must be done. Later, maybe, if the weather is fine, they will take to the moors, perhaps as far as Sladen Beck – a return walk of about four miles. They'll return in time for tea, and in the evening gather around the sitting room table just like before, to talk and work at their leisure, until they go into their father's study for evening prayers, after which he will retire to bed at nine as usual, stopping only to wind the grandfather clock in the nook on the stairs whilst they continue working at their writing desks for a while before they too retire for the night. Such could be believed of this almost magical abode that stands defiant against the threatening encroachment of the wild and imposing moorland on the one side and watches over the village's dead on the other.

Leaving the Parsonage via the irresistible Brontë Society Book and Gift Shop, I often find myself taking a moment or two to glance up Church Lane and beyond towards that imposing landscape that was so much a part of Emily, and I always have the same thought. Could it be that she too now wanders her beloved moors happy and free, just as she would have us believe Heathcliff and Catherine did after they were reunited by Heathcliff's death at the end of *Wuthering Heights*? Back down Church Lane towards Haworth's main street, I also rarely resist the temptation of making a brief detour up the footpath through the graveyard. These often-gruesome places can tell much about a place and Haworth's graveyard is no exception. Huddled together without any sort of order, the gravestones are an austere reminder of the high mortality rate in the village during the nineteenth century, especially between 1840 and 1850. The average age at death in this period was 25 years, but many were babies and children under 7 years. The cause in most cases was cholera, diphtheria, typhus or tuberculosis, which were a direct result of poor sanitation. Here there were no sewers, only open drains running down the streets; no indoor water closets, but outdoor privies shared between large numbers of families; and a polluted water supply which ran through the churchyard. Only a few houses had a piped drinking-water system, and this did not include the Parsonage, which was considered a more elaborate dwelling than most. In August 1849 a petition was sent to the General Board of Health in London for sanitary and water improvements in Haworth, and in April 1850 Patrick Brontë instigated enquiries into the water supply, but it wasn't until March 1858 that the reservoir was completed. It is said that 40,000 bodies are buried under this sod, several deep in places. I have seen this place in all seasons and to me its grimness can only be relieved by the first falls of golden leaves, which are attractive to the eye against the gnarled and blackened stones, sinking with age and now mostly invaded by a furry covering of moss creeping over the faded inscriptions of the long-forgotten dead. There were no trees to break the monotony in the Brontë years and therefore the outlook from the Parsonage could not help but be a constant reminder, as if the family needed one, that death was always on their doorstep. The trees that stand as sentinels now over their dismal charges were added by the Rev. John Wade, except for two conifers near the Parsonage which are supposed to have been planted by Charlotte on her wedding day.

Charlotte's marriage certificate is on display in Haworth Church together with various other documents relating to the family. It is a poignant reminder of Charlotte's bitter disappointment when, on the eve of her wedding, her father declared he was too unwell to attend and she had to ask her friend Miss Wooler, who she had known since 1831 when she attended her school at Roe Head, to give her away. The only other guest at the wedding was her life-long friend Ellen Nussey, who she had also met at Roe Head in the same year. It is said that the reason her father suddenly found himself indisposed was because he could not bear to lose his one remaining child and he also feared she would not be able to sustain a pregnancy due to her diminutive size. Did he have foresight, I wonder?

The church tower, although much altered, is all that remains of the church the Brontës knew. The original church was demolished in 1879 by the Rev. John Wade to make way for a new one, which was dedicated two years later. However, on a stone pillar near the chancel steps there is a plaque referring to the Brontë family vault, which is situated beneath. There is also the Brontë Memorial Chapel which was completed in 1964, and high on its wall a monument to the Brontës, originally carved by John Brown, the church sexton and a good friend of Branwell Brontë whose favourite haunt can be found conveniently situated at the foot of the church steps into the main street.

The Black Bull Hotel is where Branwell frequently found comfort and respite from his inner turmoil. In fact, the chair he used is still there, proudly displayed for all to see. Many believed him to be mentally disturbed in the months before his death. Although he is often confined to the shadows of the rest of the Brontë family, in reality he too was very talented and trained to be a professional portrait painter. One of his most well-known works is a portrait of his three sisters, which appears to have had a central figure erased from it. It is said this mysterious figure was Branwell himself and that he removed it because he was so disgusted with his life and what he felt he had become, but others report that he took the fourth figure away purely because he was dissatisfied with the crowded appearance of the overall picture. Some of his work is on display at the Parsonage and shows he did indeed have much flair, but unfortunately, at the time, there were just too many portrait painters and Branwell could not get enough commissions to give him a regular income. Besides his painting, Branwell was also gifted musically and often played the church organ – much to his father's delight.

Just across the street from the Black Bull is the apothecary which still retains much of its old-world character and charm and would, therefore, probably be very familiar to all the Brontës. Not least to Branwell, since it was here he acquired his regular supply of opium – although he would be very disappointed today as that item is definitely and permanently out of stock! Branwell's addiction to opium was not uncommon in Victorian England. It was a habit that spread across all social structures and contaminated all in its path, but this should not demean the extraordinary services afforded the public by this particular establishment. In the last century many people went to an apothecary for the diagnosis of all their ills. After all, there was no National Health Service and the doctor did not come cheap – he was only consulted in an emergency or if you happened to have enough money to pay for his services. However, you don't have to be sick today to enjoy Haworth's apothecary. As you clump over the creaking floorboards into a nostalgic world that fills your nostrils with a mixture of age-old fragrances such as Lifebuoy soap, dried lavender or lumbago ointment, your eyes are suddenly alerted to such items as metal buckets, old-fashioned shaving equipment, scrubbing boards, many long-forgotten household products that Granny would remember with pride, soothing remedies for aching limbs, oils for this and oils for that and even oils for lamps and then there are inhalants for express relief of . . . whatever you need express relief from. And so it goes on. Here there is literally something for everybody and business is thriving because people of today want what the people of yesterday had – perhaps because, as Granny will tell you, things were better in those days!

ஐ In Search of the Brontës ஐ

Haworth is situated 800 feet up in the Pennines and the main street has hardly changed since the Brontës' time. The only real difference is that many of the buildings have been converted into shops and cafés to accommodate the huge influx of tourists. Most of the houses were built around the same time as the Parsonage (1778–9) to house cottage-industry textile workers and their families. If you look at some of the upper floors of the buildings, they still have the rows of narrow windows which would have allowed more light into the rooms to assist the workers in operating their handlooms. The 1840s saw the height of domestic cloth production in Haworth before the work was eventually transferred to mills, with their water-powered machinery. Sadly, as Charlotte Brontë was well aware when she wrote her book *Shirley*, based on the Luddite uprisings, these mills were not necessarily good news for the local people, many of whom subsequently lost their livelihoods in the name of progress.

As if Haworth isn't already steeped in enough reminders of its past, a piercing, short-sharp whistle is often heard from the valley below, followed by the muted gentle rhythmic acceleration of well-oiled pistons. The railway originally came to Haworth in 1867 and, thanks to the volunteers on the Keighley and Worth Valley Railway, the old atmosphere of a regular steam-train service has been faithfully revived. There is also an engine shed that David loves to explore, given the opportunity. (As an aside this line passes through Oakworth station, famous for the part it played in the original film of that much-loved story – *The Railway Children*. It has been painstakingly preserved completely in tune with the period the film depicts and when you are there you fully expect Bernard Cribbins, who played Mr Perks, to come running out from the Station Manager's office with his cap in hand to hastily close the level crossing gates as the next train approaches.)

Although Haworth may be regarded as the home of the Brontës, it is by no means the only place that had an influence on their individual lives. However, it may well be said that Charlotte perhaps benefited most from her travels and definitely used her experiences to great effect when writing her novels. Since I have taken much of the information on the places I visited in search of the Brontës directly from my research notes, which include my initial reactions and impressions, I have of necessity written much of the remainder of this chapter as if I were seeing these places for the first time – purely because I feel by doing so I give a much more accurate representation of the impact my Brontë encounters first had on me.

Our journey begins with Wycoller (near Colne in Lancashire). This village, half-hidden and isolated in a deep sheltered valley surrounded by woodland and high moorland, has a tantalising history of ghosts and hauntings. These stories did not deter Charlotte, however, as it has been recorded that both she and Emily enjoyed walking here – and who could blame them? Wycoller definitely has a beauty all its own: enchanting houses and walls of flowering shrubs, an attractive stream which is shaded by the leafy boughs of a variety of trees along its banks.

Charlotte Brontë, knowing the village well, possibly based Ferndean Manor in her first published novel, *Jane Eyre*, on Wycoller Hall – which is the reason for our visit. It is situated at the far end of the village and was occupied by several generations of the Cunliffe family until around 1818 when Henry Owen Cunliffe, who had spent some years away, returned here to die.

Charlotte's Ferndean Manor is mentioned near the end of her novel when the now blind Mr Rochester has retreated to Ferndean after the fire which gutted Thornfield, his much more elaborate residence. According to the story, he lives as a recluse there until his beloved Jane finds him again. Charlotte's view of the old hall would have been a much more wholesome one than the one that greets us today. The years have taken their toll, and all that stands before us is a sad ruin, trying desperately to retain some form of dignity as its remaining stout stonework struggles to give its visitor a clue as to its magnificent former self. As my eyes wander from the stone-flagged floors, etched with invasive weeds, to an extravagantly wide stone arched fireplace, still very much intact but well open to the elements, and then up to the crumbling pitiful walls with a few remaining mullioned windows, a total feeling of desolation comes over me. What waste. What stories these silent relics could tell if the spell were broken and they could but speak. Perhaps they would only weep with their pain of being left to rot after serving well those that once lived here.

Notwithstanding that aspect of this old hall, there is no doubt the setting gives much to please the eye, not least the old packhorse bridge by which you leave the village road to come into the ruins of the hall.

This bridge is said to have been built between the thirteenth and fifteenth centuries and has an intriguing structure. The almost primitive arrangement of stones supported by two low, wide arches beneath gives the impression, when viewed from one of the few remaining windows of the hall, of a crocodile's head with its protruding eyes peering downstream. In truth, the bridge's crest of dubiously arranged large smooth stones with its low parapets either side has withstood the constant passage of man and packhorse trains for centuries, as well as the stormiest of weather. Although the packhorse trains are long gone, hopefully this unique little bridge will survive and continue to be used by man long into that future, when, sadly, only the coarse grasses and meadow weeds will greet it and the old hall will have disappeared without trace.

As we take our leave and I take a last look back, maybe I can believe there is some truth in those stories of hauntings.

And now I do recall
There was a presence nigh
Not dead – nor alive
Something did stir
I am very sure
But then was still
Was it good – or was it ill?

My next Brontë encounter is tinged with more than a little sadness. Cowan Bridge is situated near Tunstall on the road between Skipton and Kendal and was our next port of call. It was Reverend William Carus Wilson, an evangelical clergyman and landowner, who bought the row of eighteenth-century cottages on the bank of the River Leek and added a right-angled wing onto each end in order to accommodate a school room and dormitories. It was in January 1824 that he opened the Clergy Daughter's School, charging an unbelievably low fee, even for those times, of £14 a year for board and lodgings.

Patrick Brontë must have regarded the school with great relief – he then had five motherless daughters to think of and other establishments had proved too expensive. Thus, in July 1824 his two eldest girls – Maria and Elizabeth – both still weak from various illnesses they had suffered during the winter, were sent off to Cowan Bridge, followed by Charlotte a few weeks later. (Charlotte was later to recall her time at the school when she used it as the model for Lowood School in *Jane Eyre*. In her novel she makes very clear the scars that Cowan Bridge left on her.)

The aim of the school was to help prepare its pupils for working as governesses. There is no doubt the routine and discipline were without pity, the environment less than desirable and the food totally inadequate. Even Sundays brought no respite. Rev. William Wilson was not only the founder of Cowan Bridge School, but also the vicar of Tunstall. It was, therefore, expected that the girls should walk the two miles to Tunstall Church across the fields each Sunday to attend services. As winter approached, the pupils found the walk harder. They had no shelter from the harshness of the weather and the ground became more and more sodden underfoot. They arrived for the morning service cold and wet, and that was not the end of it. After the service they had to eat their meagre lunch of cold meat and bread in a room over the porch of the church and then attend the afternoon service before making the almost unbearable two-mile return walk back to Cowan Bridge, with often bitterly cold winds and needle-piercing rain or sleet hindering their every step. Today, attractive Tunstall Church, set away from the main thoroughfare of the village, has little changed and the room over the porch where the girls huddled for their lunch is still there for everyone to see. So too are the surrounding fields that bore witness to such suffering. However, in the summer sun with their lush green cloak dominating the landscape, the raw cruelness of a winter's day is well concealed.

Emily's experience of Cowan Bridge was comparatively short. She arrived at the end of November 1824, but by the following January further events were unfolding which would leave the Brontë family grief-stricken. Almost inevitably an epidemic of typhoid (or low fever, as it was then called) broke out at the school and infected the majority of pupils. The result was devastating. By February Maria Brontë had become desperately ill and was sent home, where she died on 6 May 1825 at the age of 11 years. Three weeks later her sister Elizabeth, who was also very sick, came home to the Parsonage, but within two weeks she too was dead. She was only 10 years of age. Charlotte now found herself the eldest of Patrick Brontë's four remaining children.

Fortunately, neither she nor Emily, both of whom Patrick Brontë removed from the school as a precautionary measure, contracted the illness. They never returned to Cowan Bridge.

The school, which is reported to have much improved after these events, moved to Castleton in 1833. Today the row of terraced cottages are again used as private residences. The two end wings that William Wilson added for the school have gone – destroyed by fire after they fell into disuse. On the end wall of the row of neat and flower-bedecked cottages that stand at right-angles to the main road and face the wide and substantial bridge over the pretty River Leek, there is a simple plaque reading: 'Maria, Elizabeth, Charlotte and Emily Brontë lived here as pupils of the Clergy Daughter's School 1824–5'. It tactfully makes no mention of the hardships suffered by its pupils or the tragic outcome of their attendance. Maybe it is best left to Charlotte's account of Lowood School in *Jane Eyre* to stand as a perpetual epitaph to those who suffered silently on this small piece of soil.

It was not until January 1831 that Charlotte, by the kind gesture of her godparents helping with the fees, was again sent away to school, this time to Roe Head, Mirfield Moor – only 20 miles from Haworth, in the area where Patrick Brontë had taken up his first Yorkshire curacy. The school, which was run by a Miss Margaret Wooler and her sister, was in every way a more pleasing experience than Cowan Bridge. In this large Georgian House, which commands a fine view from its bay windows of Kirklees Park and on to the Calder Valley, there were only seven to ten pupils at any one time as opposed to Cowan Bridge, where approximately seventy pupils crammed into a much smaller area. Here, with encouragement and kindness, Charlotte succeeded well in her lessons and earned prizes for her efforts. It was here too that she first met her lifelong friends – Ellen Nussey, Mary Taylor and, not least, Miss Margaret Wooler herself, who was to be called upon 23 years later to give Charlotte away on her wedding day.

It was through her 18 months at Roe Head as a pupil, her later return there as a teacher, and her frequent visits to Ellen Nussey at Birstall and Mary Taylor at Gomersal, that Charlotte gained such a sound knowledge of the area, which was commonly known as the Heavy Woollen District. I decided to follow in her footsteps to explore for myself the places she had seen which provided her with so much inspiration for the setting of her second novel, *Shirley*.

Set in the year of 1812 – a time of Luddite riots, the Napoleonic Wars and economic unrest – her father well remembered the events of the period, a little before Charlotte herself was born, and so she drew on his knowledge to help her with much of the factual detail she needed to provide the backdrop to her book. She then set out to portray, skilfully and accurately, how the troubled times took their toll on the lives of her leading characters and irreversibly affected their futures.

Charlotte Brontë writes a very detailed account of the home of her heroine, Shirley Keeldar, which she refers to as 'Fieldhead'. In reality it is a very accurate description of the Elizabethan manor house, Oakwell Hall, visited by Charlotte in the 1840s whilst staying with her friend Ellen Nussey at Birstall. At the time it was being used as a girls' boarding school run by a widow, Mrs Hannah Cockill, and her three daughters, one of whom had been at Roe Head School at the same time as Charlotte and Ellen. The Cockills were related to the Nusseys.

'This was neither a grand, nor a comfortable house,' wrote Charlotte of Fieldhead in *Shirley*. Obviously she was not impressed with this fine Elizabethan mansion. Maybe she was right to describe it thus – we shall see. Looking at it now – dark, imposing, mysterious and beckoning – it would look just right in one of those old horror movies. You know the type, reader. Dead of night, leaves blowing off the trees in a raging storm, house being lit up by flashes of blue lightning and a spindly thin butler opening the heavy oaken door which creaks on its hinges with a spine-chilling groan. No such association, however, is made by Charlotte, but when describing its outward appearance, she does comment on 'its irregular architecture'. I have to agree with her. Whilst it cannot be called rambling to any great degree, being of modest size, its numerous gables accentuate its non-uniformity of shape and totally defy the intruder to contemplate the layout of its interior which is further kept secretively obscured by its lattice windows.

I also agree with Charlotte when she uses the word 'picturesque' to describe the whole aspect of the building. For, despite my initial comments, it is an excellent example of the type of Manor House built for the minor gentry in the sixteenth century, and this one was linked exclusively to one family – the Batts (not the belfry kind, I hasten to add) – who purchased it in 1565. Much altered and improved in the first half of the seventeenth century, it has little changed since that time. It stands surrounded by beautifully maintained gardens which both in layout and detail are totally in keeping with the period of the hall. Beyond the grounds lies the superb rural landscape of Kirklees Park.

On entering the house (the door does not creak, by the way), I cannot not fail to be impressed by the Great Hall. From the diagonally arranged stone flags on the floor, to the oak-panelled walls, to the tall mullioned window, to the grand fireplace, to the open gallery above displaying, invitingly, the upper storey, I am totally captivated by the entire arrangement. Springing back in time to those days when gallant gentry and their ladies used these rooms to resume their family life, I can feel nothing other than a certain admiration for the quality of workmanship and design with which they were associated then. Here was character and charm, working hand in hand with a simplicity and elegance that we have lost forever. How we should mourn their passing. However, I believe I do understand why Charlotte felt compelled to describe it thus: 'Very sombre, it was long, vast and dark, one latticed window lit it but dimly. The gallery on high was seen but in outline.' I, too, feel a little strange as my eyes follow the path of the oak panelling, dulled by age, creating indiscernible darkened corners, nooks and crannies, which all seem to be listening to the echo of my footsteps on the stone. Even the ornate staircase over in the corner by the fireplace, back lit by a window which immediately throws it into silhouette, has my imagination working overtime. What of the balcony above, which to Charlotte would indeed have been obscure, since she was notoriously short-sighted. In Charlotte's life there was so much darkness that if she had felt as I do now (she too had a rich imagination), it might well have reflected just a little too much of how she felt inside, which, for a moment gave her an irrepressible longing for escape to something brighter and of more cheer to conquer the burden she carried so bravely on her young shoulders. It must be remembered, after all, that when Charlotte was writing *Shirley* it was a time of great personal grief, having suffered the sickness and subsequent loss of her brother Branwell and then her two beloved sisters, Emily and Anne. No such reasoning applies to me, but I have definitely lingered here too long and having spooked myself a little decide it's time to move on.

The Grand Parlour is next. (All downstairs rooms, whatever their use, were referred to as 'parlours', while all upstairs ones were called 'chambers'.) This is a pleasant room, well lit and airy and of moderate size which Charlotte Brontë well describes in *Shirley*. She remarks on the panelled walls having been painted over in pink paint, and how this would be easier to keep clean. This was indeed true until recently, when the room underwent restoration work to return it to its former glory of the late 1600s. As the paint was carefully removed, superb detail in the general panelling was revealed and more especially, over the mantel, intricate landscape paintings became apparent that had been cleverly etched into the wood. Charlotte would truly have been impressed by them and it would probably have made her wonder, as it did me, why anyone should want to paint over them in the first place. The crowning glory of this room was its elaborate plaster ceiling with the Batt Coat of Arms and flowers embossed over its entire surface. Unfortunately, during a great storm in December 1883, a chimney came crashing down through the roof into the Grand Parlour Chamber above this room, where a lady was sleeping. It didn't stop but continued its downward path through the floor of that room bringing the bed (and the lady) down with it to the Grand Parlour below, completely destroying the prized ceiling. The lady survived, without serious injury, on a musical note. She landed on the grand piano!

It is not only the Grand Parlour that is trapped in the 1600s. Climbing the stairs to the upper storey and getting a first glimpse of what awaits me, it is clear that, as near as possible, each room has been expertly tended, with attention paid to the detail of that period, so that the visitor is immediately drawn back to a time when Charles II would have been on the throne following the restoration of the monarchy after the death of Oliver Cromwell in 1658. The Grand Parlour Chamber, now with roof and floor intact (but no sleeping lady!), contains the only *garderobe* (toilet) in the house, built out so that a chute may deliver the goods to the ground below! Viewing each chamber with its old timbers, low doorways, uneven floors and jumble of antiquated wares, there is little doubt as to how they were used by the household. A tremendous amount of credit has to be given to those people who have contributed to presenting Oakwell Hall to the public with such a high standard of accuracy wherever possible.

It must be remembered that it may have been Oakwell Hall's link with Charlotte Brontë that brought me here, but this magnificent building has a history all its own which is far removed from Charlotte's nineteenth-century *Shirley*. During the seventeenth century, England festered in bitter civil war that resulted in the country being splattered by the blood of so many of its people. The Batt family were indeed Royalists, but in this part of Yorkshire it was the Parliamentarians who had the sympathy of the people. It would have been a period in history that Charlotte, no doubt, would have been well aware of, and, notwithstanding the date over the front door of 1583, she would have been well able to date the house approximately from its outward appearance. However, the interior would not have been the museum piece it is now and she would not have had the pleasure of seeing the reconstruction that visitors witness today.

A mile from Oakwell Hall is a dwelling of a very different outlook – Red House, Gomersal. After purchasing the relevant map from Oakwell Hall's gift shop to help find the way, I decided to do as Charlotte would have done and walk through the fields, leaving the car at Oakwell. Mind you, I soon discovered that my jeans were far more practicable for such an exercise. Heaven knows how those ladies of Charlotte's time coped with those long full skirts, bustles and whatever else. They must have been ripped to shreds on the undergrowth or soaked through at least in the wet. Doesn't bear thinking about, especially when you think it was still in an era when ladies were expected to be just that – neat and proper at all times – and lifting your skirts was just unheard of. However, the walk was refreshing and rewarding.

Red House was the home of the Taylor family, in particular Mary Taylor, who became friends with Charlotte in the days of Roe Head. Charlotte visited it often in the 1830s and thus when she came to write *Shirley* she not only based the Yorke family on the Taylors, but used Red House as the model for the Yorke's home of 'Briarmains'.

It is situated in what I would describe as a 'secret garden'. You enter the garden by a door in the wall that now runs along the edge of the A561. According to Charlotte, the house was built 'ere the highway was cut', which is probably true, but also proves that there has been a road here at least since Charlotte's time. Once in the garden, the close cut lawns, majestic trees and shrubs all seek to encompass the visitor with a complete feeling of peace and tranquillity far removed from the bustle of the thoroughfare on the other side of the wall. The neat paths lead the eye to the house itself. No fuss, no trimmings. It stands open to criticism, unashamed and uncomplicated by any obstruction to obscure the view. Built in 1660 by William Taylor, it could never be dated by first sight as accurately as Oakwell Hall. Abandoning the traditional local stone, it has been built of red bricks – which probably gave the house its name – but the reason it may fool most of us with regard to its date is that, apparently, the frontage and interior were structurally remodelled in the eighteenth century, which explains its tendency to the Georgian neat, square lines as opposed to the frills and fancies of some earlier buildings. It remained the property of the Taylor family until as late as 1920, although no Taylor has lived here since Jane Lister Taylor died in 1887.

Behind its unpretentious front door, Red House is displayed as it may have looked in the 1830s when, as I have mentioned, Charlotte Brontë was a frequent visitor. At that time it was the home of Joshua Taylor, owner of the mill at Hunsworth, his wife Anne and their six children, four boys and the two girls – Charlotte's friend Mary and her sister Martha. Sadly, Martha died of cholera in October 1842 while at school in Brussels with her sister Mary and was buried at the Protestant cemetery there. At the time, Charlotte and Emily were also in Brussels and were able to offer Mary some comfort. Much later, when Charlotte was writing *Shirley*, in which, as I have said, she based the Yorke family on the Taylors, she actually used this sad experience when predicting the future for Mr Yorke's youngest daughter, Jessy.

Mary Taylor, determined not to rely on her family's fortune, left England for New Zealand in 1845 to earn her own living. She set up shop and eventually earned enough money to return to England in 1859 (four years after Charlotte's death) when she had her own house built in High Royd, Gomersal. She lived there until she died on 1 March 1893. She is buried in St Mary's Churchyard, Gomersal.

Red House obviously very much appealed to Charlotte and she records her impression of it: '. . . lights from the windows shone vividly – this was no dark or lonely scene, nor even a silent one . . . curtains did not muffle the voices and laughter'. Here was obviously the cheeriness of family life which encouraged a sense of excitement in Charlotte. Here too there was the bitter-sweet reminder of something she had once had that was now gone, the companionship and happiness from within the family unit that needed no outsider to enhance. Around the time of her visits here she would still have had Branwell, Emily and Anne. However, when she was actually writing *Shirley* and recalling these memories she was alone.

My immediate reaction to Red House is 'I could live here'. Leading off the entrance hall to the left is the parlour, which would have been the 'best room' of the house, where visitors would be received and entertained and afternoon tea would be served. Comfortable, elegant and totally uncluttered, here one could perhaps relax with some needlework whilst listening to Mary Taylor playing the piano over in the corner. A door from this room leads conveniently into the kitchen quarters of the house.

The scullery, or wash kitchen, is separate from the main kitchen, an arrangement that I think is totally sensible and would suit me fine. The former room is exactly what the name implies. Here the laundry is laboriously processed. How the poor maids must have suffered! Wash day hands must have been a permanent complaint. Scrubbing, starching, ironing for the whole family, I assume, and think of the amount of water they would have needed to boil. One or two mod cons would have to be added here, I think. I wonder how scullery maids of the nineteenth century would have regarded that great invention of our age – the washing machine – if they could have seen that far into the future. A blessing from heaven, I am sure. It would probably have frightened the life out of them at first, bearing in mind there was little automation in their world and certainly no electricity!

Now to the main kitchen. There are none of your conventional modern units here, reader. Instead, one wall of the main kitchen is given over to a very attractive dresser arrangement displaying its tempting assortment of kitchenware in copper, pewter and ceramics. The open range, the oak food cupboard, the large central wooden kitchen table, with rack beneath and the long case clock together with various other pieces of furniture and curious implements of the period, feed my imagination to bursting point. Here I could play for hours. Yes, of necessity, I would have to add some modern equivalents, but to dress this room without touching the basics would bring it in line with my idea of a dream kitchen. I can almost smell the freshly baked scones straight from the oven in the range, hear the kettle singing on the hob, and see the large kitchen table laid for Sunday tea. What of convenience when cosiness and character are lost? What of speed when there is no time to enjoy? I suspect, however, that the lady of this house, Mrs Taylor, would have spent little time here. She had two staff to enjoy these surroundings and would probably have only been seen in here giving directions to the cook or maid on her requirements.

The room Charlotte refers to in *Shirley* as the 'back parlour', which was 'the usual sitting-room of an evening', has been reconstructed as a formal dining room with the table beautifully set for a candlelit dinner. Here also can be found the stained-glass windows of Milton and Shakespeare, which Charlotte describes in detail. As with the parlour, there is a simple elegance about this room which would challenge the most critical eye to find fault with it.

The tour of the downstairs of Red House finishes with Mr Taylor's study which, amongst its many items of interest, contains a bookcase that originally belonged to Ellen Nussey, a friend of Mary Taylor and, of course, Charlotte. The upper storey of the house continues the theme of an unassuming, quiet, tasteful simplicity that makes me feel that, apart from one or two modifications to suit our modern-age requirements, it is more or less ready for occupancy.

However, do not misunderstand me, this house, as with Oakwell Hall, has been faithfully and beautifully restored, with special attention to the minutest detail, to bring to all its visitors a glimpse back into an era, which as you may have gathered by now, totally enthuses the writer. It is also an age which has had a great influence over our present and probably our future too, and I do not believe I am in the minority in finding it as fascinating as I do. Whereas Oakwell Hall is a masterpiece representing an age we have read about and can only try to imagine, we do find it easier to relate to the nineteenth century which is not so far removed. In fact it has become fashionable of late to reproduce that age to some greater or lesser degree in our homes under that wide modern heading of 'traditional'. Red House is in no way a reproduction – it is to all intents and purposes the real thing and, as I leave it rather reluctantly, I for one am very pleased to have made its acquaintance.

❧ In Search of the Brontës ❧

Despite the fact that these few paragraphs of mine may initially indicate a tendency for the Brontës, and Charlotte and Emily in particular, to have needed outside influences, acquaintances and their own experiences to inspire them to construct their novels, there is probably only a minimum of truth in this. In fact, it could just as easily have been the reverse. From a young age they all evoked a rich imagination in one another which is illustrated by their earliest scribblings and it is far more credible that inspiration for their novels pre-empted the use of any available material to them from real life, except perhaps for Emily and her beloved moors. In truth, each of their novels was daringly ahead of its time, both in observation of life and promiscuity, and provoked much criticism from literary circles even before those circles realised that the authors were, in fact, women. They had all used pseudonyms for their works to hide their identity, which probably only goes to suggest they were fully aware of the low esteem with which their works would have been received if it had been known they were written by women in a very austere and narrow-minded Victorian England. Especially when such works include pointedly class-structured characters, underlying criticisms of the 'establishment' and romantic entwinements that would raise the eyebrow of the most liberated Victorian lady, or, worse, cause a chuckle in the smoking room of a gentlemen's club and then be thrown aside as 'profoundly unsuitable material to stand on any gentleman's bookshelf'. It has to be appreciated that at the time these books were published, they were regarded as shocking and immoral. Undoubtedly the girls were intelligent enough to realise that what they were producing may well be the harder for the readers to identify with if they knew they were the work of women – and a clergyman's daughters at that! In our terms, the Brontë sisters were fully aware that their novels could be regarded as 'politically incorrect' and the establishment would certainly not approve! Why did they write them? We will never know, but we can speculate.

Three young girls. They were not considered poor. Far from it. They lived in the largest house in the village. Modest by some standards, but seen as reasonable by most in their class. Patrick earned around £200 per annum, which, when you look at it in terms of a servant on approximately £17 per annum, seems a goodly sum. Of course, they were not landed gentry and could not compete with mill owners, etc., but to many they were well off. They could not afford their own carriage to travel about in but they did have the comfort of a fairly well-equipped and substantial home and servants to carry out the daily chores. Primarily, they would be expected to earn a living for themselves as respectable governesses but they would never work scrubbing floors. However, experience proved what they had already realised in early life, that not one of them was really primed for this type of lifestyle. In the first half of the 1840s, Anne probably had the greatest success in this direction, although she had not enjoyed her experiences, whilst both Emily and Charlotte had tried teaching but were not happy in their posts. It was then decided they would open a school at the Parsonage and to this end Charlotte and Emily went to Brussels to gain language skills which they hoped would secure the school's success. Unfortunately, despite their efforts, the idea was a complete failure. Thus the women were faced with a dilemma. They had over time come to realise they were only happiest at home and together but they needed to earn their keep. How could they achieve both in such a challenging society where being mere women could be a distinct disadvantage when you were born into such a lower- to middle-class environment? It was then they may have decided – or probably Charlotte decided for them – that they would have to put their literary talents to good use. It worked, although it took time and some disappointment, as Charlotte's initial attempt, *The Professor*, was rejected by several publishers and did not in fact go into print until two years after her death. However, in 1847 Charlotte's *Jane Eyre*, Emily's *Wuthering Heights* and Anne's *Agnes Grey* were all accepted for publication and the women were ecstatic. How they were received at the time was harder to bear, but the fact they survived and are three of the most popular classics ever written goes some way towards showing just how brilliant the Brontë sisters really were.

It was only comparatively recently that I decided to trample back again through the passage of time in search of the Brontës. This was going to be different, however, since I wanted to go back to their beginning, before Haworth, back to where they were born, in Thornton – not too far from Bradford. Patrick Brontë moved his family, which then consisted of his wife, Maria, and two baby daughters, Maria and

Elizabeth, from Hartshead where he had been minister, to take up a position in Thornton on 19 May 1815. It was here at their home in Market Street that his wife was to bear him another four children: Charlotte on 21 April 1816, his only son, Branwell, on 26 June 1817, Emily on 30 July 1818 and Anne on 17 January 1820. It was shortly after Anne's birth that the Brontës moved to Haworth, where they were to remain for the rest of their lives.

Of course, this house, the recently opened Brontë Birthplace in Market Street, probably would not attract the same amount of visitors or attention as Haworth. For to most, this is not where the Brontë sisters lived out their lives. Here there are no open moors for the girls, particularly Emily, to have enjoyed, although there is no graveyard either to have encroached on their privacy and remind them of the inevitable. Here there is no front garden to pretty on a summer's day or wild flowers and grasses for the merciless winds coming down off the moor to multiply. Here there are no hills to climb. Here you cannot be alone. But here they were born and here they were with their mother who began to die. Even here, where there are few Brontë reminders to witness, there is still present the thought that Haworth confirms what started here. The promise of a better life that never really came and stayed, the sadness of ensuing death, the hope that one day happiness would overthrow all that was locked in memory. Here, briefly, they were together – Patrick and Maria and their six children. Within 18 months of moving to Haworth the children were to become motherless and Patrick would be a widower.

When I stood before the row of neat little terraced houses, there was no obvious clue as to the significance of the end house apart from a single plaque on the wall referring to the four Brontës born here. Above the front door, which bears a passing resemblance to the one at Haworth, including the steps, I noted the builder's mark – the date was 1802, which meant the house was only 13 years old when the Brontës moved in. Despite its size and comparative newness, I would doubt Mrs Brontë had much time for organising her new home to her final satisfaction. Four pregnancies in five years, and so many little ones to care for, would have taken all her attention, I am sure. Although I had been told the house retained much of its character from when the Brontës were here, I knew it had obviously been privately owned for nearly two centuries and I was anxious to see just what had been retained and what had been sacrificed, bearing in mind when the Brontës lived here it was the Regency period, an interesting fact since even the most ardent of Brontë followers most often refer to the famous sisters as Victorian novelists, which indeed they were, but in truth these girls were born of Georgian parents into a Georgian world which influenced their young lives well into adulthood. After all, Victoria was not a year old herself when the Brontë's youngest, Anne, was born and the family subsequently left Thornton for another Georgian home in the shape of the Parsonage at Haworth. Thus it would be another 17 years before the new and innovative Victorian age would arrive. Anyway, I needn't have had any doubts about their first home. Immediately I set foot in the house it was obvious it had retained much of its old character and charm and that what had been removed was industriously being replaced to give the visitor as near as possible a true picture of how the house would have been when the Brontës lived here.

The new owner, the novelist Barbara Whitehead, has also written *Charlotte Brontë* and *Dearest Nell* and, although a very busy lady, has obviously got the enthusiasm it takes for her comparatively new project. A tour of the house inspires the imagination and you quickly come to recognise this is where it all began. Don't underestimate its relevance or importance. The cosiness of the sitting-room evokes a picture of Patrick Brontë receiving his guests on parish business or sitting quietly with his thoughts by the fire, or perhaps waiting for the telling cry of his new born (Mrs Brontë was delivered of each of their four younger children in the dining room the other side of the hallway). Undoubtedly, on such occasion there would have been much hustle and bustle about this house, especially in view of the growing number of other little ones to be tended to. Doubtless too, with home births the norm in those days, there was the perpetual fear of something going badly wrong. The dining room itself is cosy and very well arranged in a simple way. The fireplace is Georgian and the Brontës would well recognise it as it is the original. Just imagine all those kettles of water that must have been boiled over it in its time – and not just for making tea!

Although major restoration work was taking place in the kitchen, we were allowed a peep. The original stone staircase up into the servants' bedroom is still in place and a range is being installed. No doubt the servant's room was warmed by the chimney. The children's bedroom, which is conveniently situated adjacent to the servant's room, is very spacious but probably would have seemed quite cramped with six small children sharing it. Occupying the alcove on one side of the fireplace, the surround of which is original, is a huge cupboard-cum-wardrobe, again believed to be original, probably used to house all the children's clothes and toys. Undoubtedly the close proximity to the servant's room was purposeful since they were on hand to give the children comfort during the night if they needed it. The Brontës had two servants here – a fact for which Mrs Brontë must have been truly thankful. The nursemaid to the children was 13-year-old Sarah Garrs, while her older sister, Nancy, was housemaid, and both of them accompanied the Brontë family to Haworth in 1820. They remained in their service for several years until they left to marry.

With Thornton, my journey nears its end for the time being, but it is by no means the end of the list of places to be visited in search of what lies behind the fascinating world of the Brontës. I have intentionally only touched the surface here with the detail of places I visited – maybe putting more emphasis on my impressions of them, or perhaps their respective effect on the Brontë family. That is only right. I never meant this chapter to be a biography or a tour guide. As I stated at the beginning of this book, I have purely put some writings together to share with you the people and places of this marvellous county that have caught my imagination and lasting affection. This famous family, together with their part of West Yorkshire, stand as such an example.

And so I will leave them. But maybe – just maybe – readers, I have tempted you enough to want to discover this family for yourselves as I did, when my journey began at Haworth Parsonage so many years ago, 'in search of the Brontës'.

❧ SIX ❧

Stepping Stones

There is little that pleases the ear more on a warm day in high summer than the sound of water, whether it be the gushing of a waterfall, the trickling of a beck or the river lapping its encroaching banks or rushing over rocks and stones along its path. However, it is not the ear alone that can be pleased. Within the serenity of the Yorkshire countryside there is an abundance of such waterways, either contributing to the natural beauty of the panoramic landscapes or adding to the character and charm of the villages and towns through which they pass, but always giving pleasure to the eye whatever the time of year. The rivers also help to provide some of the richest grazing pastures in England and without doubt the local farmers are truly grateful.

It would be virtually impossible for me to make mention of them all within the confines of this chapter, but many of them can be found tracing their way through the superb landscapes of the Yorkshire Dales. One of these, the River Ure, is a particular favourite of mine. This temperamental river carves her way through picturesque Wensleydale and beyond. I call her 'temperamental' because she is a river of seemingly ever-changing mood – often mid-stream – but, in retrospect, maybe 'adaptable' would be more appropriate, for adaptable she certainly has to be throughout her course of approximately 45 miles from the head of the dale to her journey's end. This vital element can be bold and decisive, timid and hesitant, gather momentum and tumble over mossy boulder or gleaming stone like there is no tomorrow or steel herself and hardly appear to move at all, but whatever her mood she is always beautiful. On her ceaseless journey the river passes by or through some of the most attractive and interesting towns and villages in the Dales and, knowing them as well as I do, I refer to them as my 'stepping stones'. Together they have provided me with some fascinating encounters and I will introduce you to them in this chapter.

The River Ure begins in the high Pennines but as this meagre ribbon of water flows down from the fells she appears to glean strength and encouragement from the stark surroundings and determination fills her veins as she runs free from the head of the dale.

Said to be the highest market town in Yorkshire, Hawes lies in the rugged foothills of the Pennines and, being situated at the head of Wensleydale, is my first stepping stone. I have often thought that, compared to other villages in the dale, Hawes stands alone. I do not mean it is any less a pleasure to visit. Certainly not. We often enjoy taking a stroll down the main street, popping into the numerous antique shops or browsing around a local craft fair. It just seems different somehow. It doesn't seem to have slowly developed over generations, or have developed around a typical market square, sprawled along a winding country lane or arranged around a village green. No, it is almost as if it was purposefully planned and built, and that may well be true, for its situation determines that it must bear the brunt of some of the harshest weather in the dale. Bad weather can roll in off the high Pennines whatever the time of year and all Hawes can do is accept it. There is nothing to protect it and rarely any warning given. A heavy mist can descend out of the blue, literally; a downpour can be no less sudden, and I have driven the length of Wensleydale under a clear sky in autumn, only to be greeted by snow exaggerating the edges of the main street through Hawes.

Notwithstanding its proneness to inclement weather, Hawes is a favourite with visitors and few leave before sampling the delights of its outstanding claim to fame: the town is the home of the renowned Wensleydale cheese. It is here that the cheese is made at the local Wensleydale Creamery, where visitors are welcome to witness the process on a very informative tour of the centre. There is also the well-stocked Cheese Shop that offers a huge variety of freshly made products for sale. We often call in to collect a supply and then while away half an hour in their relaxing restaurant.

It is then that I usually find myself musing over what the monks would make of all this. Why the monks? It was apparently the French Cistercian monks who first introduced cheese to the dale, using their own unique recipe. They resided at Jervaulx Abbey in Lower Wensleydale until the dissolution of the monasteries and their product was in great demand. When they left they passed their secret recipe on to the local farmers' wives, who continued manufacturing the cheese in their own farmhouses for the next 300 years. It was then decided that because of its popularity the cheese should be produced on a much grander scale in a more organised environment, using the milk from the local farms – despite a few problems over the years and changes in management, the industry thrived and eventually became what it is today.

It was television that greatly increased the popularity of my next stepping stone: the village of Askrigg, which has beautiful Wensleydale as its backdrop. When it was decided all those years ago to adapt James Herriot's books for the television series *All Creatures Great and Small*, the legendary vet's surgery at Skeldale House had of necessity to be recreated away from its true home in Kirkgate, Thirsk. However, the building needed to be a convincing stand-in for the purposes of authenticity. The imposing three-storey, double-fronted, grey stone house with its black iron railings fitted the bill perfectly. Situated just across the road from Askrigg's old stepped market cross, it has over the years become a star in its own right and in fact has even been allowed to retain its television name officially. Of course, it was mainly used for outside filming but in a few episodes I understand the hall of the house was used and underwent some subtle alterations with the help of false wall panels supplied by the scenery experts.

Although the film crews packed up their cameras a good few years ago now, the overwhelming popularity of the series still brings visitors from all over the world to the doorstep of this fine house they all recognise as Skeldale. In fact, for a long time many believed this was the real-life one – and why not, didn't it say so in bold letters set in the glass window over the door? Of course, most people these days know where the home of the real practice used to be, but they still come here and hover on the pavement outside. They can venture no further, however, since this house is in reality a very private residence. The curious can only look and admire and not trespass. Mind you, the house itself is not too proud to be photographed and will always show the camera its best side. After all is said and done, that is how it shot to fame in the first place, isn't it?

Apart from its famous house, Askrigg is an attractive village in its own right. The predominance of varying shades of grey is usual for these parts and does not detract from the almost elegant contour of the houses, interspersed with the occasional shop, that huddle together on the gentle climb of the main street as it winds its way from around the thirteenth-century church and on past the market cross. There is no doubt that houses of these remote villages have to be solidly built to withstand the full force of a northern winter. But here, as elsewhere in the Dales, the occupants have an eye for colour and despite the fact their doors open directly onto the street, plant pots or hanging baskets, all overflowing with the rich hues of summer flowers, adorn the front of their homes to break the monotony of the grey stone walls. Here and there even a climbing rose miraculously seems to thrive. Literally planted in little more than a handful of soil at the foot of a wall, its blooms nod in the breeze almost as if they are confirming the tree's stability to any who may reasonably wonder if it can remain in place long enough to give pleasure throughout the summer months.

It was high summer when I had my first encounter with my next stepping stone – Aysgarth Falls – and I was disappointed. Oh, there can be no disputing the natural beauty of the scenes that greeted us when we descended the steep incline to the valley floor, nor that here the River Ure attracts her most ardent admirers. It is, after all, where they can witness her most magnificent performance as she gracefully drops almost 200 ft via the Upper, Middle and Lower Falls. The huge stone slabs and rocks of the falls form a massive natural staircase to ease the river's path to the bottom but as she trickled her way over the mossy steps I felt this was not what I had expected at all. As we huffed and puffed our way back up the hill I promised myself another visit one day.

This time it was autumn. I remember it to be one of those golden days, with a slight chill in the air and some dampness underfoot from the previous day's heavy rain, but a deep blue sky with only white puffy clouds held promise of the weather being fine, whilst the sun picked out the vibrant colours that only autumn can offer. At once, as we again descended the steep hill, there was something different: we could hear the rush of water. The River Ure was in full voice and I knew this time she would not disappoint me. She didn't.

We headed for ringside seats (except we stood) on the old packhorse bridge. To the left of us the Upper Falls, to the right the Middle and Lower Falls. But it was the Upper Falls that entranced us. They were magnificent. Under a canopy of golden trees, which contrasted well with the grey stone of the gorge, the beautiful Ure sparkled in the sunshine as she edged her way over the huge plateaux of solid rock and tumbled in white spray to the next level, negotiating every niche or crevice without hesitation. Forever, ceaselessly slithering downwards and onwards, purposeful and indifferent to whatever lay in her path, finding her own level on the flatter surfaces whilst her edges feathered in and out of the banks under the overhanging branches of the trees. It was whilst watching this spectacular performance that I recalled my disappointment on that hot sunny day in June and realised the truth: of course, she needs wet weather to perform like this. The rain or snow puts the blood in her veins. In dry weather she won't perform because she can't, she is tranquil and ponderous – just a whisper of her now tumbling, energetic self.

I realised I had been lucky enough to witness two very different moods of the River Ure at Aysgarth Falls – although secretly I knew which one I preferred. There were few people around that day to applaud her and, personally, I didn't mind. After all, with the onset of autumn the weather can turn very wet and cold and many feel that places such as Aysgarth are best enjoyed in the summer months. I am very glad we didn't think that on that damp, but bright, October day.

Bolton Castle, to the north of the River Ure, dwarfs the village of Castle Bolton that has grown up around it, but when it was completed in 1399 it had no such neighbours and stood formidable and alone, overlooking the ancient forests of Wensleydale. The castle was perhaps intended more as a status symbol in feudal England than as an instrument of defence but there can be no disputing that in its day this quadrangular building with its four 100 ft-high towers would have intimidated and deterred the most determined of foe. It was built by a Sir Richard Scrope, who was twice chancellor of England in the second half of the fourteenth century. The Scrope family, of Norman origins, had a long history and it appears one of Sir Richard's ancestors was even a great favourite of Edward the Confessor. Unfortunately, the royal approval does not appear to have followed down the line of Sir Richard's descendants. Despite the fact they were rich and powerful, it seems that Bolton Castle brought the Scropes little luck. Sir Richard's eldest son, Sir William Scrope KG, bought the kingdom of the Isle of Man in 1393 and was appointed Treasurer of England in 1398, but then his luck ran out. In the following year, as Bolton Castle was being completed by his father, he was losing his head on the block. Subsequently, further Scropes met a similar fate: there was Archbishop Scrope of York, who crowned King Henry IV and then saw fit to be involved in a plot against him; and a Sir Henry Scrope, who rebelled against King Henry V – both lost their heads.

You would think after that the Scropes would have learnt to err on the side of caution as far as their sovereigns were concerned, but that was not the case. The third Lord Scrope of Bolton Castle was married to a Margaret Neville, whose sister happened to be married to Richard of York who saw it as his birthright to challenge the Lancastrian King Henry VI for his very crown; hence the Wars of the Roses. So the Scropes once again became involved in yet another revolt against yet another Henry, only this time it was Lord Scrope's son who chose to support his uncle Richard. Sadly, Richard of York was killed, but the battle was won and his son took the Crown in place of his father to become King Edward IV. For a few years, therefore, the Scrope family were in favour whilst they had relatives on the English throne: firstly Edward and then his younger brother, Richard. However, as sure as there would be another Scrope, there would be another Henry, Henry VII this time, who proved a real problem to the fifth Lord Scrope – who fought with King Richard III at Bosworth. After the King was defeated and slain at that battle, the new Tudor king – Henry VII – was benevolent and pardoned Lord Scrope, but when, one year later, he followed the family tradition and rebelled against his new king, good King Henry had had enough and, although pardoning him a second time, confined him to living within 22 miles of London where he could obviously keep a royal eye on him. It appears after this, enough was enough and Henry VIII had a good deal more luck with the seventh Baron Scrope. For a while it seems the bad luck of the Scropes went into recession. Maybe it was something to do with there being no more 'enrys.

In fact, the ninth Baron Scrope of Bolton was captain of Carlisle and co-gaoler of Mary, Queen of Scots during her imprisonment at both Carlisle and Bolton Castles, so Elizabeth I must have regarded him with royal approval. Poor Mary was a thorn in Elizabeth's side. On the one hand she sympathised with her cousin losing her Scottish throne, but on the other hand she had a secret fear. Elizabeth knew that although she was Queen of England, she was regarded by many as the illegitimate daughter of Henry VIII and Anne Boleyn, since there were many Catholic sympathisers who felt her mother's marriage to Henry VIII had not been legal. After all, he had been married to Catherine of Aragon who was a Catholic and the Pope had refused to divorce them on any grounds. Thus Henry had made himself Head of the Church in England and, as I explained in a previous chapter, this caused much ill feeling in England at the time. So maybe Elizabeth had good cause to fear the support Mary, a staunch Catholic, may have gained in claiming the English throne. Therefore, although on the surface Elizabeth wanted it to appear she was giving refuge to her cousin and ordered that Mary must be afforded all the hospitality of her royal status, in reality Mary was securely closeted at Bolton – a prisoner who needed to be watched closely for not only her own safety from the angry Scottish lords, but for the safety of Elizabeth herself.

Now, with all that responsibility on his shoulders, Lord Scrope must have had a permanent headache. However, ironically it was Lady Scrope's brother who proved to be his downfall. Mary found she had an ally in the Duke of Norfolk and others also rallied to her support. Soon plans were being made for her escape. Apparently, she was let down through a window from her tower and horses were waiting to take her to the Scottish border. Unfortunately for Mary, one of her followers fell and this alerted the guards and Lord Scrope. Elizabeth, thus, decided that she had to find a more efficient custodian and Mary was soon transferred into the hands of the Earl of Shrewsbury. There are other legends of Mary's escape attempts from Bolton. Whether true or false, there is no real proof.

The line of the Scropes came to an end with the eleventh baron and it was his son who defended Bolton Castle on the side of the Royalists during the Civil War. Apparently they did not surrender until November 1645 when they had eaten all their horses. It was a daughter of the last Baron Scrope who married Charles Paulet and this historic castle has remained in that family ever since.

To all intents and purposes, Bolton Castle is now a shadow of its former self, but it is still a marvellous place to visit. With the help of tableaux and period furnishings in various main areas of the castle that have survived, the atmosphere of old England has returned to Bolton.

In the bedchamber, where Mary, Queen of Scots is being attended by her ladies-in-waiting, a feeling of terrible sadness always comes over me. It is said she occupied this part of the castle during her confinement and I can believe it. It's as if she is still there, still waiting, still hoping; with heavy heart she whispers the prayers of her faith by night and by day, never doubting that one way or another she will at last be delivered from her suffering. I believe Mary understood her position fully and accepted that there would be no possibility of her being freed as long as she was seen as a threat to the throne of England, which Elizabeth would safeguard at any price. I also believe that Mary knew what Elizabeth found so hard to come to terms with – that one day the Queen of England would have no option but to reluctantly put her name to the death warrant that would rid her of her rival – Mary, Queen of Scots – for ever. In other words, ironically Elizabeth would eventually find herself in virtually the same position as her father, Henry VIII, when he was faced with the decision to sign the death warrant for Elizabeth's mother, Anne Boleyn, some 50 years earlier.

Mary's confinement continued for 18 long years after she left Bolton Castle. Elizabeth could not even banish her from England, since Mary had many loyal foreign supporters who would have rallied to her cause. Sadly, the time had to come when there were no more options to explore, no more voices to be heard and only prayers to be said. The death warrant duly signed, Mary, Queen of Scots was finally executed at Fotheringhay Castle in February 1587. Mary's purgatory was over, Elizabeth's duty done. She never attended Mary's trial, although a throne had been placed there for her. In fact the two queens never met. But on the morning of Mary's execution Elizabeth wept, as did so many, for the blood she had ordered spilt for the sake of the throne she held so dear and served so well. The tears may have been genuine, but as her father had not envisaged his daughter becoming Queen of England, so his daughter had not envisaged her dead cousin's son becoming king. However, on her deathbed in 1603 Elizabeth named Mary's son, James VI of Scotland, as the legitimate heir to the throne of England. And so it was that at last the English and Scottish thrones were united and the two queens in their eternity now lay in close proximity to one another in the shadows of Westminster Abbey – for ever together in death as they never were in life.

We rarely leave Bolton Castle without climbing those final few steps out onto the roof and marvelling at the panoramic views of Wensleydale from the battlements. A landscape that has evolved over the generations, it is very hard to visualise today those thick forests long since cleared, where no doubt wild boar and deer were once the prize of the hunt. However, looking down on the period gardens now being lovingly recreated skirting the castle walls, you could almost anticipate an Elizabethan kitchen maid running out of the door to collect her master's herbs for the venison as it turns on the spit in the kitchen. Meanwhile, in the distance the River Ure, which once provided the castle with so much of its water, flows on, indifferent to time and untouched by history. The same cannot be said for Bolton Castle.

I never pass through the silent village of Wensley without the feeling that I am intruding and maybe I am. Today the peace and tranquillity of this attractively arranged unassuming village seems only to reaffirm its intention to keep itself to itself come what may, just as it has done for over 400 years since it was visited by a devastating plague. It was 1563, the fifth year of Elizabeth I's reign. Wensley was a thriving market town, regarded as the capital of the rich green dale, but the plague was no stranger to our island. Wensley was sadly just another victim. With the plague in their midst, the townsfolk untouched by the infection fled, leaving their suffering friends, neighbours and even relatives knowing only too well they would never see them again. They had no choice and nor did those that remained behind to cope alone. Of course they didn't cope. Most died and with them Wensley died too. The thirteenth-century church silently witnessed the sadness in the streets where the bereaved wept as their dead were carried away on carts to be burnt over yonder because no infected soul could be buried under holy sod. Even the homes and belongings of the dead were burned and still the bereaved wept. Outcast themselves, they never recovered – and nor did Wensley. The bustling market town had gone forever and from its ashes arose the picturesque Wensley of today within sight of the Shawl of Leyburn, the town that took its place, and the River Ure that could not wash away the tears of Wensley in 1563.

The busy market town of Leyburn is very different and one night in particular it was the most welcome sight in the world to us. It was the end of October and the day had been bright and cheerful. We had driven over to Sedbergh and, returning via Hawes, decided, just by way of a change, to take the longer route home through Swaledale. To cross from Wensleydale into Swaledale in the north we took the famous Buttertubs Pass, which, at over 1,650 ft, is one of the highest mountain passes in England, and commands some magnificent views over the Pennines. All was well. Daylight began to fade but we didn't particularly mind. We're used to it and know the roads so well that it makes little difference. By the time we approached Grinton, darkness had well and truly descended and David decided to take the road over Bellerby Moor, which would bring us back into Wensleydale and, hopefully, Leyburn. It wasn't a road we had used before, but I didn't object, not then anyway!

Unfortunately for us, however, it soon became apparent that darkness was not the only thing that had descended that night. Shortly after we had turned onto the road over the moor we were being consumed by a dense fog. I immediately thought we should turn back to Grinton and the main road, but, as David irritatingly replied, 'How?' The road was narrow, twisting and completely invisible. That the moor stretched to the left and to the right was all we knew. I offered to get out and walk in front, although I must admit I was relieved when David told me to stay where I was. We literally inched along. There were no edges to the road as far as we were concerned. Not even the odd stone or wooden post. Nothing, just a demon-like blackness and the occasional tuft of grass that warned us the moor was waiting – waiting for David to make a misjudged twitch of the steering wheel. Every now and again the road would almost twist in on itself and with the tightness of the bend it would seem an eternity whilst David tried to negotiate it with me, attempting to be helpful by hanging my head out of the window, which made little or no difference since the fog hung like a thick curtain between me and anything.

Once or twice we'd think we'd seen a light and hope would flicker on the surface, but only for a moment for then it was gone, the light and the hope. They were only the eyes of some roaming sheep reflecting our useless headlights, or so we assumed. They could be the demons of the night, for all we knew. At one point the road descended sharply and twisted at the bottom. We suddenly realised we had crossed a small bridge over a beck and nearly missed the road the other side as it ascended sharply again. Beads of sweat were appearing on David's forehead as his concentration reached a peak, and I was just plain nervous and longed for a sign that we were nearing Leyburn.

Leyburn? We didn't even know at that point whether we were still on the right road. We didn't think we had turned off anywhere, but we hadn't seen another car. Then we saw a light over in the distance. David stopped the car for a second; it didn't take much since we were only travelling at about two or three miles per hour anyway. For a second we debated: do we head towards the light on foot? It may be a farm and we can ask where we are . . . But that was only a second's madness. We couldn't leave the car. That would be really foolish. And if one went we all went, which would also be foolish. The moment of panic passed and we carried on.

Then suddenly – a good way ahead – there were a pair of red lights. 'Tail lights!' we said together. Now we felt encouraged. We had someone to follow, someone who may well know the way off this moor and back into civilisation. It is strange how a sudden surge of adrenaline can wipe away all apprehension. Our speedometer even went up a mile or two, but then our hearts sunk. Those lights were definitely getting brighter all the time but the car was not moving. It was just waiting by the roadside – and what's more it was waiting for us. As we drove alongside, the driver was lowering his window. We stopped, although I checked my door was locked, just in case, but, when we saw the elderly gentleman smile, I lowered my window too. He asked if we were going to Leyburn. David, swallowing hard, said we were.

'Oh good,' the man said, 'we are totally lost and hoped you would be locals. We want to get to Leyburn, so we'll follow you.'

With that he closed his window, still smiling, and his wife looked so relieved beside him that I, like David, didn't have the heart to disillusion them.

And so we set off again, this time with the elderly couple in tow. Talk about the blind leading the blind. We were still musing over the fact that we had hoped they would be our saviours and now it was us who were helping them, when a strange thing happened. That thick impenetrable fog was lifting before our very eyes and becoming nothing more than a mist. What is more, we had arrived at the familiar crossroads. Ahead the lights of Leyburn burned and as we descended the hill we knew we were safe – and so were the elderly couple. We left them at the marketplace and continued on our way back to Ainderby.

The mist had gone and the night was now clear under a shining moon but I felt as if something rather untoward had happened to us on Bellerby Moor. I know I have said many times I have a rich imagination, but to this day I believe there was something magical about that couple. I have even wondered if they actually existed at all – were they real? I know the fog was real. I know the fear was real and I know the relief we felt when we first saw their car. But when we later told locals of our adventure over Bellerby, although they confirmed, as we well know, that the weather can 'turn in quick' on the moor's roads, more than one also added, 'There have been some strange happenings up there on that road and some won't use it after dark.' I know someone else who won't again, either.

We did return to Bellerby, however, some days later. During the morning, I might add. David was curious to see what the road really looked like. We got a shock – it was worse than we had thought. In places it was no wider than the car and a slight move to the left or right could have meant disaster. The moor just swept away from the road and probably we would have been in serious trouble. It just didn't bear thinking about and even David said we must have had a guiding hand. Perhaps we did.

Situated high on the hillside, Leyburn commands a prominent position over Wensleydale. Its wide cobbled marketplace still plays host to a regular Friday market just as it has done for the past 300 years but with its various shops, cafés and pleasing views of the surrounding countryside Leyburn is a nice place to be at any time.

One of our favourite jaunts starts from the corner of the marketplace where a signpost reads 'To the Shawl'. In my opinion 'The Shawl' is an appropriate name for the two- to three-mile-long footpath that wraps itself around the shoulders of the hillside from Leyburn and up towards the village of Castle Bolton. But that is only my interpretation. There is much speculation on how it really got its name. Some say it comes from the Scandinavian word '*schall*', which means a collection of huts, whilst others have a more romantic notion that Mary, Queen of Scots fled along this path in a bid for freedom from Bolton Castle and supposedly caught and dropped her shawl on a bush as her captors closed in on her. Our pace is far more leisurely as we like to enjoy the bird's eye view of Wensleydale, watching miniature cars way below us as they make their way along the dale, or pointing out familiar landmarks such as the square tower of the church at Wensley and further on the four magnificent towers of Bolton Castle. The views from the Shawl confirm just how closely situated to one another the Dales communities are, and with their roots firmly fixed in the past how these settlements of necessity clung to a lifeline that served them well: the River Ure. Against the beautiful vast landscapes she relentlessly edges her way through or by each and every one and from the Shawl we watch her with respect as she gallantly flows on . . .

. . . To Middleham (as Richard III might well have said). The medieval market town of Middleham in Coverdale is still dominated by its ancient castle. Although now a shadow of its former self it was once the home of the unscrupulous Richard Neville, Earl of Warwick, most often referred to as 'the Kingmaker'. Yes, he has raised his head before in my book but now we have cause to meet him again at his ancestral home of Middleham Castle. During the Wars of the Roses, Warwick's father had lost his head at Pontefract and his uncle, Edward's father, Richard of York, had also been slain. The young earl went on to fight his cousin's cause to put him on the throne of England by deposing Henry VI. The battle was won at Towton in 1461 and Edward became king – thus Warwick's nickname.

Despite the Yorkists' victory there was still much unrest in the land and it was subsequently decided that Edward's youngest brother, Richard, Duke of Gloucester, should be placed under the protection of their cousin Warwick at Middleham. Young Dickon, as he was called, found it no hardship to grow up within the bounds of this magnificent stronghold – that is until his cousin, Warwick, turned against Edward IV, plotting and counter-plotting his downfall. He even, for a time, held Edward captive within his castle, but Edward and his brother, Richard, escaped. It was inevitable that the battlefield would settle things once and for all – and so it did when Warwick met his death at the Battle of Barnet in 1471.

His wife should have inherited his estates, including Middleham, but they were confiscated by the King and he ignored her entitlement. Instead he eventually shared them between his two brothers, George, who was married to Warwick's daughter Isobel, and Richard, who not only gained Middleham but Anne, Warwick's second daughter, who he had practically grown up with when in the earl's charge. They made Middleham their home. Richard became the 'Lord of the North' and Middleham became known as the 'Windsor of the North'. It was here that the couple were happiest and here that in 1473 their son, Edward, was born. However, ten years later, on 9 April 1483, their lives were to change forever.

At the age of only 40, King Edward IV died, leaving all he owned and ruled to the protection of his brother and this included his two young sons, the elder of whom was destined to become King Edward V. Richard's sudden responsibility for the care of his late brother's heir and realm must have been overwhelming, especially as he would have also had to contend with his own grief for a brother he had held in such high esteem. However, the dramatic events that were to follow, if he were innocent, must have shattered his world completely.

Richard had listened to his trusted advisors and housed the two young princes in the Tower of London for their own protection and safety. But in July of that same year, under very mysterious circumstances, they disappeared and, as history now records, they were never to be seen again. Richard had no choice – after all, he was now the only legitimate heir to his brother's throne. He subsequently accepted the crown of England as Richard III. Of course rumours ran riot. We must assume the rest . . .

Tongues wagged and the gossipmongers had a field day. The streets and alehouses heaved with those ready to peddle their wares and their tales, which did not only consist of what they had seen or heard. Oh,

ABOVE: Haworth – the once dusty or muddy track
that leads to the Brontë Parsonage. (Chapter 5)

INSET: The sun warms the grey stone Parsonage walls.
(Chapter 5)

BELOW: The graveyard, Haworth – its grimness only
relieved by the first fall of golden leaves. (Chapter 5)

ABOVE: The path that led Emily Brontë to 'Wuthering Heights'. (Chapter 5)

INSET: The well-worn stone of Wycoller's packhorse bridge. (Chapter 5)

BELOW: Red House – the neat paths lead the eye to the house. (Chapter 5)

ABOVE LEFT: Market Street, Thornton – birthplace of Charlotte, Branwell, Emily and Anne Brontë. (Chapter 5)

ABOVE RIGHT: Thornton – the octagonal bell tower of the old bell chapel, now a ruin, where five of the Brontë children were baptised. (Chapter 5)

BELOW: The River Ure wends its way through picturesque Wensleydale. (Chapter 6)

ABOVE: Wensleydale from Bolton Castle. (Chapter 6)

BELOW: Bolton Castle. (Chapter 6)

ABOVE: Classic Yorkshire – a brass band in Leyburn's market square. (Chapter 6)

INSET: Middleham Castle – the roofless, cavernous ruins of a Royal house. (Chapter 6)

BELOW: The Black Sheep Brewery, Masham. (Chapter 6)

ABOVE LEFT: Amanda (right), with friend Katy, at her 21st birthday party, Black Sheep Brewery. (Chapter 6)

ABOVE RIGHT: Lendal Bridge, York – the single span Victorian iron bridge over the Ouse. (Chapter 7)

BELOW: The courtyard, St Williams College, York. (Chapter 7)

ABOVE: Lady Row, York – conjures up the picture that nothing more than a dirt track once served them. (Chapter 7)

BELOW LEFT: Shambles, York. (Chapter 7)

BELOW RIGHT: Holy Trinity – tucked away behind Lady Row. (Chapter 7)

RIGHT: Pavement, York –
All Saints' crowning glory.
(Chapter 7)

BELOW: York – Georgian
elegance of the first
mansion house in England.
(Chapter 7)

no, that would be far too boring. They added supposition disguised as fact and dramatised the whole beyond recognition until they had fragmented the truth as though it was a piece of tissue paper and their gullible audiences sat on the edges of their seats and listened – and believed. The damage was done. Except that is, in the north, where Richard's loyal followers never doubted his innocence in what had occurred. They knew him best and trusted him.

Sadly, however, his new life meant that both he and Anne spent less and less time at their beloved Middleham. It was whilst they were away in Nottingham that they received the terrible news of their son's death at Middleham just a few days before his 11th birthday. Devastated by grief, they returned home, where their people wept with them as the young Prince Edward was buried in St Helen and the Holy Cross Church on Richard's estate at Sheriff Hutton. His small tomb can still be seen there today. Anne never recovered from her loss and within the year, on a March day in 1485, she followed her son to the grave. Richard's grief was insurmountable. Even Middleham could offer him no consolation, not any more. Here he had been happy. Now it only taunted him with the memories of a life he had once known and so he turned his back. He never returned and Middleham was left to mourn alone.

Richard's pain was not to last long. In the following August his life too came to a dramatic end on the battlefield at Bosworth, where he lost his crown to Henry Tudor.

Henry VII and subsequent monarchs had little time for Middleham Castle. They never honoured it with their presence and it was downgraded to purely an administrative base from where their officials could keep an eye on the turbulent north. Needless to say, this once magnificent fortress was sadly neglected and allowed to fall into gradual decline and inevitable decay. Then in 1646 came the final humiliation. After being used as a garrison and a prison during the Civil Wars it was rendered untenable and its already crumbling walls were indiscriminately blown up. The resultant huge mounds of valuable dressed stone were too much of a temptation. The people came without pomp or ceremony, without respect or regret, and took the valuable stone to build their own houses in the town and all the while the scarred but prideful remains of Richard's home looked on.

Today the great stage on which all those dramas of the last years of medieval royal lineage were set still stands and I cannot help feeling that maybe it is the saddest scene of all – the final curtain. The roofless, cavernous ruins of this renowned theatre are now only invaded by the merciless elements, no longer able to defend itself against storm or flood. Even its moat, which was fed by natural springs, has been filled in. Its stout keep remains defiant but there are no latches or locks to bar access and no one looks down to challenge you from the now decayed battlements. The banqueting hall, the site of so much revelry, is silent where once it echoed with the sound of music and laughter as maidens danced with their lords, who enjoyed the brief respite from battle. Now only the moonbeams dance across the crumbling stone that once witnessed the great pageantry of a royal house.

Naturally, Middleham as a town is still very proud of its royal connection, particularly as it represents an era of our history which has long been cause for speculation, criticism and, at the very least, curiosity by most of us who know something of the man who was so briefly King of England. So many books have been written on the subject by both those who are concerned with fact and those who are concerned with fiction. The story has been portrayed on stage, screen and television. Richard III didn't even escape the pen of the great bard himself, William Shakespeare, who wrote his great play leaving no doubt in Elizabethan England's mind as to his answer to the question, 'Did he or didn't he?' The truth is that 500 years later we still don't know what really happened for certain and nor will we ever.

'A Horse! A Horse! My Kingdom for a Horse.' Another question: did Richard III really say that? If he did then the town he once made his home must have taken it to heart for Middleham is well known to the racing fraternity. Horses have been trained at Middleham since the eighteenth century, many of them winners of such prestigious races as the Derby and the Grand National, and there are some of the finest stables in the world within a short distance of the famous Gallops. In the early morning, when the grass is still moist with dew and a fine mist hangs on the air, those fine and noble animals are often to be seen being put through their paces by their devoted trainers. The rhythmic clump of hoof on turf echoes the enthusiasm of the pair as they take advantage of their solitude in idyllic surroundings to do what they do best: work together in unison – in harmony. Oh, how much we could all learn from that!

A few years ago, we got more than we bargained for in Middleham. It was one of those awful wet days of summer that we British folk are all too familiar with. The rain is persistent; not heavy, but very, very wet. Underfoot is wet, you feel damp even sitting in your car, the sky is low and cheerless and even the colourful displays of summer flowers are soggy and limp under the weight of just too much water.

We were ascending the hill into the market square when we were suddenly confronted with a 'Road Closed' sign. A man in a very wet, glossy raincoat with droplets draining off every part of him, including his ear lobes and nose, was standing in the middle of the road guarding it. He didn't look official. Well, you can't anyway, can you? Not when you look like a drowned rat!

We decided to take a look. We parked our cars safely at the side of the road (our friends Chris and Brian were following) and continued on foot up along the side of the pub that faced onto the old market square. As we rounded the corner of the pub we noticed a group of people were intently looking up the road to our left. Our eyes followed their gaze but an old black Rover had been parked outside the pub and was blocking our view so we took a few steps further out into the road – after all, it was 'closed'. We could then see and hear an old grey tractor chugging very slowly down the hill towards the square and the group of people. There was an elderly man in a flat cap driving it and it was pulling a very tatty cart.

The whole spectacle was one of normality – and yet it wasn't. We were in the country, so a man driving a tractor was perfectly normal – albeit an old tractor. The day was wet but that didn't stop most hardened Yorkshire farmers. So why was it sparking off so much obvious attention? We looked at one another a little puzzled and were just about to walk over to find out what was going on when the man in the glossy raincoat hurriedly dripped his way over to us and, with some urgency, asked us to move 'off camera'. Totally taken aback, we just looked at him and before we could say anything he was ushering us backwards towards the corner of the pub, saying we would be fine round there if we kept as quiet as possible.

However, our eyes were now working overtime. We noticed the vans in the square, the cable threading its way through the puddles and the technical equipment. Isn't it strange how once one sense becomes overly active the remaining ones seem to get scrambled and your co-ordination goes to pot? It seemed we suddenly had no control over our mouths or our feet. The former kept opening and closing with no sound being emitted, rather like demented goldfish, and the latter seemed to have become quite unmanageable as they stumbled over one another in a vain attempt to get the owner backwards round the corner of the pub as quickly as possible. Once we were 'off camera' the poor man did kindly add that he would let us know when we could come out, but we hardly acknowledged him, I'm ashamed to say. We were too busy coming to our own conclusions about what we had just seen. Then, almost simultaneously, we remembered the black Rover. Of course, the famous black Rover! What else?

We forgot all about being quiet at that point and I think the man glared at us. For the second time we had inadvertently dropped in on the shooting of a scene for an episode of *All Creatures Great and Small* and we could hardly believe it. We did try to keep the noise down but it was becoming increasingly difficult, when we all wanted to say something. We must have looked very funny, huddled tightly together round the corner from the pub, in the pouring rain with our umbrellas bobbing about uncontrollably and the five of us trembling with laughter.

Soon the filming was over and we were allowed to venture back into the square. Men were already winding up the yards of cables, the vans were being packed up and Christopher Timothy, who plays James Herriot, and Robert Hardy, who plays Siegfried Farnon, were making a hasty retreat out of the rain. We didn't follow them. We wouldn't. However, we couldn't resist a closer look at Siegfried's precious black Rover with its camera mounting attached to the nearside front door covered in green plastic to keep it dry. I can't understand how we missed that in the first place, but then we didn't notice the filming equipment either until nearly too late. I suppose we were just too busy being nosy. Anyway after taking a sneaky picture of Amanda and Chris standing by the said Rover – just for the album – we went for a well-deserved cuppa. Even the rain couldn't dampen our spirits as we laughed and joked about how close we had come to appearing in an episode of *All*

Creatures Great and Small . . . And we laughed again when they showed the relevant scene on television because we all knew what was going on around the corner from the pub on that very wet day in Middleham.

Just south of Middleham the River Cover takes her bow as she wends her way under the Cover Bridge and becomes one with her sister the Ure. The bridge is flanked by the appropriately named Cover Inn that abruptly butts onto the road and always appears to me to be in constant danger of being over run. Nonetheless, this attractive watering hole is a welcome sight when, under cloudless skies of high summer, we have enjoyed a relaxing stroll along the Ure's grassy bank from my next stepping stone, Jervaulx Abbey.

The name 'Jervaulx' is a French derivative of 'Yorevale' or Vale of the River Yore, better known today, of course, as the River Ure. Dating back to 1156, this Cistercian abbey struggled at first to survive, leaning heavily on the abbey at Byland for support. However, after some years, due to the total dedication and hard work of the monks and lay brothers who lived within its walls, Jervaulx Abbey did prosper and eventually owned half the beautiful – then wooded – valley of the Ure. As far as the Cistercian monks and lay brothers were concerned, the fact that their beloved abbey had become both a powerful and wealthy religious house meant their future was assured as a totally self-supporting community. They sacrificed themselves to an almost hermit-type existence, observing the sacred vow of silence, and apart from being devoted farmers and very adept at making cheese (these were the monks I mentioned earlier in conjunction with Hawes), their world consisted mostly of prayer and devotion to their calling.

There is little doubt, though, that despite the calm outward appearance of these monks, the last abbot of Jervaulx, Adam Sedbar, for some reason managed to badly upset Henry VIII around the time of the Act of Suppression in 1536 that signified the closure of many of the smaller religious houses. Although this act was introduced in the name of progress and reform, in truth it was the beginning of the end for all the religious houses. In other words, it marked the beginning of the dissolution of the monasteries, which took four years to complete.

Bearing this and the abbot's vow of silence in mind, perhaps he decided that actions spoke louder than words – that it wasn't so much what the abbot said as what he did that upset His Majesty. The government had already caused a great deal of unrest in the country by the time of the new act and this unrest was particularly prevalent in the north. Many people, therefore, did not trust that the closure of the smaller religious houses was solely in the interests of reform. Instead, many suspected that the act was deliberately contrived to fatten the purse of the Crown (the Crown would quickly find new tenants for the relevant vacated properties and then pocket the revenues).

Furthermore, they believed, correctly as it turned out, that this was only the beginning of a much more drastic 'reform' that would eventually affect all monastic communities throughout the land. These suspicions, coupled with the general unrest, finally culminated in the rebellion of October 1536, which not only encouraged the dispossessed monks and nuns to return to their homes but called upon the larger religious houses to contribute generously to the cause with both men and money. Of course, many abbots obliged because they were foresighted enough to realise that should the rebels succeed in their quest then not only would the smaller religious houses be reinstated, but the future of their own more prestigious establishments would also be safeguarded. The rebellion was called the 'Pilgrimage of Grace' and although it was not purely based on the dissolution, the dissolution was the unacceptable last straw that broke the people's faith in their government and gained them the support of so many priories and abbeys. Sadly for them, the rebellion failed and eventually many died. But worse was to follow. The King turned his wrath on the larger abbeys for supporting the rebels, even to the point of advocating that the abbots should be executed without mercy. Unfortunately that included Abbot Sedbar.

The rest is history. Jervaulx was now alone, its servants had fled and the faithful few that remained had been indiscriminately dealt with by the King's men. The abbey braced itself for its own death as bravely as its abbot had done. It came quickly. First it was ransacked and then battered. Then the men shattered its walls, scattering the stone at its feet. When this was done, stripped of its glory, it sadly watched them leave, but as they rode away triumphantly its spirit sighed, for that they could never kill. It lingers still.

I will add my own epitaph to Jervaulx. It is Christmas Eve. The night is still. The moon, high in a clear hollow sky, reveals contrasting blue shadows on the pure untrodden snow. Gently the moonbeams pick out the tracery of this old abbey's remaining stone, and if you listen very carefully you will hear the monks at evensong, their musical voices echoing in the silence of the night air as they chant a Yuletide carol. Their only accompaniment is the rhythmic trickle of the Ure as she solemnly makes her way onward, leaving the abbey to celebrate the Mass of Christ as it has always done – in chosen solitude.

Notwithstanding the sadness surrounding the demise of Jervaulx, no wonder the monks loved this place so much that they stayed. To explore what remains of this grand abbey and, as I have said previously, to wander along the banks of the Ure under leafy glades of trees and shrubs thriving in soft moist turf with their angled roots embedded in the banks at the water's edge, leaves you in no doubt that this is a very special place.

The story goes that the first abbot of Jervaulx – a John de Kinstan – was travelling from Byland to Fors when he and 12 monks lost their direction in the woods. Appropriately, they were reported to have been led to safety by a vision of the Virgin Mary who told them they were no longer of Byland but of Yorevale. Thus they chose to build their abbey, and they couldn't have picked a more picturesque and peaceful place on the River Ure.

From above Jervaulx the River Ure now makes a positive decision to change direction. Up until Middleham her easterly course is not in question, but after Middleham she begins to hesitantly veer south east. Now she must head south to Masham in lower Wensleydale. Situated on the west bank of the Ure, this classic market town is a very special stepping stone which would be virtually worn away if you were to count the number of times over the years I have stepped onto it. We even have a family joke that whenever anyone asks, 'Where shall we go?' the reply often comes back: 'Masham!' It's a good job the reply was not taken seriously otherwise I might never have written this book.

Exactly why really does escape me. It has no great variety of shops and no great tourist attraction such as a castle, stately home or museum – not that we mind that – and from its plain, yet quietly attractive streets, there is no hint of a history worth noting or a story worth telling. How often looks can belie the truth. Whatever, we enjoy this unpretentious old sheep town and although we would like to keep it to ourselves, rather surprisingly it seems popular with other folk too. In the summer months, whether deliberately or just in passing, visitors come in their droves to Masham. They fill the tea shops whilst their cars fill the wide market square, except, that is, on market days when their cars are clamouring for space bumper to bumper in one half of the square whilst the market stalls fill the other half. The locals don't seem to mind the confusion. In fact, they seem to be genuinely pleased that their town is so firmly placed on the tourist map, even if they too are a little bemused as to exactly why.

Not that the town has not been used to a sudden influx of people in its long history. Quite the contrary. Once upon a time in Edwardian England Masham played host to great sheep fairs held in September, and they were a very different affair to the comparatively more orderly and subdued occasions they are today. In fact, they were famous, and farmers, traders and auctioneers came from miles around with a mind to selling or buying, bargaining or just plain nosing. They took over the town for three whole days but the locals would be making their own preparations for the event days before. Makeshift pens had to be erected in the streets and square since the first day of the fair was devoted to the auctioning of sheep, whilst the second day was made over to cattle and horses. Local shops – there were many more in the town then – prepared to take advantage of the opportunity to increase their trade whilst the ovens in most housewives' kitchens were not allowed to take a rest. In fact, the shelves in those gallant ladies' pantries positively bowed under the weight of freshly baked treats, which were not just intended for their own kitchen table but were destined to help supplement stocks at the local tea shops. The women knew full well that farmers were renowned for their huge appetites and the men at the sales would certainly need feeding, as would all the visitors to their town. Besides, if that wasn't enough there was the third day to think about. The day when the funfair would be in town and freshly baked cakes, biscuits and niceties would sell well on the market stalls, next to the cheese and eggs and other popular favourites, such as gingerbread and toffee. The third day was always special for the whole family, but especially for the children and no doubt everyone would come home feeling very hungry.

Before daylight on the first day the farmers would start bringing their sheep in from the fields around Masham to fill the waiting pens. The natural silence that usually governs night and the ensuing dawn all too soon would be brought to an abrupt end by the dull, almost rhythmic, clump of men's boots as they steered their particular charges in the general direction of the square. Although, for a while, muted by the closed and curtained windows, the intrusion was minimal to those in the town who wished to slumber on, it wasn't to last. As far as the sheep were concerned, they were completely oblivious of the earliness of the hour. As soon as the leaders caught sight of the waiting pens, they would begin voicing their disapproval in no uncertain terms and, of course, this set up a chain reaction down the ranks that even reached those who were furthest away from the market square. What's more, sheep can also have a mind of their own, contrary to belief, and start to wander. Thus their masters would have to resort to call and whistle to encourage their charges to keep pace. Now the whole town would be awake – even the most ardent sleeper – and as people peered down onto the streets their blurry eyes would be greeted with a sea of oscillating fleece as it made its way to market. Soon everybody would be up and about and whilst some men helped get the sheep organised in their makeshift pens others erected their stalls and set out their wares, for this was the day people were set on buying and the tradesmen knew it. As well as the sheep pens filling every available space, there was also a huge variety of vehicles to be accommodated too – from horse-drawn carts and wagons to trucks and tractors. There was hardly room to negotiate but somehow everybody found somewhere to be and the air would fill with the sound of men's voices as they tried to compete with one another as well as the bleating impatient sheep, the yapping of tethered dogs and the laughter of a crowd of willing listeners as a tale was told. The general mayhem would continue until, at last, there would be the familiar calls of the men who wished to be heard and as others gathered around the pens or leaned against a wall watching and listening intently there would be the exaggerated nods from the men who knew and the shaking of heads of the men who didn't. The serious business of the great sales had begun.

Sadly these great fairs came to an end prior to the First World War but there is no doubt that the King's Head Hotel, which still dominates one side of Masham's market square, would have welcomed them to boost its trade. It was ideally situated for those who wished to either celebrate striking a good deal, or drown their sorrows if they hadn't. However, had this been the first half of the 1800s some more prudent would-be patrons might well have chosen to take their refreshment elsewhere since, although faded with time, there is engraved in the stone above the doorway for all to see two words which signify another use to which this fine building was once put. It simply reads 'Excise Office' but it was regarded by many with the same respectful avoidance as it is today. Here taxes were collected from certain traders, whilst licences were issued for other privileges such as guns, dogs, horses and, of course, carriages – some things never change, do they? Licences to travel on the roads did not, as is popularly believed, come with the innovation of the motorcar; no, horses and carriages were here first and so were those excise men and since this popular hotel once served as a posting inn, where horses and carriages could be hired or simply changed for the convenience of the traveller, the officers no doubt caught many an unsuspecting soul red-handed on failure to be able to produce a current licence. This peculiar arrangement at inns was common prior to the 1850s but then excise offices were removed from such premises and I suspect a sigh of relief was breathed by both the innkeepers and their patrons.

The old coach houses and stables to the rear of the King's Head are today in a sad state of decline, save one or two now used for storage. Here gleaming carriages once awaited hire and horses took their well-earned rest, stable lads bustled about and hay littered the cobbled stone. Now they are mostly vacant, left barren and neglected. Wooden doors, naked of paint, cling onto hinges rotten with age, whilst broken panes, grimed and dim, no longer allow daylight to reveal the unswept interiors which have become littered with debris from years of idleness. Accessed by the old arch to the left of the hotel, the sign indicates craft workshops can be found here and so they can, at the far end of the yard. Among them is the Masham Pottery run by Kathy and Howard Charles. Howard's trade is one of the oldest in England – if not the world; he is a skilled potter and proud of it. In his shop he works diligently at his wheel whilst people come in and look round at his work or stand fascinated as yet another blob of clay, guided by his experienced hands, rises up gracefully into a beautifully formed vase or jug or even a bread crock. I have often thought I would love to have a go, but knowing my luck I'd probably lose control and at best end up with a squelchy mess lying as flat as a pancake on the wheel, or at worst manage to send it flying across the workshop and end up adhering itself to the face of some unsuspecting customer whence it would drip indiscriminately down that person's neck making them feel like they had suddenly been attacked by a flying octopus. . .

Howard, like many other craftsmen, not only thoroughly enjoys what he does but is using his particular skill to keep alive a tradition. I don't just mean potting. I mean the tradition of hand-crafted products. Up until the turn of the twentieth century, every town and village in England had its fair share of craftsmen. So many of the everyday necessities of life were traditionally handmade that their skills were taken for granted. Masham was no exception. There were the boot and shoemakers, the straw-hat makers, tailors, dressmakers, wheelwrights, watch and clock makers, joiners and cabinet makers, as well as the blacksmiths, who didn't just shoe horses but provided much of the town's necessary ironwork, and doubled up as the local dentist when a tooth needed pulling (one practice I'm sure none of us would like to see revived) and then there were the stonemasons who contributed much more to the town than purely the furnishings in the churchyard. The list, in fact, is endless but sadly and of necessity we have all but relinquished this way of life in the name of progress. Or have we?

Maybe for a while mass production and technology overwhelmed us and, of course, it will always have a major role to play in what would otherwise be a very tedious world, but in recent years it seems we have shown more than a passing interest in our old ways and developed a strong, nostalgic desire for their return – especially, it seems, when it comes to adorning our homes. Thus, when we come across the diligent craftsmen who put to use their incredible talents to recreate our past, we are hooked. Whether the item can be of use – such as a piece of furniture – or just sit somewhere in our home as a reminder of a bygone age, we want it and it means all the more to us because we know it has been handcrafted in the traditional way. Thankfully, as a direct result of our enthusiasm, more and more skilled men and women are finding the courage to open up workshops and follow in their forefather's footsteps, providing the highest possible standards of workmanship to customers who really do appreciate not only what they produce but the fact that they are now reviving the old traditions that we so nearly lost.

It could be said that Paul Theakston did exactly that too. Situated in a backstreet, but high enough to be obvious, and endorsed by its name being dramatically painted directly onto the brickwork of its premises, the Black Sheep Brewery proudly thrives and so it should, for despite its youth, it has a very special strength behind it . . . and I don't mean just its ale.

For five generations Paul Theakston's family had been brewing beer in Masham at the Theakston Brewery, but by 1989 Paul Theakston was faced with a stark choice. With the increasing thirst for real ale the brewery had been prospering, but too well! The big brewers became more than interested in the family concern. Paul had run the brewery from the young age of 23 when his father died and his uncle retired in 1968. By 1984 the first takeover had happened, but he was still managing the business. The second takeover, three years later, was a very different story and far more drastic for Paul. He could either accept a managerial role within the large organisation – but not at Theakston's – or go. There was no choice. Paul left. For a while he deliberated on his future, but two things were certain: one, he had no intention of moving away from Masham, which had been the home of his ancestors since the fourteenth century; and two, he needed to be his own boss, just like his forefathers. At last he came to a brave decision: to go back to brewing ale, in Masham.

Ironically, he opted for purchasing the old maltings buildings at the Lightfoot Brewery which had once been the property of Theakston's and sold by Paul's grandfather in 1919. It took two years for Paul to finally take over the property which, having been laid waste for years, was in need of a good deal of hard work. However, that was something that Paul was not afraid of, although he hadn't bargained on so many unsavoury sitting tenants – rats to us. He rolled up his shirt sleeves and with the help of just one employee set to work to get his new premises cleared out – rats and all – and scrubbed squeaky clean. Then he started on the business of finding the equipment he needed, but funds were fast running out. He hit on the idea of raising further monies by way of a Business Expansion Scheme. It worked. In fact it worked so well that it became over-subscribed.

Now Paul was in business. He finished fitting out his brewery and employed the essential staff he needed to help him to run it. There was only one problem: it didn't have a name. Inspiration came at last in the form of the Black Sheep Brewery – how appropriate! By September 1992 the brewhouse had been built within the confines of the former kiln of the old maltings and trial brews were done and sampled. At last all was ready to launch Black Sheep Ale to the trade. If there were any doubts as to how it would be received they were soon dispelled. It was an instant success. Paul and his wife Sue – who has not only supported him all the way, but is also an important member of the management team – are justly proud of what they and their happy band of helpers have achieved in so short a time.

Today the brewery boasts a visitors' centre from where it is possible to go on a guided tour of the brewery as well as pick up some gifts or souvenirs in the well-stocked shop. We can often be found enjoying the delights of good food – and good ale – in their on-site Bistro where, incidentally, we also celebrated Amanda's 18th and 21st birthdays in party style. We love the happy informal atmosphere of the place and it comes highly recommended since Paul and his family often eat there too! It seems the fifth generation of Theakstons may have had to sacrifice their name, but in keeping with their family tradition, they have found the perfect recipe – not just for their ale – and have come up trumps. I am sure their ancestors would not disapprove of the Black Sheep but wish them luck and toast them in real ale for at least another five generations!

Each year, on a weekend in July, Masham plays host to a very special event which is certain to draw the crowds. It is one of the largest and most spectacular steam and traction engine rallies in Yorkshire and well in keeping with the old-world atmosphere of the town. On the Friday evening the grand old maidens and other splendid machines can be seen gathering in a large field made over for the occasion on the east bank of the Ure. As well as the stars of the show there is a full supporting cast in the form of fairground entertainment, including side shows, stalls, amusements, bumper cars and that centrepiece of any fair and my personal favourite: the majestic carousel, rotating in time to the distinct tones of its integral organ. The air hangs heavy with that nostalgic mixture of steam, hot oil and sulphur from the combustion of good-quality steam coal. On the Saturday afternoon the great moment arrives and enthusiasts and casual visitors alike line the streets of Masham in readiness for the grand procession to start.

Yes, each year these grand old machines are fired up for their parade around the market square. Lovingly restored to their former glory with meticulous care and attention to detail by their proud owners, preserved in a condition which is doubtless far more pristine than in their natural lifetime, they make their way slowly out of the field. Negotiating their way along the road that bends sharply up over the bridge of the Ure, which dauntingly echoes its response to the sound of steel on concrete, they proceed cautiously up towards the market square. There are all types of vehicles, from the old steam lorries and buses to tractors, from steam rollers to the great iron maidens themselves – the traction engines, pipping their whistles in proud acknowledgement of the enthusiasm shown by their spectators.

To some this long procession contains many sentimental reminders of their youth, others are enthralled or just curious, but for those too young to remember or appreciate, it holds a fascination that verges on amusement that these cumbersome beasts were the forerunners of the much more sophisticated machinery they are so familiar with in our modern world. However, whatever the reactions of those who stand and stare, one thing is certain: the service these grand machines provided in their youth is now being repaid by the loving care and respect they are shown by their prideful owners. Mayhap much as their forerunners, those beautiful heavy horses who once graced our ploughs and pulled our carts to market, received the love and attention of their caring owners long after their usefulness had come to an end, in grateful recognition of their long and faithful service. They too were given pride of place at any local or county show and paraded around the arena for all to admire just like their mechanical successors that have now also been consigned to the history books. Alas, how we mourn the passing of them all. Will the same be said for our modern combines, lorries and motor vehicles? I doubt it.

Only a few miles from Masham lies one of my more secluded stepping stones. Norton Conyers is a fine Jacobean house set in beautiful parkland with the added attractions of a walled garden and stables. Originally built around the fourteenth century, although structurally it has undergone a few alterations and additions, it is essentially very much unchanged. Here, it is said, in 1632 Charles I played a game of bowls on the bowling green, which can still be seen today. Apparently the house has also played host to other royal personages such as James I in 1603 and James II in 1679, whilst in more recent times Queen Mary graced the house with her presence in 1933. For me and many others too, however, the most impressive name on past guest lists has to be Charlotte Brontë. She may not have been of royal blood, but in truth the house is probably best known for her visit in 1839, when she accompanied the Sidgwick family here as governess to their children.

Mind you Norton Conyers made some impression on Charlotte too, it seems. She is said, according to her friend Ellen Nussey, to have been fascinated by one of the legends of the old house, that of a mad woman confined in an attic room. At the time of our visit, unfortunately, access to the attic rooms, once the servants quarters, was forbidden due to the dubious condition of the floor, but on our tour of other parts of this well-preserved building I could easily believe it would have captured the imagination of the young novelist. In fact, some years later, when she wrote her celebrated *Jane Eyre*, it appears she may well have recalled the legend of the mad woman and based the mad Mrs Rochester, secured in an attic room of Thornfield Hall, on the poor unfortunate at Norton Conyers. It also seems there is more than a passing resemblance between Charlotte's description of the hall itself in her novel and Norton Conyers – for example 'the wide oak staircase, the rookery and the sunk fence' are all similar, as is its decription as 'a gentleman's manor house, not a nobleman's seat'.

I have to admit that initially it was the Charlotte Brontë connection in particular that drew me to Norton Conyers. What I did not realise was that, inadvertently, it was also to reintroduce me to one of my earlier encounters. I discovered from the Domesday Book of 1086 that the original estate here was owned by a Norman family by the name of Conyers. Are any bells ringing yet? Up until then I had not recognised the two names of 'Norton' and 'Conyers' as being separate entities but when I learned that in the fourteenth century a Roger Conyers married a Margaret Norton my suspicions were confirmed. These Conyers were relatives of my old friends the Conyers at Hornby Castle. Apparently, to cause confusion it had been her name that became the family name. Anyway, any doubts were completely dispelled when I also discovered that in 1569 they became involved in a rebellion against Queen Elizabeth I. Now, why aren't we surprised?

Remember in Chapter 1 how the Conyers family had the habit of switching their loyalties when it suited them? Caught on this occasion it seems, the Crown confiscated their estates. The house, which had been rebuilt in about 1500, was sold to the Musgrave family and in 1624 Richard Graham bought it from his father-in-law. Perhaps it was only then that it truly became 'a gentleman's manor house' in the real sense of the word, just as Charlotte Brontë described.

With Norton Conyers behind her, the Ure flows on to Ripon and as she skirts its eastern precincts there for all to see are the unmistakable towers – the reason why Ripon is indisputably designated the City of the Dales.

The Cathedral of Ripon is so openly placed that I always feel you could literally fall over it since it stands unprotected by any spacious preamble to speak of. There is no warning, you just seem to arrive at it. Its vast entrance dominates the narrow streets of this ancient city, which have little changed in layout since medieval times. The cathedral, being one of the oldest in England, also dates back to that period, although it did undergo much alteration and restoration work in the last century.

Ripon still holds a weekly market every Thursday, just as it has done for centuries, and even the old ritual of the ringing of the bell at 11 a.m. to declare the market open for business is still strictly adhered to. Each week the marketplace becomes a colourful sea of plastic canopies protecting the stalls beneath that overflow with goods of every description. Stallholders watch as people browse through their wares, either out of curiosity or in genuine consideration of making a purchase; sometimes they speak, sometimes they don't – it makes little difference. No one minds you looking, and the stallholders always seem such a friendly bunch that their usually cheerful disposition puts everyone else in good spirits too, which is obviously very good for business. Remembering that these market people are keeping alive what is after all our oldest established form of trade – even some of our great retail giants started as penny bazaars or bookstalls – it is pleasing to see that they can still attract crowds from miles around and have successfully survived the invasion of their fiercest competitors, the high-street shops. The atmosphere the market adds to Ripon on such days is one that befits this ancient city, a city that is proud of its past and unashamed of its sentiment as is substantiated by the preservation of notable historic buildings and a certain ancient tradition.

In a corner of the marketplace stands the Wakeman's house; originally dating back to the 1300s, it is now a very attractive Tudor building. Today the house is used as a museum but there is a plaque above the door that clearly states that in 1604 the last Wakeman and first mayor of Ripon resided here (he happened to be one and the same gentleman). The statement clearly suggests that, in fact, the Wakeman's job was revamped and warranted a new title – or maybe the powers that be at the time acquired a team of consultants who had to prove their worth by concocting a way of cutting working time in half by appointing one man to do double the work. Sounds familiar, doesn't it? Anyway, it seems the new job title of the man who saw to keeping their city in order may have been a cause for concern to the goodly people of Ripon, probably because they secretly feared other changes would soon be made that were not in their favour, bearing in mind the unsettling times in which they lived. Queen Elizabeth I was dead and England, through its new king, James I, was now joined to its old enemy, Scotland. It was, therefore, understandable that the majority of people throughout the land were wary of their new circumstances.

Whatever the situation in the country, however, and whatever the fears of the people of Ripon, it appears they were determined not to relinquish one of their most valued traditions: the Hornblower 'setting the watch'. A tradition that has long outlived the first mayor of Ripon, and for that matter survived the unification of the thrones of Scotland and England. Yes, rain, wind or shine, every evening at 9 p.m. a man in a three-cornered hat will stand at each corner of the market cross in turn and sound the horn, just like his predecessors. Then he will move to the front of the mayor's house and sound it again. I can't help wondering if that last blast was part of the tradition or the way the Ripon townsfolk expressed their view of the administration of the day and it has just been handed down without anyone realising what it may have meant in 1604.

Perhaps I had better explain further. The Wakeman had a special arrangement with the citizens of Ripon that was very much connected with the 'setting of the watch' by the Hornblower. You see, vandalism, opportunism of ill intent as well as professional robbery were not born of a comparatively modern age. No, in days of yore, these crimes were rife and they were born of poverty and need, deprivation and greed. Some more organised perpetrators planned their skulduggery in darkened corners of ale houses whilst other equally unsavoury characters holed up in blackened streets to take their chances and do their worst; they were never choosy about their victims. In view of these depressed times, the Wakeman provided the people of Ripon with the opportunity of having what was probably the very first form of insurance against such crimes. Householders and the like paid two pence per door per year to him and if, after the 'setting of the watch', their houses were burgled the Wakeman had to compensate them for their losses. Now, it is possible that this was an arrangement that the citizens were under threat of losing, or at least paying a much higher price for, bearing in mind, as I have said, the changes in overall management. It may be, therefore, that the retention of the Hornblower was as much to do with the townsfolk of Ripon deciding to look after their own interests as keeping alive a tradition that has now survived for 1,000 years.

A similar observation may well apply to my stepping stones. They too have withstood the test of time and throughout their long history the River Ure has never forsaken them, but kept her relentless vigil over them all. To the river they are her children. They were born out of a need to be close to her, for her waters were vital to their survival, whilst her natural course offered them a boundary of protection. She gave them what they wanted and in return they thrived. Gradually the tousled forests that shared so much of the landscape were cleared and in their place lush green pastures sprawled alongside the river, providing good grazing for sheep and cattle that also contributed to the nourishment of her children and she proudly watched as each of the small settlements grew into either village or town along her winding path. She provided them with comfort in their suffering, enjoyment in their revelries and still she nourished them, until one day they no longer needed her resources to survive, but still they wanted her and found pleasure in her company and still she stays ever watchful, ever ready to serve those she gave so much to – once upon a time.

I think it is important for my readers to realise that my 'stepping stones' are but a handful of the delightful towns and villages and other places of interest that can be found within easy reach of the Ure. Many I have not mentioned. Not because they are of any less importance, but because for the purposes of this chapter my stepping stones tell enough. As I have illustrated, they once provided the backdrop to some of the greatest dramas in our history, and if that isn't enough, the dales in which they are set consist of some of the most remarkable scenery in England. The gently undulating carpets of rich green pasture that fill the valley floors stretch as far as the eye can see.

Etched onto their landscape, with the apparent care of an artist who gives attention to detail, are the unmistakable seams of dry-stone walling. A trademark of Yorkshire, these walls have many uses, but in these dales they are most often used to divide up the land into fields which, whether by accident or design, seem to possess a similarity of both size and shape – almost as if the whole effect was pre-planned from somewhere overhead. The resultant views certainly inspire a deep sense of considerable order and immaculate neatness and with the added touches of an isolated stone byre here and there, a clump of trees, the occasional nest of farm buildings, a trickling beck or the great River Ure herself passing by, the picture is complete.

However, it is a picture that is forever changing as it adapts and responds to the uncompromising influences of the various seasons in the way it has always done. It may be delicately embroidered with the fresh sap greens of spring or bleached under the burning rays of a particularly hot summer sun, dressed in the burnished coppers and golds of autumn or transformed into a magical winter wonderland after a heavy fall of snow, but whatever its attire it never loses its identity: its essentially tolerant, ever-dominating awesome beauty. It can't. After all, these incredible dales are truly blessed with a splendour and charm that is as versatile and enduring as the people who have lived in these parts down through the centuries.

Of course, there are obvious hardships to man and beast alike when confronted with the onslaught of a harsh winter or a long, hot, dry summer, but they survive, as they have always done. As the dales resound with the overtures of spring when lambs once again fill the pastures and early morning frosts no longer adorn shrub or tree, when the glistening ribbons of the numerous becks are released from their frozen shrouds, the swallows return to their homeland for the summer and farmers witness the first signs of new life sprouting from their recently dormant fields, hardships are forgotten and a new year begins once more.

And so it is in the land of the Ure, as it has always been since man first arrived on her banks and decided to cultivate the landscape and make it his home. Away from the valley floors and beyond the comparative modesty of the softer lower fells are the ever-present reminders of how it all began: those great remnants of the ice age from which these dales evolved. The haunting, majestic mounds of the high Pennines, from which the Ure herself took her breath and began her impressive perpetual journey. A journey that stretches beyond the outskirts of my last stepping stone at the City of Ripon to edge past the grand estate of Newby Hall.

She then negotiates her way through the ancient town of Boroughbridge before flowing on to Aldborough; shortly after which she is joined by her great compatriot, the River Swale, flowing directly south from her own beloved namesake – Swaledale. Their union is significant. Many times along her path the Ure has welcomed other rivers at their journey's end. Their waters mingling with the Ure's are a source of nourishment on her tireless journey. Now her destination is nigh and the Swale does well to sustain her for the final curtain of her performance as she swiftly, inevitably allows the River Ouse to unceremoniously claim her.

However, for the Ure it is only a moment in time. Like all her sisters, she too is immortal, she too can afford to be generous and like them give of herself freely where she is needed. She is needed here and she purposefully relinquishes her combined resources to the River Ouse, which flows on . . .

❧ SEVEN ☙

. . . To York

York, second city in all England. Sacred keeper of all the great ages of our past. From Roman to Viking, from Conquest to Medieval, from the Tudors and Elizabethan to the Stuarts, from the Georgian to the Victorian and Edwardian and so to today – and even today will be remembered and eventually become an integral part of this city's tomorrow . . .

For me, York's awe-inspiring atmosphere cannot be compared to any other city I have ever visited either at home or abroad and I am sure there are many of similar opinion. I have often mused at the incredulous expressions on visitors' faces when they are obviously taking in their first impressions of York. 'Is this for real?' you can almost hear them say and perhaps for a brief moment the thought is there that it isn't. It's an understandable reaction, particularly from those who find it hard to relate to England's long and confusing history. From her comparatively meagre beginnings when the Romans first conceived their *Eboracum* – Roman York – 2,000 years ago, the city has suitably adapted to and incorporated the progressive ages of its maturity and in so doing earnt the respect and affection of all the peoples who have lived there throughout the centuries. Through those people the city has grown from strength to strength, prospered and survived, despite being the focus of some of the most dramatic episodes in England's history.

❧ Yorkshire Encounters ❧

Of course York's story is substantiated by a good deal of authenticated documentary evidence, but it is the structural facets of its past identities that provide the physical evidence for all to witness. London's streets were long ago metaphorically said to be 'paved with gold', but sadly for the majority of those who believed it, it proved a deception. However to say York's streets (or 'gates') are 'paved with history' would certainly be true. Carefully preserved within the precincts of its great walls and bars there are ancient sites confirming the significance of York's role to its earliest peoples; buildings of great age and character still serving their city today; centuries-old streets, alleys, passageways and courtyards that remain an integral part of the network of more modern thoroughfares, and if all these were not enough, there is always and forever the Minster. This is York telling its own story. The story of a life that has spanned some twenty centuries. Living proof of York's stoic endurance, silently validating its claim to that revered title of second city in all England.

It is difficult to know what to write about a city that has had so much written about it already, especially when the majority of texts appear to be specialist ones, written by people far more expert in their chosen fields than I could ever hope to be. However, this is not a book, merely a chapter, and I am no specialist. Therefore, in what could possibly be regarded as a rather unprofessional manner, I decided to do what I do best and take myself off on a midwinter stroll around my favourite city. Of course I have done this countless times before, but this time for the purposes of writing this humble offering I had pre-planned my route and, taking no chances with my over-40s memory loss, decided a notebook and pen would also come in useful. Husband David came along too, armed with his camera (and some spare notebooks). Looking back on our mini-adventure, perhaps it was as well we chose a time when the city was almost devoid of tourists or anyone else with any sense, since we must have looked like a couple of reporters who had definitely lost the plot! Anyway I hope you enjoy what follows as much as we did.

It is February and the day is cold. It has been snowing on and off for a few days now and it is obvious York has not escaped its share. However, as we make our way out of York railway station the sun comes out to welcome us and the sky is blue. It is from this point each year that many thousands of visitors take in their first sight of York – and what a sight it is. Just opposite the station forecourt from high on its grassy bank the medieval city wall has welcomed, or not, York's constant influx of people for nigh on 700 years.

Of course the railway has not been here quite as long as that! Though quite a modern invention by York's standards, the station is still very much an institution here, for, love them or loathe them, trains too have a very special place in York. Down Leeman Road (to our left as we leave the station) is the world-famous National Railway Museum, built on the site of the old railway depot. It houses some of the country's most impressive locomotives, including the famous 'Mallard' – which attained the world steam speed record in 1938 of 126 miles per hour – as well as trains from a more modern age. All are lovingly restored to pristine condition. My particular favourites are the royal carriages but there is something to appeal to everyone here and you don't have to be a railway enthusiast to enjoy it. By the way, did I mention that York's railway station is built over a Roman cemetery?

Back to the walls, which many assume are also Roman. The confusion is easily understood. Yes, the Romans were great wall builders and yes, they were the first to build a wall around York 2,000 years ago, but there is only a smattering of it remaining. The limestone walls are medieval, dating from the thirteenth and fourteenth centuries. The year of 1240 has been quoted as probably when building work commenced. By this time construction of the Minster was already underway by some 20 years, and it is not hard to imagine just how noisy, dusty and busy the city must have been, not to mention crowded with the number of craftsmen, labourers and suppliers working in such a confined space.

Within the walls bars were installed (no, not the pub variety). In York 'bars' are gates and 'gates' are streets! Anyway there were – and still are – four main bars into York: Bootham, Monk, Walmgate and Micklegate. Bootham Bar is the oldest. It stands on the site of the old Roman road that entered the city from the north-west and it is said that some parts of the bar date from the eleventh century. The much younger fourteenth-century Monk Bar is the tallest. Having had another storey added to it in the fifteenth century, it stands at 63 ft. In days of yore anyone approaching the city from the north-east who had ill-intent in mind would have found Monk Bar virtually impregnable with its heavy wooden portcullis, which is still in good working order today – so beware. Walmgate Bar to the south-east has one unique claim to fame, for it is the only city gateway in England to still retain its outer defence area, known as the barbican. Together with the portcullis it provided double protection against the enemy. Lastly, there is Micklegate Bar, probably the city's most important since it guarded the road from London and has welcomed through its archway many of England's monarchs over the centuries.

A thousand men or more, all in armour, escorted their new Yorkist king, Edward IV, as he rode towards York. In front of Micklegate stood the city mayor, officials and onlookers, sheepishly waiting to greet their new sovereign and hoping against hope that he would bear no grudge that York had once mainly been for Lancaster and supported the pious King Henry VI and his daunting and vengeful wife, Margaret of Anjou. In fact, hearing of the terrible losses of her closest allies at the battle of Towton that day, and that the victorious Edward was approaching York, they had helped her to flee the city. But that didn't matter now. York had to convince the King as he came into view that 'We are loyal, Sire'.

However, the King is oblivious of his welcome. Instead he had reined in his horse and was staring up at Micklegate Bar. There, high on pike staffs, the shrivelled heads of his father, Richard of York and his brother Edmund met his gaze, beyond recognition now – but he knew. For three months since the awful Battle of Wakefield they had decorated this bar. Three months since Margaret of Anjou, according to Shakespeare, had uttered those notorious taunting words: 'Off with his head and set it on York Gates/ So York may overlook the town of York.' The battle weary Edward could not remove his stare; silently the tears of anger and terrible sadness fell and then the order was given for the heads to be removed and honourably dealt with.

Towton lies approximately ten miles south-east of York and Edward's battle that day had been fought in a blinding blizzard. On his entry into York no doubt Micklegate Bar's stonework etched in snow would have looked similar to the way it looks to me today, except when I look up only the snow coats its battlements, not the horrors that met Edward's gaze in March 1461.

Taking to the steps of Micklegate Bar and turning right at the top makes for a pleasant walk along the city walls to our next destination:

Lendal Bridge. The path is perfectly walkable and provides a good overview of both the old and not so old York. It is especially rewarding after you turn the corner. Looking down to your left is the train station and below you, to the right, a York of more recent times, whilst underneath, as you take the gradual incline of the path over the arches cut into the walls, the traffic of modern York enters and leaves the city. However, it is the view ahead that confirms the walk was definitely worth it. On the other side of the River Ouse, which is a natural boundary, lies the city of old York, dominated, as it has been for centuries, by the magnificent sculpture-encrusted towers of the beloved Minster. We leave the wall before the river for Lendal Bridge.

This very attractive single-span Victorian iron bridge has graced the River Ouse since 1863 but apparently its cast iron predecessor did not last quite so long and collapsed. It is very difficult today to believe this wide and picturesque river lined with pleasing walkways along its banks was once the scene of a horrific Viking invasion with all the ensuing carnage and devastation. The neat and orderly character of the quays down river, especially at King's Staithe and its sister Queen's Staithe directly opposite, equally belie a colourful past. For many centuries these were scenes of perpetual mayhem where boats of all descriptions were loaded or unloaded. Merchants traded their very souls for the precious cargoes displayed on the quays or, alternatively, watched as their own wares were hauled onto waiting vessels, wondering if this time they could extract a fortune from their efforts. Yes, from its earliest times York was very much a busy inland port and these quays were the hub of its trading powers. Here there was no order, only the constant clamber for space, and competition was rife. Here men bartered for the great treasures of the world . . . but no more. Now it is the people of the world that come to enjoy the great treasures of York.

Lendal Bridge is one of four bridges that now span the River Ouse. When Edward rode into York in 1461 from Micklegate, he would have had no option but to cross the Ouse via the Ouse Bridge straight ahead of him. The oldest bridge in York, back then it was the only means by which to cross the river that divides the city in two. Of course, there were the ferrymen if you were prepared to put your life in their hands, since their boats were notoriously unsturdy and, as York's main thoroughfare, the river was always full of traffic and hazardous even in its quieter moments. Nevertheless, these enterprising men did a lucrative trade and one can only assume that, after paying their fare, their more nervous passengers could only close their eyes and pray until they were safely delivered on the other side. Unfortunately, for a few centuries similar sentiments could have been appropriate for those who took to the Ouse Bridge. Although by Edward's time someone had come up with the brilliant revolutionary idea of reconstructing the thing in stone to increase its strength and durability, it had taken a long while for lessons to be learnt and, sadly, disaster struck more than once. The first Ouse Bridge, a wooden construction, collapsed in the mid-1100s under the weight of just too many people standing on it, whilst a subsequent one, also wooden and lined with shops, met a similar watery fate and, although not officially recorded, it is accepted these were not the only two. Makes you wonder just what lies at the bottom of this mighty river, doesn't it? The Ouse Bridge remained the only means of crossing the river, except for the ferry boats, until the mid-nineteenth century, believe it or not! It then underwent a substantial rebuild in Pennine stone which, to reassure my readers, is about as tough as you can get. Subsequently it was joined by the two other road bridges: up river, the Lendal, and down river, the Skeldergate. The fourth bridge is for rail only.

Today the snow-covered banks and quays below us are deserted. Only one or two leisure boats, also covered in a thin layering of snow, give a clue as to how popular the river is with York's constant influx of visitors during the warmer months. The thought of a river trip at this time of year, however, makes me feel even colder and as we leave Lendal Bridge, our pace quickens towards the warm and inviting western front of St Peter's straight ahead.

More commonly known as simply the Minster, it is described as the largest Gothic church in northern Europe, but it is so much more . . .

We appear to be alone in the Minster. The silence is broken only by the echo of our footsteps on the cold stone, seeming to confirm that only the spiritual remains of York's past, firmly implanted in the earth somewhere below us for all eternity, know we are here. Some 1,600 years ago this had been in part the site of the principia, or fortress, which dominated the new self-governing Roman city of Eboracum, but in 410 the Romans left. Bequeathed to, but apparently ignored by, subsequent ages of York's history, this one-time pride of Rome presumably fell victim to not only the more natural elements, but also to the ravages of various tempestuous battles within the city walls. Eventually, it was Thomas of Bayeux, nearly 700 years later, York's first Norman archbishop after the Conquest in 1066, who was to recognise the wisdom of the Roman builders and choose the same site for his new Norman cathedral. Not only that, but he also decided that what had been good enough for the Romans would be good enough for the Normans too, and used much of the stone from the old principia for the walls of his building.

York had been predominantly a Christian city since the Saxon king, Edwin, had been baptised here in 627, and consequently there had been predecessors, centres of Christian teaching, but not on this site and nothing on the scale of Thomas's Minster. Sadly, Thomas died in 1105 and just over 100 years later his Minster would also begin its long journey into oblivion . . . or would it? In the crypt beneath our feet, erected over Roman dust and now redundant, are huge weight-bearing Norman pillars installed by one of Thomas's successors after a fire, to provide support to a reconfigured choir. That too is no more.

. . . And from the ashes of so much history like a great phoenix the Minster we know today arose.

Walter de Gray, who as chancellor of England under the unpopular King John had put his seal on the Magna Carta in 1215, became Archbishop of York in the same year amidst much suspicion and distrust. However, within five years he obviously proved his worth since he not only convinced the dean and chapter that the Norman Minster should be rebuilt in the new Gothic style but, recognising the enormity of the task, became the project's chief fundraiser. Unfortunately, this enterprising archbishop died in 1255, by which time only the south transept of the new Minster had been finished and it seems a fitting tribute that he was buried here. However, to 'rest in peace' might not have been a fitting sentiment, since for the first 200 years following his death and interment the Minster was primarily a permanent building site whilst the Norman Minster was systematically demolished around him and replaced with the soaring arches and ornate stonework of his Gothic vision. With only an intricate arrangement of ropes and chains operating hoists and pulleys to assist them and, of course, the carpenters' and stonemasons' chisels, it was to take several generations of skilled craftsmen a total of 250 years to finish what Walter de Gray had started. Remarkably the Minster did not close for business but maintained its role at the heart of the city's social and business life. When work began in 1220 Henry III was King of England. There would be three King Edwards, a King Richard and three more King Henrys on the English throne before it was finally consecrated on 3 July 1472. By then King Edward IV had won his crown and the Wars of the Roses were well and truly over. Within 60 years the Wars of Religion would begin.

Henry VIII appointed himself Supreme Head of the Church in England and severed his ties with Rome. As a direct result England was thrown into a long and bitter internal battle over religion that was to span the Tudor and Stuart dynasties and in its wake men were thrown into conflict and confusion or the nearest dungeon. I do not intend to relate the consequences of Henry VIII's initial actions here. I have said enough on this subject elsewhere in this book. Suffice it to say that the Minster, as a non-monastic institution, remained physically unscathed.

As the winter sun penetrates the gloriously decorated pictorial glass windows, their mysterious obliqueness from the outside, which purely enhanced the stone tracery, is forgotten as these wonderful works of art become translucent from within. So it is with all such windows. It is a fact that within the precincts of the city can be found over half the medieval glass in all of England to have survived the centuries and the majority of this can be found here in the Minster. A miracle really, when you consider the building has suffered a few mishaps and potential disasters in its life time. One of these was a horrendous fire in May 1840. It began in the south-west tower, when witnesses to the scene were treated to an involuntary chime of ten bells as one by one they were dispassionately despatched to the stone floor below. Then more horror is recorded as the fire accelerated through the medieval wooden roof of the nave. It was completely destroyed. However, someone had had the foresight to make detailed drawings of the original and now these were invaluable in the recreation of this masterpiece of architectural design and labour. Today, without knowledge of what happened here, whether the roof was the original would never be questioned except by the discerning eye! The key bosses, as with the original, depict various episodes in the life of Christ and his mother. However, the Nativity boss was just too much for the Victorian perception of what was acceptable and what was not, and breastfeeding in public was not! So Mary was given a feeding bottle to keep her modesty intact. There are no prizes for spotting it, but next time I'm in the Minster I'll be watching you!

Luckily the fire did not damage one of my favourite features of the Minster and one that has undoubtedly caught the imagination of generations of visitors. It is the choir screen. A wonder of medieval architecture dating from the late fifteenth century, the *pulpitum*, to give it its proper name, greets you at the top of the nave and is undoubtedly an irresistible focal point. Its central archway, which leads directly into the choir, is flanked on either side by the brilliantly sculptured stone statues of 15 of England's kings, from William the Conqueror to Henry VI. Divided by elaborately carved narrow pillars, the kings wear golden crowns beneath golden canopies and stand on individual plinths against a backdrop of the richest red. Enhanced by this inspirational use of colour, in their entirety they emit a warm glow of welcome that prompted me some years ago to refer to it as the 'hearth of York Minster'. This sculptural masterpiece depicts each king's supposed character, so effectively etched into his face that you could almost believe the subject posed for the artist, and to confirm the unique artistry of the work, it also incorporates the finest detail into their individual garments. 'Who's who?' identification is not too difficult since their respective names are inscribed on their plinths (in Latin!). To me, together they span the years of the Minster's creation since, whether by accident or design, the choir screen silently acknowledges by the inclusion of William the Conqueror as the earliest king that Thomas of Bayeux's Norman Minster cannot be ignored. After all, it was the initial basic concept from which Walter de Gray's far more ambitious Gothic Minster finally arose, its completion coinciding with the tragic death of the final king depicted on the choir screen – Henry VI.

There are many other outstanding features within this great building, symbolic of its long history and loyal service to its people, its city and indeed its country. However, I did not come here today to make mention of more than I have. That is not my purpose and as we leave the Minster via the south transept past Archbishop Walter's tomb, I cannot help feeling he knows that. He too had imagination, far greater than mine, for he had a vision that became a reality. He would, therefore, I am sure appreciate my comparatively simple, heartfelt interpretation of the *pulpitum* and understand why I feel that both in subject and design it ultimately represents an appropriate epitaph to all those generations employed in the creation of his Minster. It has always been a centre for Christian worship and teaching, but, as I said at the beginning, it is so much more and that is my purpose today – to illustrate that it speaks for itself, beyond any words that any writer's pen could afford. Its fame has spread worldwide. People come to York from the four corners of the globe and most often their visits are purposeful. No matter their faith, no matter their nationality and no matter why they are here, it is certain that whatever they have heard, whatever they have read, whatever their expectations were on stepping over the Minster's threshold, most will never forget what they are about to see. What better compliment could be paid to not only all those craftsmen who originally built it, but to all who have presided over its wellbeing, both spiritually and practically, ever since?

At last we must never forget that first and foremost this gentle giant, massively out of proportion to any other building in York, stands as a symbol of undaunted devotion that continues to provide hope and stability in a fragile and ever-changing world.

It is a fact that before the Reformation, there were over 40 medieval churches in York. Today 19 remain. Sadly, they are often passed by without notice, partly because many have been obscured by subsequent ages of York's maturity, but mainly because the Minster overshadows them all. Quietly they play their part in the city and many have a story to tell. During our walk I shall make mention of one or two of them, just in passing.

Having left the Minster via the south transept door under the great Rose Window, it would be easy to overlook that down to our right on the other side of the street, dwarfed by its neighbour, is St Michael-le-Belfry Church. It took its name from the bell tower of the cathedral but bears no other resemblance. It was here in 1570 that Guy Fawkes, born and bred in York, was baptised. Although his family were Protestant, when he grew up he decided to become a Roman Catholic. A risky decision at a time when religion was causing more problems in England than anything else. It would appear, however, that for a while, as far as

Guy was concerned, all went tolerably well. The Protestant Queen Elizabeth I was reaching the end of her life, however, and all too soon the remarkable, golden age of the Virgin Queen was over. On her deathbed in 1603, having no heir of her own blood, she named James VI of Scotland, son of the fated Mary, Queen of Scots, as her successor through lineage. He became James I of England. Now life was about to change drastically for Guy Fawkes and not for the better. King James I of England did not approve of Catholics and would not tolerate them. He therefore persecuted them. As a result Guy Fawkes decided he did not approve of the King or his government and he and his co-conspirators decided to give them a 'reshuffle' with a little encouragement from a keg or two of gunpowder. The scene was set for 4 November 1605, but Guy Fawkes was caught in the act. The King and his government had had a narrow escape and Fawkes was to receive the ultimate punishment, but not before the authorities had tortured him in the hope he would divulge the names of his accomplices. He refused but all to no avail because within a very short time they had been rounded up and hanged, drawn and quartered as the law allowed. As for Guy Fawkes, he was taken to Traitor's Gate in London and hanged. It has often puzzled me, even as a child, as to the significance of burning an effigy of Guy on our bonfires each year on 5 November and, I have wondered, was he really that ugly? If it is supposed to be the man himself then I don't get the plot. After all, despite the risks, Guy Fawkes didn't intend to go up in flames with those above him, did he? His plan was to set the fuses in the cellar and run (just like James Bond of a later date).

A short walk to our left past the eastern perimeters of the Minster and we arrive at the impressive facade of St William's College. Despite its initially deceptive appearance of being more Tudor than medieval, it was in fact built in the 1460s shortly before the Tudors and shortly before the completion of the Minster with which it is very much associated, since the original purpose of this attractive half-timbered building was to house chantry priests. I should explain that a chantry is an altar or other part of a church endowed for the singing of masses, often over a number of years, for the donors' souls as per their last wishes. It was the chantry priests who were specially employed to carry out this ritual. Purgatory and the horrors it conjured in people's minds at this time in religious history was a very real phobia and they were desperate to ensure they did not linger there too long, if at all, but reach heaven as soon as possible. Anyway, despite the heavy responsibilities they carried, it appears these chantry priests lived rather charmed lives and having comparatively few duties to attend to and much money in their pouches, they gained a reputation for behaving like irresponsible college lads who loved nothing better than a night on the town and all that that can lead to. They needed to be housed and kept under control and so the college was founded and a provost installed to keep them in order and away from temptation.

The college is dedicated to William the Conqueror's great grandson and nephew of King Stephen, William Fitzherbert, who was briefly Archbishop of York some 300 years earlier. Remember I related how the original wooden Ouse Bridge collapsed because too many people were standing on it? Well, it was all down to this gentleman, literally! The reason such a crowd had assembled on the bridge was to bid him welcome as he made his first official entry into the city as their new archbishop, when lo and behold the whole structure gave way beneath their feet and down they all went. (A novel form of baptism!) Once Treasurer of York Minster, William had been elected several years previously as archbishop but various religious orders in the diocese had been against the choice and the Pope intervened, much to the people's displeasure. Now he was back and the people of York showed their delight, but it so nearly turned to tragedy. However, when the archbishop saw the scene of chaos and devastation before him in the river he immediately asked God to save them all and He did. The same cannot be said for William Fitzherbert. Only a short time after his appointment, the archbishop became ill and it was suspected that he had been poisoned by the archdeacon of Richmond at Mass. It was not proved conclusively, but William did not recover. After his death, people visiting his tomb began to relate tales of miracles. In 1227 he was canonised . . . and so it seems fitting that this one-time lodging house of unruly chantry priests should be dedicated to his saintly memory, no doubt in the hope that some of his good works would rub off! I'm sure they did.

Unfortunately Henry VIII's Protestant son Edward VI, on his accession to the throne in 1547, passed an act initially on his dead father's wishes, but much enhanced by himself, that authorised the Crown to take possession of chantries. Thus the chantry priests employed to serve the various altars in the Minster became redundant, as did St Williams College.

Subsequently it was put to several uses, but none of them were in the service of the Minster. When the troubled Charles I came to York, he chose it as the site for his Royal Mint. At one point in its life it also suffered the degradation of being made into tenements and subsequently became so dilapidated and squalid that it was thought little could be done to resurrect it to its former glory, but St William must have stepped in again. Today the elegance and charm of this medieval building can be enjoyed by all and I am sure the archbishop would well approve its reunion with the Minster as the cathedral's visitor centre. On entering the main doors from the street, visitors are immediately plunged back in time by a cobbled, full-of-character courtyard where they can soak up the atmosphere with refreshments from the adjacent restaurant or wander around some of the medieval rooms open to the public in the college itself. By the way, the main doors I mentioned are of a much later date than the actual building and were actually crafted by Yorkshire's most famous woodcarver, the late Robert Thompson. Remember him from Chapter 2? His mouse is carved on the right-hand door.

Under the old gatehouse at the end of College Street we reach Goodramgate, which is both to our left and diagonally across to our right and no, the name has nothing to do with 'good male sheep'. It actually probably derives from the Viking name of 'Gutherum', so now you know! Anyway, we need to go diagonally to our right and with not a soul in sight today except for an extremely squeaky bicycle, whose owner looks as frozen as his machine sounds, we have little difficulty in crossing the road.

As with the majority of the city's streets – sorry, gates – Goodramgate is not overly wide, which seems appropriate since amidst a more modern York to our right is 'Lady Row'. A compact line of whitewashed timber-framed cottages with upper floors projecting out over the street conjures up the picture that nothing more than a dirt track once served the dwellings, and they came complete with chickens and dogs running amok in the yards around rickety carts that had seen better days. The cottages were erected in 1316 and are credited with being the oldest in the city. In addition, their structured overhang, or jetties as they are termed, have the distinction of being the oldest example in the whole of England. A special licence for their construction on the edge of the churchyard of Holy Trinity Church, Goodramgate (not to be confused with other Holy Trinitys in York), was granted by King Edward II and the Archbishop of York to the church's vicar, a William de Langtoft. Known as chantry houses, it was an enterprising scheme which endowed a chantry dedicated to the Virgin Mary within the church and supplied funds for the necessary chantry priest who offered masses for the souls of the founders and those parishioners who could raise the money.

This is probably a good time to point out what you may already have gathered. The establishment of a chantry was an expensive business and most often a privilege of the wealthy. In these times of fear of retribution, though, ordinary folk too did what they could to monetarily contribute to their parish churches in life, hoping that in death it would be here they would be buried and their souls remembered for however long their funds would allow. Ironically, it would appear, although no records survive, that these were the type of tenants who would have occupied the cottages in 'Our Lady's Row', as it was originally called, and it would have been their rent monies that would have secured the employment of the chantry priest. Seems very harsh to me that, bearing in mind these were people of very modest means, they would also have been expected to pay for him to remember their own souls. Unless, of course, they came to some arrangement, which, bearing in mind the reputation of the Minster's chantry priests, may have been possible.

However, whatever the early history surrounding Holy Trinity and this chantry, one thing is certain, that within 30 or so years of 'Lady Row' being built, whether founder or occupant, vicar or chantry priest, all would have been struck by an intolerable fear in common with everyone else throughout the land. A dreadful curse which had arrived on our island in the south was rapidly spreading up the kingdom, completely indiscriminate as to its choice of victims. No matter individual wealth, no matter class, no matter situation, no one was safe and no one could stop it.

It was early spring in 1349. Everyone in York had heard what was happening throughout England. It had gripped the south first. People were dying in their hundreds, it was said. Terrible things happened to their bodies. Sweating and sick with fever, then such great swellings as you've never seen, bursting with muck. And the stench! They've boarded some up in their homes with the rest of their family, just in case, to keep everyone else safe. Marking their doors with crosses. The dead are bundled onto carts. Then they burn, burn everything belonging to them. It hasn't worked. Many roam the streets knowing it's coming on them in search of help, or worse, are allowed out of their town. Some are making a run for it into the countryside, but who's to know who's sick and who's not until it shows itself. God, don't let them come here. Most of the cities in England have it and now Yorkshire and soon us! Don't let anyone into the city. God preserve us . . .

All in vain. The first painful deaths confirmed that the dreadful curse of the Black Death had arrived in York. Bubonic plague, to give it its proper terminology, eventually wiped out approximately one-third of our island's population. With recurring epidemics springing up time after time, it would continue to overshadow England well into the seventeenth century. Rats in the holds of ships were to blame. Whilst the ships off-loaded their cargo onto the docks, the rats off-loaded their fleas, which transmitted their deadly virus wherever they went.

Of course, in an age of comparative ignorance so far as health, hygiene and associated sciences were concerned, there was little hope of anyone discovering the plague's source, let alone how to treat it. Their nearest accurate assessment seems to have been that it was 'invisible'. After that, people could only rely on their own basic instincts of fear and a need to survive when dealing with it. Thus the isolation of victims seemed obvious. After that, in most cases no comfort or care was afforded them except perhaps by their own families. The end was nearly always the same: a lonely, intolerably painful death.

Undoubtedly both economically and socially the plague transformed York, as it did England. The recurrent outbreaks devastated industry as a whole, wiping out at least a third, and probably more, of the total population, creating great gaps in practically every walk of life, including the church. After each new outbreak there was always the uncompromising threat that next time total obliteration of the city's main sources of economic strength was entirely possible. To counteract this, the authorities in York decided they had no alternative but to positively encourage a much larger influx of new citizens into their city than they had ever done before. In this way they hoped they could not only sustain their losses in craftsmanship and maintain the city economically but also ensure continuity in all aspects of life in their often dwindling community. It was to prove a good decision, since York not only survived but also eventually thrived. As a footnote, however, I have to wonder at the sanity of these people, pursuing a new life in a city known to have the perpetual threat of plague on its doorstep.

Whether the early occupants of 'Lady Row' survived these terrible times or not we do not know. After many years of respite it was 1604 when the plague again threatened to devastate York. According to the parish records of Holy Trinity Church in Goodramgate for that September, 51 burials took place, indicating whole families had been wiped out. This was thankfully the last time this dreaded curse visited York on such a wide scale. There were mini-outbreaks, but once controlled, they did not last long and at last disappeared altogether. Despite all these years of trauma, the cottages do appear to have been continually occupied by a variety of residents throughout their long life and after the confiscation of chantries in 1547 by the Crown, they were purchased by the Corporation of York, who continued to let them. Twice in their more recent lifetime the cottages have been threatened with demolition: once in 1827, when the possibility of opening the churchyard to the street was seriously considered and once in 1912 to make way for a tramline. Thank goodness it didn't happen and now it can't. Deservedly awarded the status of a Grade One listed building, Lady Row's preservation is secured well into the future. Since 1985 the property has been privately owned and is now let for commercial use only. However, like so many other medieval buildings in this city, although its original purpose may have changed, this neither interferes with nor detracts from its overall character whilst it still continues to serve the citizens of York and all who come here.

Unfortunately, the same may not exactly be said of Holy Trinity Church, Goodramgate, tucked behind 'Lady Row' and accessed by a brick archway and gate at one end of the cottages. Although maintaining its character and indeed it is still consecrated, it is only occasionally used for services and, sadly, is for the most part regarded as redundant. But it could never be dismissed. There is so much of its history within its walls unspoilt over time. It has an air of the mystical about it that I cannot describe except to say that from its beginnings somewhere back in the twelfth or thirteenth centuries it appears to have not only maintained the physical evidence of each of its many centuries but the spiritual too. Almost as if the many people who have worshipped here have left a part of themselves behind.

The box pews fascinate me; 1600s or 1700s, I believe. They were rented from the church by families in the parish who regularly worshipped here. I can imagine them huddled in one. The gentleman looking grand in wig and waistcoat, breeches and long boots, nodding acknowledgement as the vicar preaches his sermon. The submissive, obedient wife in her long narrow dress with bonnet casting shadows over her face, trying to keep the children quiet as they point and snigger at the poorer folk, who have to make do with the narrow benches free of charge. The pulpit is of the late 1600s and originally three tiered but now two. Whatever, it is unusual and very imposing in a church of such modest dimensions. Any vicar with a stern countenance and stern message to impart would have no difficulty in convincing his congregation to heed his words from that exalted position. One of the first things I noticed on stepping into Holy Trinity was the unevenness of the well-worn stone-flagged floor which for me contributes much to the overall character of this unpretentious place. I am reliably informed that in 1674 the floor was in such need of levelling and attention that four men were paid ten shillings – 50p to us – to carry out the work. I am rather pleased nothing appears to have been done about it since. The reason for the sinkage is simple. Too many souls have been buried beneath it. Mentioning burials, I am very pleased to say there is no significant evidence of a Victorian or later hand here. Not even electricity, I am told. Personally I am relieved. Not about the electricity – although midnight mass by candlelight does rather appeal – but about the Victorians.

The Victorian age brought us much, but taste, in my opinion, was not included. When Victorians wanted to make a statement as far as ornamentation was concerned, they always managed to obliterate everything else in the process and nowhere more so than in churches and graveyards. You don't have to seek their memorials out in a graveyard. They stare you in the face, literally! From winged angels to urns, from enormous crosses to great smiling-faced cherubs complete with garland, they collectively give the impression of a gigantic forest of stone and occasional marble, jostling for space and toppling off the perpendicular. Each may be a work of art in its own right, but to me the message is lost in overstatement. Who were they trying to impress? Certainly not the departed.

By the way, talking of Victorians, which he was for part of his life, George Hudson, the 'Railway King' lived in York and Holy Trinity was his parish church where he was married in 1821. Elected lord mayor of York for no less than three terms, he was responsible for bringing the railway to York, subsequently convincing George Stephenson that the line from Newcastle should be routed through the city and not bypass it. By 1849 Hudson controlled 1,450 miles of railway, which amounted to nearly a third of England's total rail network, but disaster struck when his involvement in corruption and shady financial dealings connected with the railway were exposed. All too soon he was ruined; his reputation in tatters, he fled to France where he remained for many years, only returning to England in 1870. He died in December 1871. For many years York could not forgive the man who not only put York on the railway map, but also made it the second railway centre in England after London. The city's new industry once employed over 5,000 people and was to survive long after Hudson. However, 100 years after his death it seemed time to let bygones be bygones and acknowledge what he had done for York and so he has a street named after him, in common with Gutherum, the Viking!

This is probably Holy Trinity's only claim to fame. Unobtrusive, modest and silent in this secluded place, away from the main thoroughfare of Goodramgate, it seems right it should rest, to be visited occasionally and respectfully appreciated for what it ultimately still is: a sanctuary where peace and solitude today are offered free of charge to all who come within its walls, no matter who. How could it ever be regarded as redundant?

Continuing down Goodramgate and diagonally left across King's Square, David, at long last, admits it's time for refreshments. Thank goodness! Tucked around the corner ahead of us is the Shambles, where we know a nice restaurant.

Although only half-past two, it seems much later as thick dark clouds now obliterate the sun. It is getting colder too and we are glad of the warmth as we sit by the window in the oak-panelled room, which looks out onto the narrow street. One or two of the traders opposite are putting up their shutters already and closing, probably realising it isn't worth staying open for business on such a bleak day. The street itself is empty but the wet cobbles reflect well the warm glow of light from the shops that are still open and somehow I prefer this scene to the hustle and bustle of the Shambles in high summer. The Shambles is aptly named, some might say, with its buildings all askew and, being of terrible age, given to the appearance that each one definitely depended on its neighbour for support as together they tumble out over this medieval street. Some, not all, are of early Tudor style, their three storeys conforming to the architectural design of their day, which dictated that each level should extend a little further over the street than the one below, whilst their characteristic gnarled ribs of greying oak take the strain of their seemingly precarious bow just as they have always done throughout the centuries of their age.

However, in truth this byway of York does not owe its name to the outward appearance of the houses that line its course. 'Shambles' comes from the word '*shammels*' and shammels there were in plenty along here for they were the benches on which meat was displayed and this was the street of the butchers.

The Shambles is the only street in York to be mentioned in the Domesday Book of 1086 and, according to the records, by 1270 there were some 17 butchers trading here. Just imagine the mayhem with all those bits of carcasses 'hanging' about! After all, in medieval England, butchers' shops were not the havens of hygiene they are today. Your taste buds were not tempted by row upon row of special cuts of nice red, or, for that matter, white meat being artistically arranged on clinically clean white trays, and the convenience of such assets to the trade as cling film and cold stores were nearly 700 years into the future. No, the best these highly respected tradesmen could do was to rely on a few handfuls of straw strewn about to absorb the messier side of the butcher's lot. Meat was meat in those days, salted perhaps, but nevertheless meat in its most basic form, with every part of the beast being considered for sale – head to trotter, nose to tail. The butcher would serve his customers from the open window behind the wooden shammel where his meat lay very much open to the elements and whatever else dropped in on it!

However, there had been some deliberation on one aspect of this problem: the effect of sunlight on the butchers' delicate produce, since the Shambles was apparently built as a very narrow street for the express purpose of shielding the meat on the shammels from the sun. Naturally, the extended upper floors of the buildings also went some way to achieving this end but, unhappily, I suspect some occupants of those upper storeys also provided their family butcher with another problem by way of following a rather disturbing habit of medieval times. Many people were not averse to using the quickest route for ridding themselves of their unwanted household waste and so they tossed it indiscriminately out of an open window down into the street below. Not surprisingly, everything in its path was at risk. In fact, it was that awful ritual that gave rise to the quaint custom of a gentleman always walking on the outside of a lady down a street. I suppose she had the shelter of the buildings whilst he took whatever was coming to him. I bet that could put a 'dampener' on their evening out.

It is said that at the narrowest point of the street if a person leaned out of the attic window beneath the steep gabled roof of one building he or she could shake hands with a neighbour at the corresponding window opposite. However, remembering the meat below and the fact that a deep gully ran down the length of the street carrying the butchers' unwanted scraps of offal, etc., as well as the dubious variety of other waste products already referred to, perhaps this exercise would have best been avoided by those with nostrils of a more sensitive nature. After all, the narrowness of the street may well have kept much of the sun out but also kept a good deal of the stench in.

Talking of attics and butchers brings to mind the story of Margaret Clitherow. She was a butcher's wife who lived at Number 35 in the Shambles. Today the little house is dedicated to her memory, for this lady was very special; in fact, on 25 October 1970, 384 years after her tragic death, she was made a saint. She was born in 1556 and married at 15. A staunch Catholic, she followed the beliefs of her true faith and in an England where the Roman Catholic religion was no longer tolerated, she frequently came to the aid of Catholic priests, hiding them in her attic until it was safe for them to leave undetected. Of course, she was caught and, after her trial, she suffered the most gruesome death on 25 March 1586. A wooden door was placed on top of her – not one of your lightweight hardboard variety, oh, no, the real thing, and in Tudor England that was solid English oak. If that wasn't enough to flatten the poor woman, it was then systematically laden with rocks. Unfortunately the authorities of the day were determined that an example should be made of anyone found to be defying the law of the land and maintaining loyalty to the Church of Rome. By so doing they believed others would be fearful and take heed. Sadly Margaret Clitherow and her horrific death were meant as one such example.

Having finished our meal, we leave the restaurant. The heavy sky, now beginning to darken as early evening approaches, is just visible between the high-pitched gables and shows promise of more snow. Just as the thought comes so do the first tell-tale white fluffy flakes. How Dickensian, I think to myself. Here, with no one in sight, other signs of life can only be assumed by the orange glow from an occasional window penetrating the darkening street. There is nothing to date the timeless scene. Should a woman suddenly appear from the other end of the street dressed in the style of Victorian England, her long skirts soaking up the wet from the pavement beneath her feet, her bonnet strings tied firmly under her chin and her cloak fluttering about her as she hurries on her way, she would not look out of place. Then again, nor would a group of young street urchins, grimy and ragged, huddled around the meagre remains of an iron street brazier, its glowing embers giving some warmth and comfort, whilst dulled eyes stare out from frozen faces into its flagging depths, hoping it will not falter too soon.

Whoops, I forgot: the street lamps. In Dickens' time few streets were afforded such a luxury and they would have been gas. Electric public lighting didn't arrive on York's streets until about 1900. Still, they are discreetly mounted on the walls, since there is no room down here for free-standing ones. Anyway, some licence can be allowed, for as they offer a yellowish tinge to the already impacted snow etching ledge and sill, kerb and roof, the scene before us is just too similar to that which often adorns a particularly nice Christmas card to let a minor detail bespoil the thought. In fact, it is a ready-made set for that Dickens seasonal favourite, *A Christmas Carol*, and Scrooge himself would look most 'at home' shuffling his way along this narrow pathway of cobbles, now being gradually obliterated by the thicker and more persistent fall of fresh snow. However, by the time Dickens was creating Scrooge, the number of butchers in the Shambles had risen to some 30 or more. Undoubtedly the trade by that time (the mid-1800s) would have been a far more sophisticated affair than in the days of their medieval predecessors and the shammels may well have fallen into disuse as the butcher no longer served his wares from the open window behind them, but allowed his customers to enter his premises to make their purchases.

Sadly, today there are no butchers in the Shambles, the last one having left a few years ago, leaving this famous thoroughfare solely to those traders more likely to draw custom from the thousands of visitors that pass this way each year. Glancing at the shammels that remain, being gently caressed by the fresh flakes of snow falling thick and fast now from a blackened sky, I cannot help wondering how many of those visitors even notice them, let alone realise their very real significance to this, the most celebrated street in all York.

Towards the end of the Shambles is a narrow passageway leading to Whip-ma-Whop-ma-Gate. The shortest street in York; hence the shortest paragraph in the book!

Leaving the Shambles, we are now in Pavement. The first street to be paved in York, hence its name. This is where the wealthier citizens lived. Bypassing the fine house opposite we go left into the alleyway, grandly named Lady Peckett's Yard. (It's lit, thank goodness!) Her husband was a mayor of York in the early 1700s and her yard is one of many fascinating byways in York that hide behind more obvious thoroughfares. They double as atmospheric shortcuts and we are now in Fossgate. Turning right we come to another little pathway which is conveniently signposted to the Merchant Adventurers' Hall, situated virtually on the banks of the River Foss.

Originally, in 1357, some of York's wealthier and more influential citizens joined forces and established themselves as a religious fraternity. Thus, with their own funds they built the hall. Completed in 1361, it catered for all their needs: an office from which to transact their business, a hall for more social gatherings and a place to pray. It was here too, in the undercroft, in 1373, that they set up a hospice for the poor and sick. No longer able to look after themselves, they were attended by chaplains who provided them with comfort and prayers to ease their end. By 1430 membership of the fraternity predominantly consisted of prosperous merchants and mercers (traders in textiles) who had successfully invested their own monies in overseas trading ventures, which is what defines a merchant adventurer. Incidentally, with their knowledge of trade, the merchants were able to transact their overseas business using bills of exchange as opposed to shipping out coinage, and it was this entrepreneurial approach that was to eventually become the foundation of our present-day merchant banks. Realising it could be to their mutual benefit to form an alliance, the merchants and mercers founded their trading association, or Merchant Adventurers' Guild, and subsequently became a force to be reckoned with, especially since many of them 'wore two hats' as the saying goes.

Not only were they traders, they were also mayors, councillors and the borough's representatives in the parliamentary Commons. In other words, they not only contributed greatly to York's prosperity and ultimately the prosperity of much of the north of England, through their own expansion and establishment of trading powers far beyond the city walls, but they also controlled the city from within, administering its internal and external affairs. This arrangement was not unique to York. Merchant Adventurers, despite other smaller guilds, usually held the monopoly and, with it, the power.

The city's élite, these wealthy families intermingled, intermarried and interfered with just about everything, but not necessarily purely in their own interests. In the world in which they lived, where fear of retribution in the afterlife was never very far away – in fact it was many of them who endowed the chanceries – coupled with the prevailing fear of plague and the resultant sudden decline in York's economic growth a real possibility, they saw it as their duty to take proper control of certain facets of the city's economic and social structures, whichever hat they were wearing, to safeguard its future. They encouraged young men into business by starting them off with grants. No new shop could be opened without first applying to them for permission. They ensured fair trading by keeping a close eye on weights and measures. Apprentices were also given a fair deal by being provided with a contract between them and their employers to ensure both sides were treated fairly. All sounds a bit like a modern-day parliamentary manifesto, doesn't it? In real terms, however, we cannot overlook essential facts that historically have been proven. Throughout all their commercial enterprises, both at home and abroad, and their internal administrations and other responsibilities, York did thrive. Also, they never lost their perception of Christianity, their commitment to God and responsibility to care for the poor and sick members of the community. Eventually becoming the Merchant Adventures' Company by royal charter in 1581, remarkably, their hospice did not close until 1900.

Although no longer a trading association, the Merchant Adventures' Company still have a modern-day role to play. Administering charities and holding services in the chapel, they retain their ownership of the hall but now they are the proud trustees who welcome visitors to spend a while taking in the atmosphere of this great York antiquity where once much of the wealth of the north was established. It had taken 1,000 years for the city to again use bricks in constructing a building. Then it had been Eboracum, Roman York. Now it was medieval York and they were to be used for the Great Hall's undercroft. Above, in the Great Hall itself, would be the great double-naved timber-framed roof, assembled at ground level first so that each piece could be marked to show its relevant position once hauled up to roof height. The reason the roof had to be double naved is essentially down to the width of the hall and a lack of English oak timber of the span required. According to records, it took 100 standing trees to build the hall and, in a sense, those trees have remained standing for nearly 650 years. Of course, some additions would be made throughout the great ages of history to the original building, but essentially it was destined to remain intact. In fact the hall, in its entirety as a Scheduled Ancient Monument, listed Grade One, is the only medieval guild hall in Europe to have retained its business room, hospice and chapel and still be under its original ownership. Quite a legacy.

Leaving the Merchant Adventurer's Hall we return to Fossgate and walk back towards Pavement, bypassing Lady Peckitt's Yard. Turning left into Pavement, we cross at the junction, keeping to the left of All Saints' Church, Pavement, straight ahead of us. All Saints' has had a long association with York's leading guilds and, not surprisingly, bearing in mind what I said before about Merchant Adventurers wearing two hats, there are said to be no less than 39 lord mayors buried here, which may or not prove the point. Not an overly large church, it dates from the 1300s, and, surrounded on three sides by modern York's roadways, gives the appearance of an elaborate, if unusual, traffic island. Sadly, for this reason it is often overlooked as traffic and pedestrians alike navigate round it to reach their destinations and it is not until glimpsed from a distance that people finally appreciate its most outstanding, or should I say upstanding, feature, which evokes curiosity: its impressive octagonal lantern tower, which definitely is All Saints' crowning glory. Although it makes for a uniquely attractive church tower, it once served a far more necessary purpose. Records confirm that once 'a large lamp hung in it, which was lighted in the night time'. It was indeed a beacon to assist travellers finding their way to the city through the dense Forest of Galtres, which surrounded York in medieval times. Today, of course, it could be deemed redundant, but this is York! The lantern tower is still lit up at night, but now it acts as a poignant memorial to all those who gave their lives in two world wars that took place in but one small century of York's long life.

Directly opposite the tower, to our left, we enter the modern, open-to-the-elements, shopping precinct of Coppergate Walk. No, it was not the Viking street of 'coppers'! They weren't invented until Sir Robert Peel, home secretary at the time, established the Metropolitan Police in 1829. Later to become prime minister, his force were known as 'bobbies', after him. Where 'coppers' came from, I'm not sure. As usual I have digressed. 'Coppergate' may derive from old Scandinavian and mean carpenters or joiners but my favourite, probably because it seems most appropriate, is that it derives from the Danish '*koopen*' or 'to bargain' (i.e. this was 'the merchants' street'). It is also very apt today since it boasts such 'ancient sites' as Marks & Spencer, Boots, Clintons, Fenwicks and other leading high-street names. Well planned, this unobtrusive acknowledgement of our modern world neither detracts from, nor intrudes on, the more historic architecture of this fine city. But there is more to Coppergate than immediately meets the eye. It has a hidden story to tell.

Coppergate is situated on the banks of York's second river, the Foss, not far from where that river joins the Ouse and, as I mentioned earlier, it was on the triangular piece of land formed by this natural union that, many centuries ago, York had its beginnings. Much of the England in AD 71 was part of the vast Roman Empire. The great Roman armies had invaded our island and subsequently established strategically placed settlements throughout the south. However, there was increasing concern about the marauding tribes creating havoc in the north and it was, therefore, decided to despatch a legion to the area to hopefully alleviate the problem and at the same time incorporate the north into the empire. Apparently this was the famous Ninth Legion, although to be honest I had never heard of them until now and why they were famous also escapes me. Understandably, this expanse of land, conveniently hemmed in by the junction of the two rivers and the Forest of Galtres, was considered by the Roman governor – a Mr Quintus Petillius Cerialis (I know, but that's what the history book called him!) – to be an ideal site to set up his camp. Well, the legion must have done a good job discharging their duties, perhaps that is why it was famous, since it was soon decided by the Roman authorities to make this outpost a more permanent structure. It was then given a name too, which I have mentioned before, Eboracum.

It was around this time the Ninth Legion were replaced by the Sixth. Probably the building detachment! Limestone was quarried from nearby Tadcaster and stone walls replaced the wooden structure around the perimeter of the stronghold. In the walls four fortified gates were also constructed at the points where the main roads entered the garrison and Eboracum was now firmly established as the military base of the north, with some 4,000 men stationed there. Eventually villages began to spring up too and the settlement thrived just like its counterparts in the south. However, despite its rise in status to a colonia, the highest grade of self-governing Roman city, and despite its ever-increasing wealth and power over three centuries, Eboracum's decline was rapid from the end of the fourth century, and Rome had troubles of its own. By 410 the Roman troops, who were pretty old by then, were called back to defend Rome. England was left to its own devices and after 350 years of Roman occupation Eboracum, with its people gone, was left to cope alone, but not for long. York had been born and would rise again. Such was the city's destiny.

What happened to it in the years immediately following the Roman evacuation is mostly speculation. Even the best historians and archaeologists have a tough time putting together the pieces, so to speak, so what chance do I stand! What we do know for certain is that eventually the Anglo-Saxons, who had infiltrated our shores in the hope of colonising new lands, chose Eboracum for one of their prime settlements and gave it a new name: Eoforwic. It was here the King of Northumbria lived and in 625 married a Christian princess from Kent. This was the seventh century and Christianity was now becoming firmly established in Saxon England. Consequently King Edwin's wife at last, after much coaxing and no doubt a little nagging too, persuaded her husband to relinquish his pagan gods for the Christian faith. He ordered a wooden church to be speedily built on a site, probably in the vicinity of that now occupied by the present Minster, for his baptism on Easter Day, 627. In fact it wasn't just his baptism as it turned out, since he instructed the rest of his family and all his court to also be baptised into the new faith. Obviously he believed in safety in numbers. The church, later replaced by a stone one and often referred to as the first Minster, was dedicated to St Peter the Apostle, a tradition that, unlike Edwin's pagan gods, has never been relinquished and still continues to this day. It was his wife's priest, Paulinus, who performed the ceremony and he is regarded as York's first archbishop, although the Pope did not officially grant York the pall of an archbishop until 735. York subsequently became second only to Canterbury in so far as religious importance was concerned. It still holds that privilege today. The city also prospered during this period of unusual peace, trading with Europe and making a name for itself.

By the beginning of the ninth century, however, England had fallen victim to sporadic raids by Danish pirates who burned, pillaged, raped and slaughtered their way around much of England's southern and eastern coastlines. They were so feared that the English had their own name for them: the Vikings. Over the ensuing 50 years these random assaults escalated, becoming more purposeful infiltrations by larger forces that were no longer returning to their homelands for the winter but remaining in England – an obvious and ominous indication to the English of their real intent, which was confirmed when in 865 even larger armies fought mean battles for supremacy throughout the Anglo-Saxon kingdoms of the south and east, culminating in the Vikings establishing large settlements in the areas they conquered. There was no doubt now: England had arrived at its Age of the Vikings.

Meanwhile, way up in the north lay the kingdom of Northumbria and its Saxon king, Aelle, had problems of his own to contend with. He had managed to overthrow another king, Osbert, because the throne of Northumbria was only big enough for one. Osbert had not given up easily and was still a real headache for Aelle. What is more, poor Aelle was not very popular with the Vikings either. He had once succeeded in capturing a great Viking leader by the name of Ragnar and subsequently dispensed with him by placing him in a pit that came complete with poisonous snakes – and we call the Vikings barbaric! Knowing the state of unrest in Northumbria and knowing that Aelle resided in its capital, Eoforwic, the Viking warriors decided the time was right for revenge. Aboard a fleet of longships, the bold Danes made their way up the River Ouse towards their goal, the oars of their great vessels confidently, rhythmically, licking the angry surface of the water. Knowing no fear, their adrenaline at fever pitch, the warriors, led by the sons of Ragnar, had no hesitation in coming ashore. They chose their moment well. They met with little resistance in the unprepared, bewildered town, King Aelle fled and overthrowing the Saxons, the Vikings took Eoforwic for their own, renaming it Jorvik. Now it was the capital of a Viking kingdom.

Of course the Vikings had a terrible reputation, and, with names like Eric Bloodaxe – the last Viking king – in our history books, who can blame us for believing there is a great deal of truth in the stories that have been handed down of their barbaric ways? We must remember, though, that this was the world of 866, a world where the status and power of a kingdom had always been judged on the lands it succeeded in conquering, occupying and subsequently accumulating wealth from, not on the methods used to achieve those ends.

Bearing this in mind, perhaps we should regard the Age of the Vikings with a little more tolerance and respect, especially when we take into account that the Viking settlements in England, subsequent to their invasion, were just that: settlements of a people who wanted nothing more than to farm, trade and exist in harmony with their neighbours. Nowhere else was this more true than in Jorvik. Following their victory they built single-storey wattle-and-daub houses and set up home with their women. Contrary to popular belief, your average Viking was not a bearded beast, constantly wielding an axe and wearing a two-horned metal helmet all his waking hours, but a talented craftsman who would far rather wield the tools of his particular trade and wear the plain tunic and hose of a peace-abiding citizen. They used animal hides that went through a tanning process before being made into shoes, scabbards and belts; worked bone and antlers into decorative fastenings and combs; ironsmiths made weapons; bronze craftsmen made artistic jewellery and finery; and then there were the carpenters who produced most of the household necessities such as cups, bowls, buckets and furniture. There is no doubt these Vikings were a self-sufficient, talented people who not only did well for themselves, but contributed all they could from their various industries to ensure their Jorvik continued to prosper as a reputable trading centre renowned throughout many countries of their world.

They also rebuilt the old Roman town which the Saxons had little altered, giving it a completely new street layout – much of which is still incorporated in the York of today – and extended the Roman walls to make for a larger and more prominent town. It could almost be taken as a well-earned mark of respect that York has retained the suffix 'gate' at the end of its road names. Derived from the Scandinavian *'gata'*, as I mentioned before, it is often used in preference to the Saxon equivalent of 'street' – and why not in the city a community of Vikings made their home for nearly a century?

To have recalled very briefly the sequence of events in York's first millennium with particular reference to the Vikings in the city is very relevant to Coppergate. As I intimated earlier, this is much more than a modern precinct and the story I have related is much more than pure conjecture. It literally arose from deep in the earth beneath my feet. Across the way from the all too familiar high-street stores is a building of similar modern architecture called Jorvik Viking Centre. It stands adjacent to St Mary's Church and although in itself is of no religious connection, to me there is a peculiar similarity between it and its neighbour that I find almost awesome. Several feet below its floor, entombed in the earth like a huge crypt, the remains of a community have quietly slumbered under the bustling streets of a York that has survived a further 1,000 years of history since its demise. Its last memories locked with the sound of the sword and the sight of the torch, as the merciless armies of William the Conqueror came to claim the city for their king during his 'Harrying of the North'. The Normans subsequently fiercely and indiscriminately defended their new garrison against a ferocious attack by Danes and other retaliating northern peoples. It was 1069 and now it was the turn of the Normans to occupy this ancient site, this York. Pillaged and largely burned, Jorvik faded into history, destined to be implanted further and further into the earth by the debris and decay of all the great ages of York's history yet to come, until now.

In the mid-1970s, before the new precinct had been built, a massive excavation programme was undertaken by archaeologists of the Yorkshire Archaeological Trust to uncover part of this community – this Jorvik. No one had any idea just how much would be gleaned from the laborious task ahead, but gradually it became obvious that the compacted earth had done its job well. Preserved in its resilient clutches were the substantial remains of various buildings, such as dwelling houses and workshops, incredibly, defining the street layouts. Tentatively, painstakingly, filtering their way through the layers of earth, the archaeologists slowly peeled back the years of this fascinating city's life, uncovering a vast number of artefacts as well as other debris. It was soon clear that this magnificent find was a living museum, telling the story of the lives of these ancient people who once lived here, and it naturally followed that the trust decided, after five years of hard work, that they must now resurrect Jorvik in York to tell the Vikings' story for itself. They did just that, using the original excavation site to build on what they had, and what they had was more than enough to be accurate. The result is the magnificent Viking Centre where one literally travels back through time to the Age of the Vikings, to find them hard at work, living out their daily lives amidst all the noise, bustle and aromas of their Jorvik.

Tonight Jorvik is silent, safely locked away from our world back into its own where the snows of yet another winter cannot reach it. Maybe it is because I have never known Coppergate to be so empty, it is usually so alive with shoppers, locals, tourists and, of course, those who are patiently awaiting their turn to visit Jorvik. Or maybe it is the crispness of the night and the stillness, but an eerie feeling seems to hang on the air as if someone else is listening to our footsteps growing fainter as we take our leave via Coppergate Walk ahead. It is almost as if we aren't quite alone. Once again my imagination is not doing me any good, but I wonder – really wonder – is there any truth in those stories about the immortality of the Viking spirit? No, there can't be . . . but then again I have been to Jorvik!

We are now in Tower Street and the great bulk of Clifford's Tower dominates our view. Adrift from the main thoroughfares of the city, it stands alone and exposed midway between the Ouse and the Foss, just above where those two rivers meet. Of little character or style, but purpose built, it reveals nothing of the appalling tragedy that took place here in the time of its predecessor, out of whose ashes it arose. A tragedy that so deeply penetrated the soil on which it now stands that although it is of later date and has taken the brunt of many further episodes of human suffering in its lifetime, the very sight of it always prompts the most ghastly story of human sacrifice to once again be recalled, just as it has always been down through the pages of history, so that all know exactly what happened here.

It was our old 'friend' William the Conqueror in the latter half of the eleventh century who first ordered a tower to be erected on this site when he chose York for his northern military base. Despite the fact it was made of wood, as was the practice back then, it long survived William, that is until the gruesome night of Friday, 16 March 1190. In these turbulent times Jews were a persecuted race in England and they suffered much at the hands of the authorities who had little or no respect for them. Often money lenders by trade, generally they were a peace-loving people who lived within their own communities, clung to their own beliefs and attracted as little attention as possible to themselves. Rarely were they left alone for long, however, and so it was that on the night I mentioned, 150 Jews found themselves at the mercy of a riotous mob. Like hounds with the scent of blood in their nostrils they chased their pitiful, helpless prey through the narrow byways of York, brandishing cudgels and other unsavoury weapons and bearing torches aflame that lit their otherwise darkened path. They did not relent. Their leader was a Richard Malebiss and some say that many in the mob were in fact citizens who had borrowed money from the Jews, but it appears the cry on everyone's lips that night was a religious one.

The hunters called for the Jews to save themselves by agreeing to be baptised and thereby publicly renouncing their own faith whilst the hunted prayed a silent prayer of their own for salvation and so they fled, finally seeking safety within the walls of the wooden tower from which there was no escape.

Outside the wooden castle they were surrounded by the bloodthirsty mob and incited by their leader, cries could be heard, threatening to slay all the Jews if they did not come out quietly and do the mob's bidding. The poor Jews must have been petrified. Some tried to escape but were instantly, horribly, slain. The remainder realised their fate was sealed. There were no options to consider and, more to the point, the mob were now so restless that they were beginning to vandalise the Jews' vulnerable sanctuary. Time was running out as silently they made the last and most sacred decision of their lives that they must now each and every one of them die by their own hands rather than throw themselves at the mercy of their hungry predators. Silently they made their pact and silently they carried it out. When the mob realised the Jews had made their own voluntary journey to their Maker, and thereby deprived them of any form of victory, their anger was at boiling point and they turned their aggression onto the tower itself. Thus they razed it to the ground to mingle with the blood of the 150 Jews who had so tragically died that night.

It was some years later that its more substantial stone successor was built and formed the keep to York Castle, but still it was the site of suffering, and indeed its name is derived from one of its 'victims': Roger de Clifford, a Lancastrian, who, having lost at the Battle of Boroughbridge in 1322 paid the price by being hung in chains from the battlements. He was not the only one to meet with such a grim death. Robert Aske, who led the Pilgrimage of Grace, also met such a fate here in 1537 and the story goes he took many days to die. You would think that there had been enough torturing of men's souls on this small piece of York soil, wouldn't you? But no. After the Civil Wars in the 1600s it was once again doomed to become a centre for much human suffering, this time in the form of a prison. The filth and stench in which the cruelly neglected, half-starved victims of mischance came to find themselves in the prisons of that period of our history, cannot be imagined by our society today. Suffice it to say the crime was of no consequence in those far-off times, innocent until proven guilty was the least of the authorities' priorities and even the most basic of human dignities were not afforded man, woman or child in those flea-infested, squalid places where not even a self-respecting rat would linger for long. Sad, but true, the innocent were thrown in with the guilty, women were raped, men were tortured, fever was rife and children died. The hangman's noose was often a welcome relief, despite the fact the crimes of many who dangled from its fatal knot did not deserve such drastic punishment.

Talking of hangmen's nooses, Clifford's Tower was eventually destined to become part of a much larger prison complex with the construction of the new Debtors' Prison just across the green, completed in 1705 – the very same year as its most famous inmate was born. It was here in 1738 that the notorious highwayman, Dick Turpin, was imprisoned and his cell can still be seen today, although now this beautiful Georgian building no longer serves as the county gaol but the fascinating York Castle Museum. Poor Dick was his own worst enemy. Using the name John Palmer, the story goes, Turpin, a much wanted man, escaped capture in London and fled to York. His crimes were said to be numerous but included killing a man – supposedly in self-defence – highway robbery and horse-stealing and there was a price on his head for any information leading to his arrest. Two hundred pounds, in fact, which was a lot of money back then. Legend would have us believe he made the ride for his life in a single day on Black Bess, but with time this has proved to be false, although romantic.

Anyway, York proved to be his downfall. Dick could not keep out of trouble and was initially arrested for shooting his landlord's cockerel and then threatening the landlord himself. Later he was in hot water again for his old habit of horse-stealing. In those days, when horses were very much a way of life for the citizens of England, horse-stealing was regarded as a very serious offence and if caught the offender could face the most severe penalty of all. Dick knew that but, ever the optimist, and knowing the authorities at that time had no idea of the prize they had under their roof, he undoubtedly hoped he would charm his way out of yet another tight corner and avoid the ultimate punishment.

However, sadly for Dick, his luck was about to run out. A former schoolmaster identified Dick's writing from a letter he had written in prison and declared his name was Turpin, not Palmer. His fate was sealed. Oh yes, of course, he was tried: on 22 March 1739 at York Assizes, just across the green from his prison cell, but it was a foregone conclusion that Turpin would not escape the hangman's noose. And so it was that on 7 April 1739 at the age of 33, Dick's life came to an abrupt end just outside the walls of York at 'The Mount'. His final resting place in St George's Churchyard, Fishergate, is marked by a simple stone. Tonight, however, it is far too cold for us to contemplate paying our respects as we would have to continue our walk down Tower Street and over the bridge that spans the Foss in order to reach St George's.

Instead we retrace our steps through Coppergate Walk and, crossing the road, follow the pathway opposite, turn right past All Saints' Church, Pavement, now on our right, which takes us back to the junction, where we turn left into the commercial thoroughfare of Parliament Street. The snow is falling again with renewed vigour as we cross St Sampson's Square. Still there is that silence: it reminds me of Christmas Eve as a child when I lay in bed listening for those magic sleigh bells that only ever came when my eyelids had grown too heavy for my ears to listen any more.

Across the Square, we follow Davygate, which opens out into St Helen's Square, sharing its name with the little church to our right that can easily be overlooked, tucked into the seam of the corner. To our left, looking no less impressive in the street lighting, is the Georgian elegance of the very first lord mayor's official residence to be built in England. The Mansion House, built in Italian Palladian style, which was fashionable at the time, was completed in 1726, ten years ahead of its London equivalent. Dominating the square, its imposing fascia suggests three storeys. In fact there are only two. The third is an illusion. A little like the King at the time. A German, King George I, had inherited the throne from Queen Anne. That poor lady had given birth 17 times, but to no avail. All her children died in infancy. King George, although only distantly related to the royal family, was the best we could get at the time, since after the Act of Settlement in 1701, we could only be ruled by a Protestant monarch. Anyway, he could well be described as an 'illusion' because he was rarely in England. German through and through, he wanted to keep popping home. Understandable for ordinary folk, but as our king, it wasn't altogether a very acceptable arrangement. Nor was the fact he did not put himself out to get a good grasp of the English language and as for governmental matters, he left it all to a particular minister to deal with, whose only credential had to be that he was able to achieve a positive vote when it came to negotiating the royal salary. This was, in fact, the advent of our getting into the habit of having a prime minister. Didn't have much to thank this illusive, reputedly bad-tempered and rude king for, did we? Anyway, he died on his way back to Hanover the year following the completion of the Mansion House in York, so that was that.

Georgian York, however, through the reigns of George II, III and IV which take us to 1830, was certainly not an illusion, but first we must travel back in time to 1642 just prior to the outbreak of the Civil Wars in England between King Charles I and his mainly puritan Parliament.

Unfortunately the King was not popular with the Scottish parliamentarians either, which didn't help matters. The Scots had already been causing problems in the north and this was undoubtedly a contributory factor to why the majority of York's citizens would have much preferred it if the King had not chosen their city as a refuge in March 1642 for not only himself, but his family, his court and his many ambassadors. The mood in the country generally was nervous. They knew civil war was inevitable and imminent. York would now act effectively as the capital city of the kingdom whilst the King was in residence, but there was little pride, only anxiety and a large helping of embarrassment. There were a number of puritans by this time in the city and propaganda from both sides, but despite this York was Royalist and loyal to its king. It just wished he would go somewhere else!

He did. Nearly six months later and six days after that, on 22 August 1642, he raised his standard in Nottingham.

England was now entrenched in the bitter Civil Wars and York had been transformed into a Royalist stronghold complete with army. Hostilities came to a height in 1644. The Scots were infiltrating Durham on their way south and in the West Riding an army of 5,000 English Parliamentarians under Fairfax were threatening York. The Royalist army in York marched out of the city to meet the Parliamentarians at Selby. They were heavily defeated. It was 11 April.

Soldiers sent to Durham to help stop the Scots returned to York, followed by the Scots who bypassed York and met up with Fairfax and his army in Tadcaster. Joining forces, their combined armies were 20,000 strong and now they turned their attention to York. It was 23 April. For ten weeks they remained in position. Meanwhile the York garrison of 4,000 men was costing the city a fortune in ammunition such as musket shot, various food preparations, tending the injured and burying the dead, not to mention paying for soldiers to guard their precious Minster. Various negotiations were from time to time entered into between the city and their enemies but eventually it was again the battlefield that was to decide the outcome.

York had known they were coming, and opened its gates to welcome, hopefully, its Royalist saviours in the form of Prince Rupert and his army. It was 1 July. Truly believing at last they would be freed of their enemy still lurking outside the city, one of the most well-known and decisive battles of the Civil Wars took place on Marston Moor. Sadly for York, the Royalists were defeated and the Parliamentarians returned to continue their siege of the city. Now there were only 500 soldiers remaining in York and there was little choice. This time negotiations were fruitful. Fairfax had much influence in the city and he assured them the Parliamentarians would be prevented from running amok and destroying several centuries of York's heritage. He kept his word. He was made governor of the new Parliamentarian stronghold. It was 16 July 1644.

The King and the country's traumatic years of enduring the Civil Wars were abruptly ended when Charles I was executed in London in 1649. Many of England's people believed that Charles' death was an unnecessary miscarriage of justice but it was wisest not to voice the thought. For the ensuing 11 years England was ruled by a Huntingdon squire, Oliver Cromwell, who had led the Parliamentarians to victory. He now led an England that had overnight become a republic for the first and only time in its history. Supposedly offered the crown, he subsequently refused it. However, after his death in 1658 there was one very big problem. His son was not considered worthy to follow his father and the country began to look around for options. It came in the form of what is referred to as the Restoration. In 1660 Charles' son, also Charles, who had been living in exile, was asked by Parliament to return to England and accept its Crown. He did, amid a blaze of welcome. The monarchy had been restored and England now had a Charles II.

York had suffered through the wars and under the influence of the Parliamentarians, who had subsequently dominated the north. It had lost much of its earlier status as essentially a prosperous trading centre and its political standing was negligible. Whilst some aspects of its social structure remained virtually unscathed, the same could not be said for its religious base or its administrative council, both of which had been forced to conform to the new regime. After the Restoration, however, the city had a new archbishop, the Minster was restored to its former glory and the civic preachers were dismissed. Local administration began to conform to the demands of a new age and despite the fact it had lost its seat in government, the city retained its role as the county's administrative centre.

The fact that much of York had not suffered substantial structural damage as a result of the Civil Wars, although merciful historically, was not entirely in its favour. Other provincial cities had taken the opportunity to give themselves a new look, ridding themselves of many timber-framed dwellings and replacing them in stone. London's Great Fire of 1666 necessitated that city being virtually rebuilt. In comparison, York gave the appearance of being behind the times, out of date, dull and prompted many of the more arrogant critics of the time to remark on the fact, in very uncomplimentary style. But York refused to be hampered by unrealistic 'bad press'.

The city had two very significant advantages in this new age: its location and its reputation. Post-Restoration England had been released from the shackles of the Civil Wars, invasion and dictatorship and with this new-found freedom came the redistribution of lands and wealth and a new class structure. York's close proximity to some of the most affluent and influential land owners in the north, who were already frequenting the city's racecourse on Clifton Ings, gave the city the opportunity it needed to once again adjust to a very different age. Only this time it would become a goods and services provider to the new society that had taken its new monarch's lead and sought leisure and pleasure in whatever form it was likely to take. One fact is indisputable: within a very short space of time these new leisure classes found all they wanted within the walls of York since it was described in late-Stuart England as 'the place to be'! Thus what the Stuarts had started, the Georgians would continue and, like I said at the beginning of this piece, it was no illusion . . .

The Georgians were notorious for their extravagance, vanity and snobbery. Although it was the Stuarts who had sown the seeds of a very different class structure in England, it was the Georgians who plucked the fruit and flaunted it. Despite the fact that for most of the period England was in and out of war, mainly with France, York was largely a remote outstation to these events and although the names of Nelson, Napoleon and Wellington were undoubtedly bantered about in conversation, they meant little to most. Meanwhile, York continued to capitalise on its popularity with those who took advantage of its hospitality. Stonemasons, silversmiths, dressmakers, wigmakers – yes, an essential fashion accessory for men as well as women – tailors and many others found their skills in great demand as they pandered to their wealthy patrons' expensive tastes. We mustn't forget the musicians – this was an age of music and dancing and they were always in demand for entertainment. When they weren't, they composed or provided instruction to those who wished to learn. In fact, the city catered for most new cultural levels, which included lawyers and scholars of learning and idiots who hoped to learn! There was an abundance of bookshops to meet their needs. Shopkeepers in general were now selling new goods, many of them imported from the colonies, and shopping became a hobby for all those who could afford it – the plague of men, the joy of women – and still is! Trade was also boosted by the arrival of that great innovation, the stagecoach.

Of course, where there is affluence, there is also poverty. It is unfortunately the wont of society that whilst the rich get richer, the poor get poorer and York had its share of poverty. Whilst fashionable society was not only enjoying the city's benefits but building their impressive houses within and beyond the city walls to entertain their equally influential associates, the poor lived beneath the breadline and suffered silently. The corporation attempted to support these lower reaches by finding them work and providing them with the basic necessities of life, even exempting them from paying taxes to help ease their burden. Boarding schools for orphans, hospitals for the sick and workhouses were set up, often by bequests, to help.

But whilst these poor unfortunates still had their slums, many others within the city had found new wealth in their prospering trades and were able to live to a far better standard than they had hitherto. Many seized the opportunity to reconfigure their houses to improve their facilities and living accommodation. An improved lifestyle within the city was one thing but as a result of these years of increasing popularity, York was beginning to suffer an increase in population that would only be satisfied by the provision of new and better-equipped houses over and above the locals' modest requirements. Already Georgian buildings such as the Mansion House had been slowly appearing within the city but most were purpose built for the social side of life. Only a minority of the wealthy had established a residence within or just outside the city boundaries but now it was time for York to expand and acknowledge the full extent of Georgian influence on its life. Thus the familiar fascias of Georgian townhouses began to line the streets both within and outside the city walls. It was the birth of the suburbs which would continue into the Victorian age, especially with the advent of the railway.

Inevitably, by the end of the eighteenth century York had outlived its attraction as far as the 'fashionable society' it had cosseted was concerned. In fact, many of them had also been consigned to the inevitable socialite dustbin as times were changing and the far less flamboyant, more refined and often colourless Victorian era approached. York didn't mind. It was used to accommodating strangers within its walls, being adapted to suit their needs, being forsaken when all its usefulness for them had gone.

As with all the preceding ages of York's past, the Stuarts and then the Georgians had stamped their identities on the city and they would form an integral part of the city's future. With a positive increase in business and commercial enterprises, York was ready to face the Victorian age.

It cannot be denied that the Victorian era of our history literally bulges with well-known names of men and women whose dedication to their work was eventually to touch virtually every facet of life in England. By the end of Queen Victoria's long reign, many of the great gaps in our social landscape had been filled. Industry, science, engineering, medicine, nursing care, law enforcement, railways, education, the publication of literary works, hygiene and the long-awaited flushing loo, to name but a few! Sadly, however, great areas of progress had a price and it was paid once again by the poor and the weak.

For example, children had long been an essential part of the great labour forces needed to help maintain Britain's now very lucrative cloth-manufacturing trade. This was very evident in the north of England. In the cotton mills of Lancashire the clatter of the spinning frames could be heard from 5 a.m. to late at night and when they fell silent many of the children would crawl into makeshift beds under the benches with little to eat to rest their frail and weary bodies for the new day tomorrow. Over the border in Yorkshire the prosperous woollen mills were little different. In fact, Bradford had long been a successful woollen town and by the 1800s was the wool capital of the world, but children were still the mainstay of its workforce. That is, until the advent of the Industrial Revolution, which put many of them out of work and predestined them for either a miserable existence back in their squalid homes that testified to how intolerable their plight had become or the equally squalid conditions of the dreaded workhouse. This did not purely apply to Bradford. Make no mistake, it was a virus like the plague and it had spread to the outer reaches of our kingdom. Ironically it was a Bradford MP, W. Forster, whose 1870 Education Act finally put an end to the neglect of England's children. It insisted every child should receive an elementary education. Now they at least had hope of a future.

Suffice it to say, where York was concerned it coped despite the problems inflicted on it by an age that on the one hand could boast it had revolutionised almost every aspect of life in Britain but on the other completely lacked any real appreciation of the fact that the ever-increasing numbers of lower-class citizens were being pushed further and further towards poverty and deprivation. Of course, these problems of the poor had, to a certain extent, been allowed to escalate over several generations by the constant neglect of responsible authorities to address the problems. Nevertheless, the gap had widened so dramatically between the now firmly established classes of our British way of life that by the mid-nineteenth century it was left to literary geniuses such as Charles Dickens to use the power of the pen to illustrate a more concise overview of life in Victorian England through his acclaimed novels such as *Oliver Twist, David Copperfield* and *A Christmas Carol* to name but a few.

It seems a preferred habit of chroniclers from many ages of our English history, the Victorians being the last, to bestow on us the triumphs and virtues of their age with little reference to what they may have regarded as insignificant detail of their lower social structures. To substitute 'insignificant' for 'more realistic' or 'eye-opening' may be nearer the truth. It is in fact often left to later historians to piece much of this social history together to try and compensate for the huge gaps such information would have no doubt filled. In reality, until the comparatively pampered society of the twentieth century unfolded after the two world wars, it could be argued that the greatest battles of all were fought within the community by the lower classes, constantly struggling to come to terms with the ever-changing face of a society they could no longer associate with to any great degree. It raises the question: would we have interpreted our history in exactly the same way if these long-suffering people could have, by some miracle, contributed their own views on events in their time and included their own demoralising stories? Would we have gleaned a much more accurate impression of what it was really like to live in Stuart, Georgian or Victorian England, for example? It would have made fascinating reading. Perhaps that is why the paupers were mostly kept illiterate. So they couldn't tell us the real story behind our history!

Leaving St Helens' Square and the Mansion House we turn right into Stonegate. Originally the Via Pretoria of Eboracum, it led directly into the garrison, now forever lost beneath the footings of the Minster. Up this street in 1220 huge stones were hauled, by equally huge men, no doubt, to build their Minster. The stones had arrived at the city by boat and this was the shortest route to the waiting building site. This is the most apt explanation of the street's name.

It is not difficult to imagine Stonegate in late medieval and Tudor times. It still bears much of the character of its age. Now itself paved in stone, it would still be most acceptable to the elegantly attired men in their short cloaks and hose as they wandered through it in search of the very newest invention, the York printing press. In fact, this street was to become the home of a number of printers and associated bookshops in the ensuing years after the Restoration, publishing fine theological works as well as other works of a scholarly nature, and we must not forget the promising literary geniuses – Laurence Sterne's masterpiece *Tristram Shandy* was first published here between 1760 and '67.

No doubt these great men of learning could partake in refreshment either in Ye Olde Starre Inne, reputedly the oldest surviving public house in the city, or in later times, the coffee houses where they could glance over a newspaper, not yet delivered to your door, or discuss business and political implications of their age. Talking of coffee and newspapers, on our right we have arrived at the entrance to Coffee Yard. Many passageways and courts or yards lay behind the fascia of Stonegate and this is one of them. If you have any doubts about its exact location, look up. Perched on the wall is the squatting impish effigy of a bright red printer's devil, complete with horns, tonight protected from the snow by the projecting eaves. To me he is a cruel representation of the little lads, known as 'devils', who used to carry the hot type in pans for the printers. However, he is appropriately placed since it was here in Coffee Yard that York's first newspaper was published in 1719. The Yard is also the home of Thomas Gent's coffee house, by the way, which presumably helped give the Yard its name.

As we continue our walk up Stonegate directly ahead we catch a glimpse of the now floodlit southern walls of the Minster. Usually obliterated by the number of visitors that frequent this thoroughfare, it signifies the end, but not quite, of our journey through time . . . and of our walk. Straight on from Stonegate and through the narrower Minster Gates passageway we are now opposite the Minster's south door, from which we emerged some hours ago. Directly to our right, also floodlit, are two reminders of where our journey and indeed York's story began. The impressive statue of the Roman Emperor Constantine reclines on his plinth and, opposite, a huge Roman column has been erected on its plinth. It was one of many that once graced the great Roman hall that once stood on the site of the Minster. One point I should mention, however, is that it has actually been erected upside down! Maybe that is why Rome wasn't built in a day. Certainly York wasn't.

Leaving the Minster, Constantine and the column behind us and retracing our steps towards Lendal Bridge and the station, the snow crisp and freezing under our feet, our virtual solitude throughout the day in a city that usually vibrates with life now seems totally unreal. Even on a winter's day York may be quiet like many cities but there are always many more people about than we have seen. It is as if we were meant to have York to ourselves and, unhurried and uninterrupted, that I be allowed to tell its story as I saw it . . .

. . . and as we stop for a moment to watch the soft flurries of snow, highlighted by the warm glow of the lamps, making their way to the blackened river below us, I cannot help feeling that all those souls of her great age who I have thought worthy of mention are falling with them. Their names may have been lost in time, but each is silently confirming they have been well rewarded for the role they played in ensuring their beloved city at last thrived on this small piece of Yorkshire soil; ultimately their blood was well spent. At that moment I realised today I had not been alone. They had been there in the shadows with me all the time listening to my Winter's Tale of a City called York.

> How best to describe what some have never seen
> And still others might not know
> Falls to me to be their eyes in winter's drifting snow
> If I have given some the heart to see what I can see
> Then my job has been well done and that well pleases me